ReFocus: The Films of Joachim Trier

ReFocus: The International Directors Series

Series Editors: Robert Singer, Gary D. Rhodes and Stefanie Van de Peer

Board of advisors:
Lizelle Bisschoff (Glasgow University)
Stephanie Hemelryck Donald (University of Lincoln)
Anna Misiak (Falmouth University)
Des O'Rawe (Queen's University Belfast)

ReFocus is a series of contemporary methodological and theoretical approaches to the interdisciplinary analyses and interpretations of international film directors, from the celebrated to the ignored, in direct relationship to their respective culture – its myths, values and historical precepts – and the broader parameters of international film history and theory.

Titles in the series include:

ReFocus: The Films of Susanne Bier Edited by Missy Molloy, Mimi Nielsen and Meryl Shriver-Rice

ReFocus: The Films of Francis Veber Keith Corson

ReFocus: The Films of Xavier Dolan Edited by Andrée Lafontaine

ReFocus: The Films of Pedro Costa: Producing and Consuming Contemporary Art Cinema Nuno Barradas Jorge

ReFocus: The Films of Sohrab Shahid Saless: Exile, Displacement and the Stateless Moving Image Edited by Azadeh Fatehrad

ReFocus: The Films of Pablo Larraín Edited by Laura Hatry

ReFocus: The Films of Michel Gondry Edited by Marcelline Block and Jennifer Kirby

ReFocus: The Films of Rachid Bouchareb Edited by Michael Gott and Leslie Kealhofer-Kemp

ReFocus: The Films of Andrei Tarkovsky Edited by Sergey Toymentsev

ReFocus: The Films of Paul Leni Edited by Erica Tortolani and Martin F. Norden

ReFocus: The Films of Rakhshan Banietemad Edited by Maryam Ghorbankarimi

ReFocus: The Films of Jocelyn Saab: Films, Artworks and Cultural Events for the Arab World Edited by Mathilde Rouxel and Stefanie Van de Peer

ReFocus: The Films of François Ozon Edited by Loïc Bourdeau

ReFocus: The Films of Teuvo Tulio Henry Bacon, Kimmo Laine and Jaakko Seppälä

ReFocus: The Films of João Pedro Rodrigues and João Rui Guerra da Mata Edited by José Duarte and Filipa Rosário

ReFocus: The Films of Lucrecia Martel Edited by Natalia Christofoletti Barrenha, Julia Kratje and Paul Merchant

ReFocus: The Films of Shyam Benegal Edited by Sneha Kar Chaudhuri and Ramit Samaddar

ReFocus: The Films of Denis Villeneuve Edited by Jeri English and Marie Pascal

ReFocus: The Films of Antoinetta Angelidi Edited by Penny Bouska and Sotiris Petridis

ReFocus: The Films of Ken Russell Edited by Matthew Melia

ReFocus: The Films of Kim Ki-young Edited by Chung-kang Kim

ReFocus: The Films of Jane Campion Edited by Alexia L. Bowler and Adele Jones

ReFocus: The Films of Alejandro Jodorowsky Edited by Michael Newell Witte

ReFocus: The Films of Nuri Bilge Ceylan Edited by Gönül Dönmez-Colin

ReFocus: The Films of Claire Denis Edited by Peter Sloane

ReFocus: The Films of Steve McQueen Edited by Thomas Austin

ReFocus: The Films of Yim Soon-rye Edited by Molly Kim

ReFocus: The Films of Annemarie Jacir Iqra Shagufta Cheema with Stefanie Van de Peer

ReFocus: The Films of Joachim Trier Anne Gjelsvik

edinburghuniversitypress.com/series/refocint

ReFocus:
The Films of Joachim Trier

Anne Gjelsvik

EDINBURGH
University Press

Edinburgh University Press is one of the leading university presses in the UK. We publish academic books and journals in our selected subject areas across the humanities and social sciences, combining cutting-edge scholarship with high editorial and production values to produce academic works of lasting importance. For more information visit our website: edinburghuniversitypress.com

© Anne Gjelsvik, 2024 2025

Grateful acknowledgement is made to the sources listed in the List of Illustrations for permission to reproduce material previously published elsewhere. Every effort has been made to trace the copyright holders, but if any have been inadvertently overlooked, the publisher will be pleased to make the necessary arrangements at the first opportunity.

Edinburgh University Press Ltd
13 Infirmary Street
Edinburgh EH1 1LT

First published in hardback by Edinburgh University Press 2024

Typeset in 11/13 Ehrhardt MT by
IDSUK (DataConnection) Ltd

A CIP record for this book is available from the British Library

ISBN 978 1 3995 1712 6 (hardback)
ISBN 978 1 3995 1713 3 (paperback)
ISBN 978 1 3995 1714 0 (webready PDF)
ISBN 978 1 3995 1715 7 (epub)

The right of Anne Gjelsvik to be identified as the author of this work has been asserted in accordance with the Copyright, Designs and Patents Act 1988, and the Copyright and Related Rights Regulations 2003 (SI No. 2498).

Contents

List of Figures	vi
Acknowledgements	viii
Prologue	1
1. Mimesis and Memory	13
2. Fractured Narratives	31
3. Sculpting Time	47
4. Oslo	59
5. Closures and Openings	73
6. The Human Condition	89
7. A Good Picture	106
8. Voices and Words	118
9. Moments and Movements	134
Epilogue: An Interview with Joachim Trier	147
Filmography: Joachim Trier's films	158
Filmography	162
Bibliography	165
Index	175

Figures

1.1	The Frogner Baths in winter. From the prologue of *Oslo, August 31st*.	15
1.2	The Frogner Baths in summer. From the epilogue of *Oslo, August 31st*.	18
1.3	Aksel reflects on how, towards the end of his life, he is only looking backwards in time.	21
1.4	Phillip and Kari negotiating their memories of their relationship.	23
1.5	Conrad's memory of playing hide and seek and hiding from his mother.	26
1.6	Isabelle pretending not to see Conrad.	26
2.1	Thelma's father considering shooting his own daughter.	33
2.2	Erik and Phillip fantasising about future fame as authors.	39
3.1	Aksel pouring his coffee as the world freezes in *The Worst Person in the World*.	51
3.2	Julie running through the streets of Oslo while the rest of the world stands still.	52
4.1	Julie overlooking Oslo from Ekebergåsen.	59
4.2	Anders at Åpent Bakeri.	66
5.1	Anders framed in his own darkness.	78
5.2	The performance, *Sleight of Hand*, functions as a visualization of Thelma's panic attack.	83
5.3	Thelma recovering from her panic attack at the opera house.	84
6.1	The awkwardness of invasive questions from strangers.	89
6.2	Conrad resting on the memory of his mother.	96
6.3	Thelma and Anja.	98
6.4	Julie, a woman with the gaze.	99

7.1	The comic *Gaupe* in *The Worst Person in the World*.	108
7.2	A picture of Gene: 'She thought that was a very good picture of me'.	109
8.1	Erik and Phillip when it all begins.	123
9.1	A short glimpse of bliss.	135
9.2	Isabelle Huppert as Isabelle and herself in the long close-up.	138
9.3	Cheerleaders in *Louder Than Bombs*.	142

Acknowledgements

I would like to start by thanking the series editors of 'ReFocus: The International Directors', Robert Singer, Gary Rhodes, and Stefanie Van de Peer, for their enthusiastic and supportive response when I approached them with a proposal for a book on Joachim Trier. The same thanks go to Gillian Leslie at the Edinburgh University Press for her always-swift responses and never-failing support. EUP's position as a leading publisher within film studies is in large part thanks to you. My thanks also go to editorial team members Sam Johnson and Kelly O´Brien, for always being available for questions big and small.

Several other people have helped this manuscript on its way to the finished book. Special thanks go to colleagues and friends Sven Østgard, Eirik Frisvold Hanssen, and Jørgen Bruhn, who have read different parts of the manuscript and offered valuable advice. I owe you. I am also indebted to another friend and colleague, Anne Jerslev, who has been important for my work on Trier ever since we co-edited a special issue on him for *Journal of Scandinavian Cinema* in 2019.

A warm thank you to my colleagues and students at the Department of Art and Media Studies at the Norwegian University of Science and Technology (NTNU), for interesting discussions about Joachim Trier's films over a number of years. I also received valuable feedback and suggestions from my colleagues in the film and television group at the Norwegian Association for Media researchers conference when I presented one of the chapters there in 2022. I also owe a great deal to the Linnaeus Centre for Intermedial and Multimodal Studies (IMS), for hosting me as their 2022 Lars Elleström Memorial Guest Researcher, and for giving me valuable time to concentrate on my writing in beautiful Växjö. The feedback I received from the colleagues there when I presented my research at the IMS seminar has been valuable.

I have had the privilege of writing for the column 'Analysen' in Norwegian film journal *Montages* for more than a decade. I have learned a lot from writing about Norwegian cinema on a (for an academic) tight deadline, and from my discussions with editors Lars Ole Kristiansen and Karsten Meinich, and ideas from my articles in *Montages* on *Louder Than Bombs* and *The Worst Person in the World* have found their way into the chapters here. I have also written on *Louder Than Bombs* in *Cinema Between Media* (Edinburgh University Press, 2018), and my co-author Jørgen Bruhn will probably recognise some ideas from our chapter there as well. The chapter 'Closures and Openings' is a rewritten version of an article I published in *Journal of Scandinavian Cinema* in 2019.

A warm thank you goes to Joachim Trier for his generosity in sharing his thoughts and reflections on filmmaking and his own films. Several of the ideas in this book are the results of conversations with Joachim from when he was an 'Artist in Residence' at the Department of Art and Media Studies at NTNU in 2017. I felt lucky to be his host during his stay with us in Trondheim. I am happy and proud that Joachim trusted me when I told him about this book, and thankful that he agreed to give the interview which has become its Epilogue.

Last but not least, a very warm and special thank you goes to Marta Eidsvåg, who has played an important and special part in the writing of this book. Acknowledging that my writing is freer and more inspired when I write in my native language, I decided that I wanted to write this book in Norwegian and have it translated into English. Without having one's own translator in the family, such a thing would not have been possible, and I am thankful that Marta accepted this special task and performed it with patience, knowledge, and creativity. The book is much better thanks to you.

* * *

I have received funding to write this book from The Norwegian Non-Fiction Writers and Translators Association (NFFO), as well as financial support from Department of Art and Media Studies and Faculty of Humanities, NTNU.

* * *

Written in Norwegian for Edinburgh University Press and translated into English by Marta Eidsvåg.

Prologue

I like telling stories, I like characters, I like observations of people, but I am not the guy who just wants to tell a story. I am interested in making cinema, somehow, and exploring what cinema could be.

Joachim Trier.[1]

The Worst Person in the World's success made Joachim Trier (born 1974) a household name on the international film scene. The film premiered at the Cannes film festival in 2021, where its star, Renate Reinsve received a Best Actress Award. The film was subsequently nominated for a number of international awards, including two Academy Awards (Best Original Screenplay and Best International Feature) and two BAFTAs (Best Leading Actress and Best Film Not in the English Language). It received near-universal praise from international critics, toured several other festivals between Cannes and the Academy Awards, and picked up several other awards along the way. It was distributed internationally to an extent that is near unheard of for a Norwegian film and saw record audiences abroad.[2] In 2022 it was included in the influential Criterion Collection (on both DVD and Blu-Ray), and made widely available for streaming. In sum, the success of *The Worst Person in the World* has made Trier the most internationally recognised and celebrated Norwegian director to date.

However, while it is fair to say that *The Worst Person in the World* brought about Trier's definitive international breakthrough, he had long been a favourite among both Norwegian and international film critics. Even as a student, he made award-winning shorts: *Pietà* (2000), *Still* (2001) and *Procter* (2002) and his debut as a feature director, with *Reprise* (2006), was long awaited.[3] *Reprise* saw him hailed as a talent who would shape Norwegian cinema for years to come. Descriptions like 'never seen a braver debut', 'a debut in a class of its own', and 'a pioneering work in Scandinavian cinema' are illustrative of his instant breakthrough at home.[4] Film historian Gunnar Iversen has called it one of the few Norwegian movies not similar to any other, and an instant classic.[5] *Reprise* was deemed an unusually ambitious and accomplished debut film abroad as well; it received, among a long series of accolades, an award at the Karlovy Vary film festival, was sold to more than 28 countries, was picked up by Miramax for American distribution, and Manohla Dargis of *The New York Times* described it as 'a blast of unadulterated movie pleasure', and 'an exuberant, exhilaratingly playful testament to being young and hungry'.[6] The *New York Times*' critic was also likely the first to mention Joachim Trier and the Academy Awards in the same sentence, when acting nominations for Anders Danielsen Lie and Espen Klouman Høiner, and a Best Original Screenplay for Trier and Eskil Vogt were among her predictions at the end of the year.[7]

When Norway's biggest newspaper, VG, listed its top films of the decade in 2009, *Reprise* took the number one spot, and in 2011, when film scholars and journalists were naming the best Norwegian films ever made, Trier's second feature, *Oslo, August 31st* came third, this in the very year of its release.[8] This film also premiered at Cannes (in Un Certain Regard) and brought Trier both international attention and further awards. An indication of the position this film holds in contemporary Norwegian culture is that the Oslo Cinematheque screens it every year on the last day of August. Two of Trier's next films, *Louder Than Bombs* (2015) and *The Worst Person in the World*, were subsequently selected for the main competition in Cannes. The latter was the first film in Norwegian since Anja Breien's *Arven* (*Next of Kin*, 1979). Between these two features, he made genre flick *Thelma* (2017), appealing to a somewhat different audience than his other works. With five feature films, a number of advertisements, short films, and a documentary *Den andre Munch* (*The Other Munch*) (2018)) under his belt, Trier is established as a leading figure in Nordic and European cinema, winning increasing fame even outside of cineaste circles.[9] An example of this is that he is the only director who has been nominated for the prestigious Nordic Council Film Prize five times (for all of his five feature films!), a prize he won for *Louder Than Bombs*.[10]

Trier is considered one of the, if not the, most important representative of what has been called a 'norwave' in Norwegian film history, meaning a time of more artistically ambitious and stylistically confident film production than what was seen in the small, national industry before the new millennium. The term was coined by *Variety* in 1997, after two Norwegian films directed by debutants, *Insomnia* (Erik Skjoldbjærg) and *Junk Mail* (Pål Sletaune) were screened at Cannes as the first Norwegian films in a long while and is a wordplay on Norway and the French New Wave.[11] The term encapsulated a sense of 'tensions between global and local identities' in the way Norwegian film production was evolving, with new Norwegian directors attempting to make films that could reach international audiences while remaining rooted in Norwegian film tradition.[12] Multiple Norwegian directors have seen critical or commercial success in the wake of this short-lived wave. While some have garnered more recognition at home (like, for instance, Dag Johan Haugerud and Erik Poppe), others stepped beyond the Norwegian borders, through either Hollywood careers or the international television industry (such as Morten Tyldum, Joachim Rønning, Espen Sandberg, and Anne Sewitsky). Joachim Trier has found greater success than these, both at home and abroad.

In an early interview with the *New York Times*, Trier stated that critics described his debut film as un-Norwegian, and that though he did not know what that meant, he took it as a compliment.[13] Throughout his career, the Norwegian director has been labelled original and 'untypically Norwegian', and yet was immediately also seen as a director very much of a particular time and place. An example of this can be found in Gunnar Iversen's *Norsk filmhistorie* (*Norwegian Film History*): 'Trier's film [*Oslo, August 31st*] is both original and very much of its time. It is unlike anything else, and simultaneously entirely typical of Norwegian film in 2011'.[14] In the same breath, author Gunnar Iversen compares Trier's debut with Erik Løchen (1924–1993), often considered Norway's most important modernist filmmaker, despite having only made two feature-length films, *Jakten* (*The Hunt*, 1959) and *Motforestilling* (*Remonstrance*, 1972). Løchen's debut was selected for the main competition at Cannes, but he also made his mark on Norwegian cinema through a number of shorts, scripts, and other positions held in the industry. Løchen was Joachim Trier's maternal grandfather, and though he died young (at fifty-eight) when Trier was only nine years old, he clearly influenced his grandson's ambitions and approaches to filmmaking. Both directors would, for instance, explore the medium's inherent possibilities through experimentation with narrative structure and voice-overs. Trier's parents were also in the film industry. His Danish father, Jacob Trier, was a sound engineer, and his mother, Hilde Løchen, worked as a script supervisor, among other things within film production before she pursued a career with the NRK (Norwegian Broadcasting Corporation).[15] There were visual artists and musicians on both sides of the family, and the Triers were influential in different areas of Danish public life, including leftist politics.[16] Joachim Trier has described himself as 'an inbred guy', and he grew up with kitchen table conversations about film and film politics.[17] He has said that he always has known that he wanted to be a filmmaker.[18] Growing up, he would play around with Super 8 and video tapes. His first films, as a teenager, were skateboarding films (1991–1992), and he was himself active in what was then an underground Norwegian skater scene, as skateboards were banned in Norway from 1978 to 1989. He got his own professional start on the ground floor, as a cable puller for game shows at the NRK. This was also where he met Eskil Vogt, who would become his closest collaborator.

Trier's ability to be part of a particular wave in Norwegian film history, while at the same time also being distinct from and somewhat outside of it, stems from the fact that he has been heavily influenced and inspired by international film history and culture, while he has grown up, lived, and done most of his work in Norway. Four out of five of his feature films were shot not just in Norway, but in Oslo, featuring Norwegian actors speaking Norwegian in a contemporary, Norwegian reality. All of his films, including his English-language feature *Louder Than Bombs*, which is set on the American East Coast, were produced by Norwegians and have received funding through The Norwegian Film Institute.[19] At the start of his career, Trier did not feel like he belonged in the Norwegian film industry, and he and his collaborator Eskil Vogt both applied to film schools abroad (see the epilogue on this as well). Vogt to La Fémis in Paris and Trier the European Film College in Denmark (1995–96) and then the National Film and Television School in London (NFTS) (in 1997, graduating 2001). Trier was only 23 when he was accepted as a student at NFTS and has described his start there as somewhat of a challenge. Being used to film with his own film camera and being inspired by Michelangelo Antonioni and films like *Hiroshima mon amour* (1959) and *Don't Look now* (1973), thinking as a director and learning about storytelling and character development within a British tradition was quite a transition.[20]

Trier will often praise the training and contacts he came away from NFTS with, but his aesthetics also stand out from the British, realist school of filmmaking in which he was taught. His work is more often compared to and analysed in terms of the French New Wave, and for good reason: *Reprise* is obviously inspired by both the films of Jean-Luc Godard and François Truffaut's *Jules and Jim* (1962), and *Oslo, August 31st* is a remake of Louis Malle's *The Fire Within* (*Le feu follet*, 1963).[21] Trier can clearly be placed within art cinema traditions, but his sources of inspiration go far beyond just European modernism. Every interview with him is nearly overflowing with references to the films and filmmakers held high in his regard (see epilogue). In a video made for the Criterion Collection Closet Picks series, he praises directors as diverse as Paul Schrader, Eric Rohmer, Bob Fosse, Akira Kurosawa, Andrei Tarkovsky, Victor Sjöström and Jan Troell, among others.[22] His genuine enthusiasm for auteurs like these is demonstrated through his ability to recount, in great detail, exactly what about a certain creator (Claire Denis's use of *mise-en-scène*) or a film (the structuring of Kurosawa's *High and Low* (1963)) he has learned from and wishes to carry forward in his work. He is also clearly inspired by contemporary peers like Mike Mills, Paul Thomas Anderson, Mia Hansen-Løve, and Céline Sciamma.

Trier's own auteur status derives from distinguishable formal and thematic traits that are consistent throughout his filmography, from his early shorts and through his most recent output.[23] Central topics in Trier's oeuvre are identity and relationships (friendship, love, family, loneliness), memory, and the importance of art (cinema, literature, and photography especially), particularly in the construction of a sense of self. His films are generally acknowledged for their nuanced takes on existential themes, and often feature troubled characters seeking to understand themselves. His characters always generate engagement and empathy in the viewer, not least because they all share a sense of disconnectedness or inferiority. Despite the range of characters, settings, and plotlines, all five feature films can be described as works about people in some kind of existential crisis.[24] Despite this, they are also all filled with sparks of life and humour. This simultaneous consistency and variation can be seen in a brief summary of the main plot points of his five features:

Reprise (2006) is about two young men seeking to become acclaimed authors, one of whom experiences a serious mental health crisis. *Oslo, August 31st* (2011) traces the final day in the life of a young man just out of rehab. *Louder Than Bombs* (2015) depicts the lives of a father and his two sons three years after the mother's sudden death. In *Thelma* (2017), a young female student with supernatural powers is struggling to break free from her family and her past. And *The Worst Person in the World* (2021) is an existential romantic comedy about a woman in her late 20s struggling to make definite life choices. Although both themes and moods are quite varied in these five films, it is also safe to say that Trier's films to date all have several elements in common. He has himself has described *The Worst Person in the World*, as a coming-of-age movie for grownups, and one might argue that the concept of growing up or finding your true self is a common denominator in all the films. The investigation of these themes is then combined with some kind of investigation of different cinematic genre and possibilities. 'It was kind of a buddy movie', Trier has said about his debut film. '*Oslo, August 31st* was inspired by the modernist novel and ideas of solitude. With *Louder Than Bombs*, I wanted to make something like a psychological family drama like *Ordinary People*. With *Thelma*, I wanted to make a supernatural thriller'.[25] And one can add, after that he went on to explore the rom-com genre with *The Worst Person in the World*, adding melancholy and existentialism to the traditional mix.

Trier and close collaborator and co-scriptwriter Eskil Vogt's approach to filmmaking has been described as a contemporary approach to modernist topics in a realistic yet self-reflective style that foregrounds character development and dialogue over plot.[26] All of Trier's films combine realistic, contemporary stories with formal experimentation, often featuring meta-cinematic qualities and a distinct ability to capture a sense of place, time and zeitgeist, as well as human behaviour. His work always displays complex narrative structures, employing pauses, flashes-forward, montages, and voice-overs in investigative ways, drawing inspiration from both art cinema traditions (such as the French

New Wave) and contemporary Scandinavian and American cinema, including well-established genres such as the thriller, the romantic comedy, and the family drama. Trier has stated in interviews that he is deeply interested in human beings (how we think, feel, and see), but also how he, as a modern director, can explore the art of cinema.

While Trier is one of few Norwegian directors who can claim the title of 'auteur', an important foundation for his career has been close and sustained collaborative relationships with others. First among these is scriptwriter Eskil Vogt, who has co-written all of Trier's films, including the shorts produced during his time as a student. Vogt, who is himself a trained director, has influenced Trier's work profoundly, as can be seen in the published scripts, and in comparisons with Vogt's own features, particularly *Blind* (2014).[27] And Vogt's second film *The Innocents* (*De uskyldige*, 2021) about children with supernatural powers shares a clear and close kinship with *Thelma*. The two collaborators made Norwegian film history by each participating with a film at Cannes in 2021, Trier in the main competition and Vogt in Un Certain Regard. Trier and Vogt were both inducted into the Academy of Motion Picture Arts and Sciences (also known as the Oscar Academy) in the scriptwriter branch in 2018.

Other close collaborators have also been important to Trier's career: Swedish Jakob Ihre has been his cinematographer since *Procter* (2002), which was Ihre's final project at NFTS, and *The Worst Person in the World,* shot by Danish Kasper Tuxen, was Trier's first feature not to be shot by Ihre.[28] Olivier Bugge Coutté has been Trier's editor since they met at the European Film College, and Gisle Tveito and Ola Fløttum have been the sound designer and composer, respectively, for all of his feature-length films. He has, additionally, had an on-going collaboration with set designer Roger Rosenberg and costume designer Ellen Dæhli Ystehede. In other words: an established and experienced production team come together to make a Trier feature. One exception to the rule is producers: Trier has changed producers over the years, with Thomas Robsahm (*Louder Than Bombs*, *Thelma* and *The Worst Person in the World*) being the most stable one. With a new feature film (number six) in the making, Trier has yet again changed production companies: this time to growing Norwegian production company Mer Film together with newly established Eye Eye Pictures, the latter company's producer Andrea Berentsen Ottmar being the link between films number five and six.[29]

Despite his towering presence in contemporary Norwegian cinema culture, exemplified by Norwegian film magazine *Montages*' extensive coverage of his work, Trier's filmography has to date not been extensively examined in academia.[30] His films have, however, established a prominent position in modern Norwegian film history, particularly in Gunnar Iversen's representations of newer Norwegian cinema.[31] A handful of master's theses have been written on one or more of his works.[32]

English-language literature on the most internationally renowned Norwegian director is scarce, with the exception of some articles in *Montages International Edition* and a special Issue of *The Journal of Scandinavian Cinema*, 2019 (JSC; edited by Anne Jerslev and myself).[33] The articles in *The Journal of Scandinavian Cinema* concern formal aspects of Trier's work, such as his structures and close-ups, but they also cover genre characteristics, the coming-of-age themes, and his parental and female characters.

Other academic output consists mostly of case studies of different cinematic elements and approaches, including sound,[34] intermediality,[35] memory,[36] film and emotion,[37] trauma,[38] and film and mental illness.[39] In addition the website Seventh Row has collected several reviews and interviews in an e-book.[40] This current book is thus the first full-length academic study of Joachim Trier's films, his styles and themes. Unlike many other single-director studies, this book is not organised film by film, but is structured thematically, with some chapters focusing on specific themes in his films, others on modes of narration or style. Throughout the next nine chapters, I will look closely at selected tropes across the director's filmography – such as memory, time, and identity – and also narrative structure, the use of voice-over, and different settings.

I have chosen this form because I wish to highlight certain unique characteristics that span Trier's oeuvre as a whole, and I believe my choice will enable me to delve deeper into these than mere analyses of individual works could. I will pursue a selection of different themes and techniques that recur throughout several of his films.

Though each chapter can of course be read on its own, here is a brief summary of the thematic trend of this work:

Chapter 1, 'Mimesis and Memory': The first chapter investigates the importance of memories. Memory and remembrance are recurring topics in all of Trier's films, both in the form of individual and private remembrances, and collective and shared recollections. Taking the opening of *Oslo, August 31st* as my starting point, but engaging with selected scenes from all five films, I will in this chapter discuss Trier's films as ways of thinking of and talking about memory. The chapter will lay out some chief characteristics of all the films, focusing on plot, and will therefore also function as an introduction to Trier's filmography and some of the other central themes.

Chapter 2, 'Fractured Narratives': Two characteristics of Trier's narrative style are investigated in this chapter. First: the rapid and inventive montages used to portray characters or describe periods of time. The openings of both *Reprise* and *The Worst Person in the World*, along with a central scene in *Louder Than Bombs*, are used as examples. Secondly, the use of non-chronological structures, most developed in *Reprise* and *Louder Than Bombs*, are also discussed here.

Chapter 3, 'Sculpting Time': Following up on the previous chapter, this chapter moves from narrative structure to a broader discussion of 'what cinema is', but the analytical focus is on one scene in particular. As foregrounded in the previous chapters, ideas about time – past, present, and future – are both central to Trier's films and closely related to the very idea of cinema as a time-based art form. This chapter provides a close study of the chapter in the film, 'Bad Timing', and the innovative use of 'frozen image' in *The Worst Person in the World*, in order to discuss how time is, in fact, captured in Trier's films. I have called this scene a 'time sculpture' in a previous analysis, and will provide a more detailed study of it here.[41]

Chapter 4, 'Oslo': Four of Trier's films share Oslo as their location, and three of them (*Reprise, Oslo, August 31st,* and *The Worst Person in the World*) constitute a series referred to as the 'Oslo trilogy'. Taking these three films as its main examples, this chapter will discuss the use and meanings of different aspects of *mise-en-scène*, and particularly the use of specific places. Trier has described Oslo as 'his matter', and I aim to demonstrate the meaning behind this statement.

Chapter 5, 'Closures and Openings': *Oslo, August 31st* chronicles the final day in the life of a depressed drug addict, before he commits suicide. In *Reprise*, two aspiring writers face multiple challenges when one of them suffers a mental breakdown and is hospitalised. In *Louder Than Bombs*, three family members try to process their trauma and loss after their mother's sudden death, and the main character in *Thelma* struggles with emancipation while at the same time suffering from strange seizures, seemingly caused by some unidentified psychological issue. In this chapter, I argue that mental health and mental illness are important topics in Joachim Trier's films, and will use *Thelma* and *Oslo, August 31st* as my main examples.

Chapter 6, 'The Human Condition': *Reprise* is a movie about friendship, *Louder Than Bombs* a movie about family, and *The Worst Person in the World* about romantic relationships. Simultaneously, these films are all about identity. In this chapter, I will investigate how identity is negotiated as something created in relation to others in all the films, with a focus on family, friendship, and romantic relationships.

Chapter 7, 'A Good Picture': I argue that art is an important topic in Trier's films as well. Art (literature and photography in particular) is also part of what shapes the identities of Trier's characters, and how they see themselves in relation to others. This chapter discusses the importance of other art forms in Trier's films, with a special focus on photography.

Chapter 8, 'Voices and Words': Trier's approach to filmmaking has sometimes been described as novelistic,[42] and this chapter will investigate the prominence of words, writing, and voices in his films. Drawing on the published scripts (co-written with Eskil Vogt), I will look at the roles of writing, the construction of characters' inner worlds (particularly how thoughts are depicted through streams of consciousness), and his inventive use of voice-over.

Chapter 9, 'Moments and Movements': In this chapter, I will try to capture the significance of Trier's work to date, particularly his visual aesthetics, through looking at how he draws on film historical inspirations (both American and European) while simultaneously developing his own personal style. This chapter will try place Trier within different film traditions, ranging from art cinema to popular genre film, and to capture his cinematic style in a more general way, drawing on previous chapters, in order to form a sort of conclusion on the director's style.

The 'Epilogue' is an interview with Joachim Trier.

An extended filmography, featuring all of Trier's work, can be found at the back of the book. This features an overview of the other chief creatives behind each film, including the actors in the most important roles. Throughout the chapters discussing the films, the actors' names will only be provided the first time a character is mentioned – this to avoid unnecessary repetition. Kindly use the filmography as a reference beyond this.

NOTES

1. Truls Lie, 'Joachim Trier on Being a Director', 16 September 2015, https://vimeo.com/140561626.
2. The film was in particular successful at the box office in Denmark and France, a result both of his standing in these two countries as well as the role of co-producers and distributors.
3. For more on Trier's short films, see Dag Sødtholt, 'Tre enigmaer av Joachim Trier', *Montages*, 27 August 2015, https://montages.no/2015/08/tre-enigmaer-av-joachim-trier/; and Eino Aleksander Kerr, *Minner og melankoli en auteurstudie av den norske filmskaperen Joachim Trier* (Trondheim, Institutt for kunst og medievitenskap, NTNU, 2013).
4. Birger Vestmo, 'Reprise', NRK P3, 8 September 2006, https://p3.no/filmpolitiet/2006/09/reprise/; Marius Lyngar, 'Fra Revolt til Reprise? – Joachim Trier og den franske nybølgen', *Z Filmtidsskrift*, 6 October 2011, http://znett.com/2011/10/fra-revolt-til-reprise-joachim-trier-og-den-franske-nybolgen/. The reviews from *Aftenposten* and *Berlingske Tidende* are quoted from Lyngar.
5. Gunnar Iversen, 'Tiden leger ingen sår "Reprise"', in *Den norske filmbølgen: Fra Orions belte til Max Manus*. (Oslo: Universitetsforlaget, 2010), 267–90.
6. Manohla Dargis, 'Two Friends, Two Novels, One Mailbox: Lives at the Speed of Ambition', *The New York Times*, 16 May 2008, https://www.nytimes.com/2008/05/16/movies/16repr.html.
7. Manohla Dargis, 'For Your Consideration, Academy', *New York Times*, 3 January 2009, https://www.nytimes.com/2009/01/04/movies/awardsseason/04oscars.html.
8. Rushprint (ed.), '"Jakten" er tidenes norske kinofilm', Rushprint, 21 December 2011, https://rushprint.no/2011/12/jakten-er-tidenes-norske-kinofilm/. On this list *The Hunt* (*Jakten*), directed by Joachim Trier's grandfather, came first.

Pinchcliffe Grand Prix (*Flåklypa Grand Prix*) (1975) came second, and Trier's father did the sound for this film.

9. The documentary *The Other Munch* (2018), about novelist Karl Ove Knausgårds curating a Munch exhibition, was co-directed with his brother Emil Trier.
10. The list of awards given to Trier is substantial. His films have been nominated for and won a lot of prizes at the Norwegian Film Awards, including the 'Amanda', as well as the Norwegian Society of Film Critics' awards through the years. Among the accolades he has received following *The Worst Person in the World* are the Anders Jahre Culture Award 2022 (the largest culture award in Norway, shared with three other film directors), the German Academy's Der Grosser Berliner Kunstpreis 2023 (the first Norwegian ever to win this) and a seat on the jury at the Cannes film festival (2022).
11. *Insomnia* was remade by Christopher Nolan in 2002 with Al Pacino and Robin Williams.
12. Ellen Rees, 'Norwave: Norwegian Cinema 1997–2006', *Scandinavian–Canadian Studies* 19 (1 December 2010): 88–110.
13. Dennis Lim, 'Joachim Trier's "Reprise": Cinematic Life in Oslo (Where Else?)', *The New York Times*, 11 May 2008. https://www.nytimes.com/2008/05/11/movies/11lim.html.
14. Gunnar Iversen, *Norsk filmhistorie* (Oslo: Universitetsforlaget, 2011), 316.
15. Trier was born in Copenhagen and speaks Danish. Danish film critic Christian Mongaard opened a public interview with Trier in Copenhagen in 2022 by joking that that both Trier and *The Worst Person in the World* were Danish.
16. Lars von Trier's original surname comes from the same family line (he has himself added on the nobility marker 'von'). Von Trier grew up believing Ulf Trier to be his father, but on her deathbed, his mother revealed this not to be the case, and disclosed the name of his birth father. The two directing Triers are, thus, not truly related.
17. Daniel Kasman, 'Representation of Self: Discussing "Louder Than Bombs" with Joachim Trier', MUBI, 29 May 2015. https://mubi.com/notebook/posts/representation-of-self-discussing-louder-than-bombs-with-joachim-trier. Joachim's brother Emil is a film director (music videos, documentary) and his sister Elli a photographer.
18. Kjersti Nipen, 'Joachim Trier: – Alt jeg gjør, er ekstremt personlig', 14 September 2017. https://www.aftenposten.no/amagasinet/i/92Gxd/joachim-trier-alt-jeg-gjoer-er-ekstremt-personlig.
19. The Norwegian Film Institute (NFI) is a public institution operating under the authority of the Ministry of Culture. NFI is the government's executive body for the film sector, and its advisor on film policy issues. In a small country and linguistic area such as Norway, nearly all film production, excepting that produced by commercial streaming services, is at least in part publicly funded. NFI is the chief provider of such funding.
20. Joachim Trier, 'Masterclass with Joachim Trier in Conversation with Anne Gjelsvik'. Department of Art and Media Studies, NTNU, 18 September 2017.
21. Malle's film was itself an adaptation of the novel *Le feu follet* (*Will O' the Wisp*) by Pierre Drieu La Rochelle (1931).

22. 'Joachim Trier's DVD Picks', 2016, https://www.youtube.com/watch?v=qF3qYnnuGxI.
23. Even some of his advertisements display hints of his distinct signature. See Kerr, *Minner og melankoli*, on this. For example *Life in Reverse* for the Norwegian bank Sparebank1 which can be found on YouTube.
24. This is also the case with his short films.
25. Tara Brady, 'Making The Worst Person in the World, an Oscar-Nominated "Unromantic Comedy"', *The Irish Times*, 19 March 2022, https://www.irishtimes.com/culture/film/making-the-worst-person-in-the-world-an-oscar-nominated-unromantic-comedy-1.4824526.
26. Søren Birkvad, 'Analysen: Oslo, 31. August (2011)', *Montages*, 14 September 2011, http://montages.no/2011/09/analysen-oslo-31-august-2011/; Iversen, *Norsk Filmhistorie*; Jørgen Bruhn and Anne Gjelsvik, *Cinema Between Media: An Intermediality Approach* (Edinburgh: University Press, 2018), 51–69.
27. All of Vogt and Trier's Norwegian scripts (that is all but *Louder Than Bombs*) have been published by Norwegian publisher Tiden Norsk Forlag: Eskil Vogt and Joachim Trier, *Reprise. Et filmmanus*. Oslo: Tiden Norsk Forlag, 2007; Eskil Vogt and Joachim Trier, *Oslo, 31. August, Filmmanus*, Oslo: Tiden Norsk Forlag, 2011; Eskil Vogt and Joachim Trier, *Thelma*, Oslo: Tiden Norsk Forlag, 2017; Eskil Vogt and Joachim Trier, *Verdens verste menneske: filmmanus*, Oslo: Tiden Norsk Forlag, 2021. In addition, the three Oslo scripts are also collected in Eskil Vogt and Joachim Trier, *Oslo-trilogien. Filmmanus*, Tiden Norsk Forlag, 2022.
28. See, for example, Jakob Ihre's master class on this collaboration: 'Masterclass with the Emmy Award Winner Jakob Ihre, Director of Photography', Kulturakademin Gotenburgh Studios (2020) https://www.youtube.com/watch?v=b2ZzPRLeL_g.
29. For more, see the Filmography, and Chapter 9.
30. See https://montages.no/filmfolk/joachim-trier/ for an overview of articles both in Norwegian and English. Film critic Dag Sødtholt has written in detail and depth on Trier's work for *Montages*, and I will draw on several of his articles here. See, for instance, the richly illustrated article Dag Sødtholt, 'Focus of Faith: Joachim Trier's The Worst Person in the World', *Montages International Edition*, 27 March 2022, https://montagesmagazine.com/2022/03/focus-of-faith-joachim-triers-the-worst-person-in-the-world/
31. Iversen, 'Tiden leger ingen sår Reprise'; Iversen, *Norsk Filmhistorie*.
32. Guro Johansen, 'Sted og selvrefleksivitet: en adaptasjonsanalyse av Oslo, 31. August og Le feu follet', Oslo, Universitetet i Oslo (2012). https://www.duo.uio.no/handle/10852/38132; Vilde Bjørnødegård, 'Film og sanselighet: Affektfremkallende egenskaper i "Louder Than Bombs" (Joachim Trier, 2015)', Oslo, Universitetet i Oslo (2018), https://www.duo.uio.no/handle/10852/63219.
33. Anne Gjelsvik, 'In Focus: Joachim Trier', *Journal of Scandinavian Cinema* 9, no. 2 (1 June 2019): 191–96, https://doi.org/10.1386/jsca_9_2.191_1.
34. Gunnar Iversen and Asbjørn Tiller, *Lydbilder: mediene og det akustiske* (Oslo: Universitetsforlaget, 2014).
35. Bruhn and Gjelsvik, *Cinema Between Media*.
36. Benjamin Bigelow, 'Acts of Remembering, Acts of Forgetting: Architecture, Memory and Recovery in Oslo, August 31st', *Journal of Scandinavian Cinema*

10, no. 1 (1 March 2020): 7–24, https://doi.org/10.1386/jsca_00011_1; C. Claire Thomson, 'Louder Than Films: Memory, Affect and the "Sublime Image" in the Work of Joachim Trier', *Arts* 8, no. 2 (2019), https://doi.org/10.3390/arts8020055.
37. Tarja Laine, *Feeling Cinema: Emotional Dynamics in Film Studies* (New York: Continuum, 2011).
38. Tarja Laine, 'Trauma, Queer Sexuality and Symbolic Storytelling in Joachim Trier's Thelma', *Journal of Scandinavian Cinema* 12, no. 3 (1 September 2022): 291–305, https://doi.org/10.1386/jsca_00077_1.
39. Anne Gjelsvik, 'Openings and Closures: Mental Health in Joachim Trier's Cinematic Universe', *Journal of Scandinavian Cinema* 9, no. 1 (1 March 2019): 75–88, https://doi.org/10.1386/jsca.9.1.75_1.
40. Alex Heeney and Orla Smith, *Existential Detours. Joachim Trier's Films of Indecisions and Revisions*, vol. 5.1 (Toronto: Seventh Row, 2024).
41. Anne Gjelsvik, 'Sculpting Time: Joachim Trier's The Worst Person in the World', *Montages International Edition*, 17 December 2021, https://montagesmagazine.com/2021/12/sculpting-time-the-worst-person-in-the-world/;
42. Bruhn and Gjelsvik, *Cinema Between Media*.

CHAPTER I

Mimesis and Memory

While Joachim Trier is often described as a director who captures the zeitgeist, his movies also tend to have a retrospective and nostalgic feel to them. Remembrance and reminiscence is, I argue, a recurring topic in his work, one he approaches from a number of different angles. He has explored attempts to recreate feelings from the past (*Reprise*), the ways different people remember things differently (*Louder Than Bombs*), the deliberate act of forgetting or trying to forget (*Thelma, Oslo, August 31st*), the ways we think about how we will look back on something in the future (*Louder Than Bombs*), and pasts that have been lost (*The Worst Person in the World*). Trier has himself referenced this preoccupation with memory in several interviews, making statements like: 'It's why I'm interested in cinema; it's the art form of memory'.[1]

Trier is not alone in considering cinema the medium of memory, nor is cinema the first or only medium to be compared with the human process of memory formation. The photograph in particular has held such a position.[2] But as memory studies scholar Susannah Radstone points out, two theoretical paradigms have clung to film and memory since the birth of the medium: 'Memory has been conceived of by analogy with cinema, and in a reverse move, the cinema – and specific types of film – have been understood to be analogous with or even to be modes of memory'.[3] Though this quotation comes from a different context, it captures something that I consider essential about Trier as a filmmaker. He makes films focusing on memories, while simultaneously exploring the film medium as an art form of memory.

Taking the opening of *Oslo, August 31st* as my starting point, I will discuss Trier's oeuvre as a means of thinking and talking about memory and memories, both in the form of individual and private memories, and as collective and shared recollections. I will look at how this theme creates what has been described as a melancholy sweetness in *Oslo, August 31st* and how this situates Trier within a European modernist film tradition. The act of remembering is present in all of Trier's films, and this chapter will engage with selected scenes from all five. It will also provide a short introduction to all his feature films.

'I remember thinking "I'll remember this"'.[4] In *Oslo, August 31st*'s prologue, a number of unseen, anonymous narrators share their memories of Oslo. This specific memory, though, or rather this montage of memories, is not just about Oslo, but also about the very act of remembering. We see aerial shots of the city: archival footage of empty Oslo streets from the past (the 1960s, 70s, and 80s), when cars, buses, and shop signs all looked just a little bit different.[5] And we hear these young voices (both women and men, speaking different regional dialects) sharing their memories of being children, of their parents, friends, parties, feelings, and different places around the city. Almost all open with the line 'I remember. . .' They all share a sense of light, summery nostalgia that is exemplified by the very first recollection: 'I remember that the first Oslo-fjord swim of the season would always be on the 1st of May'. And then, next: 'I remember so well that feeling of coming back in, Sunday afternoon-evening, as the sun was setting; we'd be coming from Son into an Oslo that was empty'.[6]

Then the images change, from archival stills to private video recordings accompanied by music: a young woman holding her hand up in front of the camera, squinting at the sun; some children skiing; a young child making faces at a kitchen table; a girl dressed in bunad;[7] a skater falling over; a boy in a yellow jumper racing around on his tricycle. The memories shared on the voice-over turn from descriptive to more reflective, focusing on things related to Oslo, what was felt in the moment, and what this has come to mean since: 'I remember we moved to Bislett . . . we felt extremely mature', 'I remember how free I felt the first time I came to Oslo. Then I realised how small Oslo is', and 'I remember every football match that I've ever played since I was six years old, and they were all with friends that I still have today, and that is because I am from Oslo'.[8]

Next comes a series of memories that feel more personal and emotional, a feeling that is enhanced by the fact that the accompanying images appear in a more rapid succession: 'I remember his laughter', 'I remember the way her hair smelled when we'd been to the beach', and then, a bit later, 'I remember being sad'. Last, but not least, this montage contains a few reflections on the nature, or character, of memory itself: 'I don't recall, I don't remember Oslo as such, it's people I remember', 'That was the last time I saw him', 'I remember how he insisted "melancholic" was a cooler word than "nostalgic"', and, finally: 'I remember thinking "I'll remember this"'.

In interviews, Joachim Trier will often offer similar reflections on what memories are, and what it really means to remember. On several occasions, he has shared a specific recollection from his own childhood: 'I remember, as a child, being really preoccupied with memories...When I was like five, in nursery, I have this really clear memory of this moment where I'm sitting on a tricycle, and I'm thinking: oh, I've decided to remember this. This will be a memory.'[9] This acknowledgement, by a child, that the moment being experienced will not exist in the future but can be carried forth in the form of a memory, has been influential, Trier believes, on his work as a filmmaker: 'I think that experience of the importance of remembering ties in with filmmaking'.[10]

The prologue of *Oslo, August 31st* combines that very memory – a boy on his tricycle (shown) – with musings on what it is to remember (spoken). This type of contrast between what we are seeing and hearing – someone talking about one thing while the images on the screen show something else – is, as we shall see, a recurring feature of Trier's films.

Figure 1.1 The Frogner Baths in winter. From the prologue of *Oslo, August 31st*.

Much can be said of this prologue, which only vaguely relates to the film's protagonist, Anders (Anders Danielsen Lie). We do see places in the prologue that he will visit during his day in Oslo, most notable the open-air swimming pool Frognerbadet (The Frogner Baths). But *Oslo, August 31st* is not explicitly about childhood, or youth, nor an Oslo that no longer exists. The film follows Anders through a day and a night, the last day of summer, and his first overnight stay outside of the rehab facility he is an in-patient at. What should be the first day of his new, sober life, ends up being his last.

Twenty-four hours, from sunup on the 30th of August until sunup on the 31st, is condensed into what feels like the past, present, and future combined. The past is present through the people – relations from his life before – Anders meets (but also fails to get in touch with) throughout the day. We first see him after a rather unsuccessful date with an ex-girlfriend (Malin), and we then watch him make an unsuccessful suicide attempt and have an unsuccessful job interview. We tag along as he moves through Oslo, going to see an old, close friend (Thomas), attending a party at the home of another friend and ex-partner (Mirjam), meeting up with an acquaintance (Petter) and partying on with him. He meets a new girl (Johanne) and attempts three times to reach another ex-girlfriend (Iselin) on the phone. He is rejected by his sister, who does not wish to see him and sends her girlfriend (Tove) in her place. The people closest to him (Iselin, his sister, and his parents) are the ones he cannot reach.[11] In contrast to the prologue, the rest of the film is, above all else, a here-and-now kind of story, told chronologically throughout the day, with no retrospection to explain how Anders ended up where he is when we see him.

There is one important exception to this: At one point, the film is visually in the present – Anders heading through Oslo, on his way to his childhood home – while the soundtrack looks back in time – Anders talking, or thinking, about what his parents were like, what their values were, what they taught him. One of these memories that we can hear him narrate is: 'They were both from Oslo and had memories from the places we'd walk past'. Anders's personal history and private recollection is thus tied, both visually and auditorily, to the collective chorus of the prologue, a connection that is strengthened by Olav Fløttum's music, which is present in both sequences.

This very connection, between individual and collective memory, is often highlighted when theorists discuss cinema as the medium of memories.[12] A film can simultaneously follow a single person (Anders) having their personal memories, and show us a collective space (Oslo) filled with and tied to the memories of many people. Anders's journey throughout the city takes him down old roads and back to old haunts, but it is a look at it through new (sober) eyes. The city space is shared, collective, but the images of Anders in its streets and parks show him looking very alone and private, even as he is surrounded by people. His loneliness and isolation are made especially poignant in a scene, early on, in which he exits a café where he has been sitting and listening to the lives and dreams of others. To Anders, Oslo is a place full of memories, but unlike the people whose voices he can hear all around, he has no visions of any kind of future.

The film draws a close connection between memories and places, a connection most notably demonstrated in the opening. In his discussion on the connection between memory and the architecture of Oslo in *Oslo, August 31st*, Benjamin Bigelow claims that 'Oslo is depicted as a memory-saturated space where the canon of active memory is constantly reshaped and maintained, just as urban space is the site of a never-ending renewal project. Anders's return is marked by nostalgia and melancholy.'[13] When film scholar Claire Thomson writes about how Trier's films deal with memory, she opens with her own recollections of Oslo, its icy winter streets, the cold, the fjord, the colours, and the hills surrounding the city.[14] As Birgit Neuman puts it when describing how literature depicts memory:

> Fictions of memory may exploit the representation of space as a symbolic manifestation of individual or collective memories. Space may not only provide a cue triggering individual, often repressed, past experiences; it may also conjure up innumerable echoes and undertones of a community's past.[15]

As such, the film not only looks back on a time before Anders inhabited Oslo, but also features several nostalgic moments of him retracing his own steps there, walking streets and paths that he has walked before. As the title itself suggests, in *Oslo, August 31st* memory is tied closely not just to place but to time. The final day of summer is, particularly to people in places where a change of seasons means a great change in conditions, itself a moment evocative of nostalgia. And so the title carries with it a notion of something coming to an end, of the summer that was.

Nostalgia can, as per Svetlana Boym's definition, be described as 'a sentiment of loss and displacement' and 'a longing for a home that no longer exists or has never existed'.[16] More than longing for a place, nostalgia is a longing for another time, Boym asserts, and, though it often is, that time does not strictly have to be behind us. The feeling of nostalgia is, unlike melancholy, anchored in and caused by something concrete, and it is often tied up with identity, both on an individual and a collective level. Definitions of what constitutes a memory often focus on both the temporal aspect (something about the past), and the very process of remembering.[17] In daily usage we tend to use the two terms in much the same way. Summer is coming to an end, but Anders's life is also coming to a close. The melancholy mood Bigelow describes in his analysis of *Oslo, August 31st* does, however, I'd argue, not fully strike until the end of the film. Here, the prologue and main story are tied together through an epilogue.

At the dawn of this final day, Anders, having returned to his childhood home which his family is in the process of leaving (as the result of drug-related debts), deliberately overdoses. Following his death, the film moves, in reverse chronological order, through all the places he has been during the previous twenty-four hours: his parents' house, the Frogner Baths, Mirjam's balcony, the exterior of the café he visited, the bench where he sat with Thomas, his room in the rehab facility, the lake where he attempted to end his life, the hotel room where we first encountered him. The film's final image is of the open window in this dark bedroom, capturing the balance between light and darkness that makes this film both devastating and comforting. The sun rises on a new day in Oslo (the 31st of August), but it is a day without Anders.[18]

This closing sequence, with the empty spaces, seems to paraphrase the closing scene of Richard Linklater's *Before Sunrise* (1995), in which the places visited by lovers Jesse and Celine (Ethan Hawke and Julie Delpy) during the one day they spent together in Vienna are left empty, without them, as the sun rises. *Before Sunrise* is also a film about a city, and about loss and missed opportunities; although the goodbye here is less final – as the two characters, though separated, will live on with the memories of the day they spent together.[19] In *Oslo, August 31st*, the images in the epilogue also become depictions of the memories created in the viewer, and though the spaces look empty, the audience fills them in with their recollections of Anders, of a life that was. Similarly, the film becomes a collection of memories of Oslo as it was. Watching it now, more than a decade on and after it has become part of a trilogy (together with *Reprise* and *The Worst Person in the World*), the ways in which the city has already changed again become evident, and this, too, incites a sense of nostalgia.

Figure 1.2 The Frogner Baths in summer. From the epilogue of *Oslo, August 31st*.

Trier employs this same move – flashbacks revisiting important places from the film but with an important character missing – in *Thelma*, though this time to a different effect. The 2017 film represents a change in style for Trier: it is a plot-driven and spectacular genre movie, existing somewhere in the space between thriller, horror, and coming-of-age story, with supernatural elements and an erotic mood. Above all else, it stands out from the rest of

Trier's filmography in how it is told. Horror scholar Christer Bakke Andresen describes it as 'a plot-conscious psychological horror movie'.[20] *Thelma* is structured chronologically, with some exceptions to this, the most important of which are three crucial jumps back to when the eponymous character was six years old. Here, we are not talking about bittersweet moments of nostalgic retrospection, but of painful memories that are traumatic, even when they are repressed.

This film tells the story of a shy young student, Thelma (Eili Harboe), who has just left her over-protective religious parents (Henrik Rafaelsen and Ellen Dorrit Petersen) and small hometown in the south-west of Norway behind, and moved to Oslo to study biology. While working in the study hall at the university centre at Blindern, she unexpectedly experiences what looks like a violent epileptic seizure, and is sent for medical evaluation. Under much emotional stress (emancipating herself from her parents, starting her new life as a student, seemingly suffering from some unknown medical condition), she meets Anja (Kaya Wilkins), to whom she is immediately deeply attracted. Falling in love with a girl adds to her anxiety (or even causes it), as this goes against both her own and her parents' values. With her background, Thelma cannot permit herself to act on such feelings, and Anja already has a boyfriend. We learn that there is 'something wrong' with Thelma; not only does she experience fits, she apparently has psychokinetic powers that enable her to draw Anja towards her (both emotionally and literally), but that also, unbeknownst to her, caused her little brother's death many years earlier, when she was only six.

Thelma undergoes a series of examinations in hospital, and her doctor tells her that to find the source of her seizures and make a diagnosis, their tests will have to take her some uncomfortable places. During an EEG test, hooked up to several sensors measuring her brain activity and reactions, Thelma is asked whether she can remember anything from what her chart describes as a breakdown that happened when she was six years old. She says she does not, and no reaction is detected. Thelma not recalling anything about her brother's death (or her mother's subsequent suicide attempt) suggests that her memories have been repressed.

The doctor instructs her to 'think of something painful' and she thinks of Anja. Her memories of sharing a bed with her love interest, touching Anja's hair, and kissing her, flash past. And with them comes a powerful epilepsy-like seizure. The scene depicting Thelma's seizure is crosscut with one showing Anja mysteriously disappearing from her flat. If we choose to understand this film literally, that is, to accept, that is, that Thelma has some form of psychokinetic ability, it follows that her thoughts, or more precisely her memories, are what cause Anja to disappear.[21] Anja's disappearance is followed by images of the rooms where she and Thelma saw each other (the lecture theatre, the study hall, the library), but this time without Anja in them. Each image is held for a shorter amount of time than the similar ones in *Oslo, August 31st*, and while the spaces left behind by Anders are serene, Anja leaves a void that is unsettled.

Because we are watching a thriller, there is tension and excitement in not knowing what has happened, whether Anja is dead or could possibly return. Anja's disappearance is one of the film's most intense scenes, one that, aided by music and strobe lights, incites a sense of dread or terror in the viewer.[22] The audience is, as such, likely to experience the memory sequences in these two films quite differently. The images of the voids left by Anja in those rooms appear to be Thelma's memories, though we do share in her discomfort and anxiety. But the voids left by Anders feel like our own memories, and though we feel sad for him, we also experience a more general, existential sense of loss.

Both *Oslo, August 31st* and *Thelma* can be seen as films about attempting to forget the things that hurt us. But while memories in *Oslo, August 31st* come in both good and bad varieties, in *Thelma* they are more or less unequivocally bad. Anders has things he prefers not to think about; Thelma has memories she has repressed entirely. The thought that she as a little girl could have deliberately caused her little brother's death, and as a young adult caused Anja's, through the power of her mind, is utterly unbearable. The plot centres on the repression of very specific bad memories, but *Thelma* can also be interpreted as a story about the need to free oneself from a traumatic past more generally and universally. And in this film, memories and flashbacks also function as important plot devices. Thelma's buried memories (her brother drowning under the ice, her parents believing that she deliberately moved him there with her mind power, her mother attempting to kill herself) are kept hidden from the audience, and thus become a tool with which Trier can create suspense.[23]

Though a sense of uncertainty is present in both places – can we or can we not believe what we are seeing? – the different memories depicted in the film do function differently. In the case of Thelma's childhood memories, the uncertainty makes us potentially less willing to trust and sympathise with her. Did she, intentionally or not, kill her brother? The memories of Anja that Thelma actively tries to repress, on the other hand, are used to make us connect and empathise with her.

For several of Trier's characters, memories and trauma are closely connected, and the notion that memories can hurt runs through all his films. In *Louder Than Bombs*, *Reprise*, and *The Worst Person in the World*, too, they are tied to something that is lost and gone. These films show us attempts at keeping the memories of a mother who has passed away alive, efforts to revive a relationship long lost, and the struggle to hold on to life itself. In all three cases, though, the goal is to retain rather than to banish the memories. They show memories as precious and important.

Memory is less present in *The Worst Person in the World* than in Trier's other works, and on the whole, it is a film that feels in the present. Still, there are elements of looking back, most notably represented by the voice-over narrator introduced in the prologue, but also by one of the film's most moving scenes. *The Worst Person in the World* follows Julie (Renate Reinsve) through a handful of years just before and just after she turns thirty. She has yet to find (or figure out) exactly what she wants in terms of an education, a career, or a partner. She falls for cartoonist Aksel (Anders Danielsen Lie), a decade her senior, and moves into his flat, but when she meets Eivind (Herbert Nordrum), who is her own age, at a party, she falls in love again and leaves Aksel for him. Aksel later receives a terminal cancer diagnosis, and Julie comes to see him at the hospital. They share an emotional and nostalgic conversation, and Aksel talks about how he now only looks backwards. He describes how important cultural objects have been to him: VHS tapes, vinyl records, and comic books. He remembers what the shops he used to go to looked like, what it felt like to sift through stacks of comics or records: 'Now it is all that I have left. Knowledge and memories of stupid, futile things nobody cares about'. He says in jest that it is only natural for a person dying of cancer to be looking back, but then the gravity of the situation overtakes him:

> In recent years. I reached a point in life when suddenly . . . it just happened. When. . . I began to worship what had been. And now I have nothing else. I have no future. I can only look back. It's not even nostalgia. It's fear of death. It's because I'm scared.

Figure 1.3 Aksel reflects on how, towards the end of his life, he is only looking backwards in time.

Not only does this scene function as an emotional peak in Julie and Aksel's story, it also strikes right at the heart of the existential questions present in all of Trier's works. As he says himself in the interview he gave for this book, when talking about which films are worth making: 'It's got to be about something existential, some greater ideas – time, identity, existence'.[24]

Even when Trier directs adverts, these great, existential questions shine through.[25] In *Reversed Life*, made for the Norwegian bank Sparebank 1 (2006), we see a person being buried alive, while a voice-over says, 'First you are nothing, then you are born, then you take your first steps.' We see an old man, in a home, with a walker, and now the soundtrack and the images move in opposite directions, through a human life. On the soundtrack, this life is told chronologically, while the images show it in reverse. This short advert is almost a more extreme version of *Oslo, August 31st's* epilogue. Discussing literary depictions of memory, Birgit Neuman writes that just such breaks with and shifts between different temporal levels are typical of how authors attempt to convey the nature of memory: 'The constitutive characteristic of all fictions of memory is therefore their operating with co-present time perspectives: The multi-temporal levels of the past and the present intermingle in manifold and complex ways'.[26]

This is a common way of describing memory. When someone looks back upon their life – at the end of it, for instance – the various memories are unlikely to arrange themselves neatly and chronologically like pearls on a string. As we have seen, Trier explores memory in all his films, but he also explores cinema's ability to portray how memories work, not least through intermingling the past and present in complex ways. While the examples I have provided so far are relatively conventional in their use of flashbacks and voice-overs, Trier is much more experimental in the last two films that I will discuss here. I will also pursue both how he structures his narratives and his use of voice-over later on in this book. Both *Reprise* and *Louder Than Bombs* feature memory sequences that blend past and present, real and false memories, and showcase Trier's interest in exploring the narrative possibilities of his medium.

In *Reprise*, promising young novelist Phillip (Anders Danielsen Lie) goes to extreme lengths to recreate his memories from when he and his ex-girlfriend Kari (Victoria Winge) visited Paris while freshly in love. While the film centres on the relationship between Phillip and Erik (Espen Klouman Høiner) and their dream of becoming celebrated novelists, the relationship between Phillip and Kari is also of vital importance. Phillip's quest for this reprise stems from the fact that he cannot accept that the relationship is over, and now a mere memory. In the year following their trip, he has been severely mentally ill, hospitalised for psychosis, and instructed by his doctor not to see Kari at all. But in an attempt to find his way back to what they once had, Phillip takes her back to Paris, where he tries to reconstruct every single thing that they did, down to the most minute detail: they travel on the same date, stay in the same hotel, he wants to take the same photos, with her posing in the same ways, and for them to have the same conversations and sex at the same times. At first, he is struggling to remember, and asks Kari: 'What did we do the next day?', 'What was the weather like?', 'What did we talk about?', 'What was I like?', 'Was I happy?' 'Don't you remember?' she responds. 'Sure', is his less than convincing answer. And yet he is the one chasing the reconstruction, a reprise of the happiness, the infatuation, the sex. Such desperate attempts to recapture lost time, lost affection, are of course doomed to fail. When Phillip nit-picks Kari's posing in the Jardin du Luxembourg, she says that sitting the way he wants her to is uncomfortable. But the root of her discomfort lies elsewhere, and after an attempt to recreate the first time they had sex, she ends up crying on the toilet. As Audun Engelstad puts it:

> Phillip's attempt to replicate the actions of the past shows with utmost clarity that even if a repeated series of events takes place with great precision, the experience and emotions cannot be replicated. This becomes obvious when Phillip counts down from ten to zero. This exercise is an attempt to freeze a moment, a golden flash of time in which something specific happens. Such a moment is impossible to replicate except in memory or the imagination.[27]

But still, I argue, such attempts to freeze a moment is a recurring goal for Trier himself.

Trier uses his technique of the places with and without the main characters in *Reprise* too, but in this case, the absent/present dichotomy has been turned

Figure 1.4 Phillip and Kari negotiating their memories of their relationship.

on its head. We first see the Paris locations Kari and Phillip visited before, and then we see the pair in those places. In parts of this sequence, the past and present blur together somewhat. When Kari sits on the bed and removes her bra, we cannot easily recognise whether that is a flashback in Anders's memory, or part of his actual reconstruction. The pair do not remember everything in the same way either, because that is how people are. Different people will have different recollections of the same event. And so the reconstruction of a memory can also become a debate – or a negotiation – about what is true.

This is the case in *Louder Than Bombs*, where three people also remember their mutual past differently: this film depicts an American east-coast family, comprising father Gene (Gabriel Byrne), a former actor turned high school teacher, and his two sons. Jonah (Jesse Eisenberg) is around thirty and teaches sociology at a university in another state; Conrad (Devin Druid) lives with Gene and is a student at the high school where his father works. Their mother was world-famous press photographer Isabelle Reed (Isabelle Huppert), and she died three years before the story takes place. This film is about living on after a mother and spouse has passed away. We might say that Isabelle is only present in it as a memory, or more accurately as memories, that are different in the minds of the three bereaved. This is shown mainly through a series of flashbacks, in which Isabelle appears with each of the three men. We get particularly familiar with youngest son Conrad's memories, and these are slightly more intricately told.

One scene stands out as a particularly subtle exploration of what memories can be – both in the context of Trier's own filmography and in film history more generally. We are with Conrad in his high school classroom, listening as Melanie (Ruby Jerins), the girl he has a crush on, reads from a novel.[28] She reads about a man who appears to be drowning, about his thoughts in his final moments, and how they do not turn to important memories from his life: 'Instead his thoughts travelled to the other reach of his memories, small events long forgotten. He remembered a sentence he had read in a newspaper a few days ago and did not understand.' As she keeps reading, we see Conrad's gaze move away from Melanie, his attention pulled into the world of his own thoughts. The narrator says: 'He thought about an old suitcase in his uncle's attic. A brief glimpse from a stranger', and then we are shown what we understand to be Conrad's mental images. These could be memories or pure imagination. Along with the description of the very moment of death in the novel – 'Seconds that were not seconds anymore but stretched out to minutes. Time suspended' – Conrad's thoughts go to his mother, and to her final moments. He imagines her driving at night, falling asleep behind the wheel and hitting a lorry head on. The line from the book is repeated, and Isabelle's drive is repeated, but this time Isabelle crashes because she is swerving to avoid a deer. In the moment of her death, the narration changes into: 'What could she have been thinking. What went through her mind when she realised the accident was unavoidable', and we see an extreme close-up of Isabelle's eye, her gaze on the headlights rushing towards her. The impact, the glass shattering, Isabelle being thrown forward – these are all shown in slow motion. 'She remembered lying on the beach.' A close-up of an arm on a sandy beach. 'Dozing off, feeling the wind blow and grains of sand on her face. Thinking that if she lay still long enough it would end up covering her.' Glass hitting her face in slow motion. We hear 'Maybe she remembered places. The house. Our hallway. The living room', and see Conrad's image of their home. Again we see empty spaces, like the spaces Anja and Anders left. Again, memory is tied to place, and the missing to empty spaces, voids. 'Maybe she even thought of him, some little thing. Something he himself had forgotten. He was hiding. Listening to her calling out his name'. We see images of a small boy hiding behind sheets hung out to dry in the garden. He is clearly visible, but his mother pretends not to find him.[29] Conrad smiles to himself in the classroom as he remembers and learns something new by revisiting the memory.

Compared to the other depictions of memory I have highlighted, this is a much more complex and sophisticated scene.[30] There are these subtle shifts in who the narration is referring to: first it recounts the final moments of a nameless, unknown character in a novel, but then the very same voice-over ends up being about Conrad too, or perhaps *just* about him. Conrad certainly feels that the text is about him, and that the words follow his visual imaginings. Finally, there is a pronoun shift, making the narrator's subject a woman rather than a man, just as we are seeing Conrad's mental images of his mother's death.

Moreover, this short (three-minute) sequence consists of a series of internal images that are very different in character. Conrad's stream of consciousness includes everything from fantasies and musings on an old suitcase to ruminations on his mother's death and memories of playing hide and seek with her when he was a little boy. There are also his visions of what he thinks she might have remembered at the time of her death. This scene thus captures something crucial about collective memories. Memories are not strictly personal things, but when different people share experiences, their memories of them are not identical either. They are shaped by each person's respective perspective. Both Conrad and his mother may remember the game of hide and seek, but while he remembers her not seeing him, she might remember doing so, but pretending not to find him. When Conrad revisits this memory, in the presence of the film, he realises her ruse. 'He realised now she must have seen him, all the time he was just standing there, she just pretended not to'. And if he is to re-remember it again, his memory will have changed.

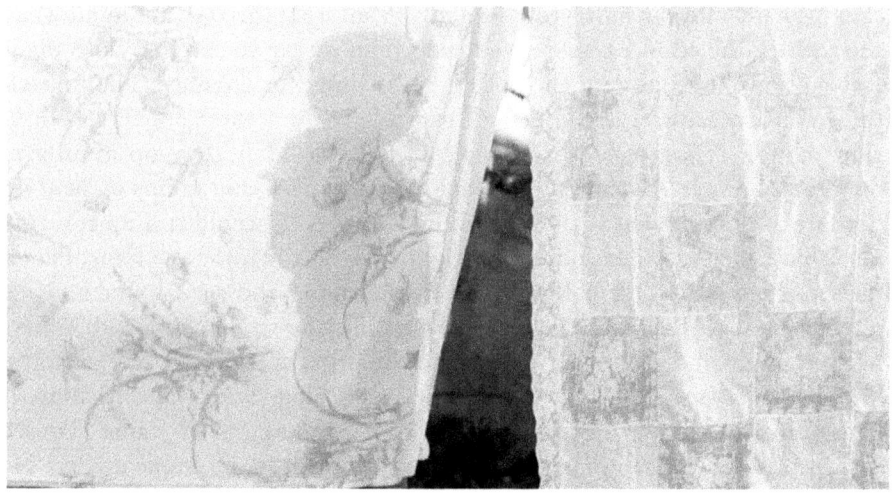

Figure 1.5 Conrad's memory of playing hide and seek and hiding from his mother.

Figure 1.6 Isabelle pretending not to see Conrad.

This scene can also be read as a meta-depiction of how a person's inner reality, and particularly their memories, can be depicted. The novel being read out is itself about how memory will jump from one thing to the next. The fictional novel excerpt displays a stream-of-consciousness technique (and deals with subject matter) found in the works of modernist writers like Virginia Woolf and James Joyce. Here, the film also visualises how certain words can trigger concrete images in us, and how a person's train of thought can itself present as a visual montage.

Both the text of the novel and the cinematic montage here thus approach modernist modes of expression, both in literature and in cinema. inspirations from film history for exploring memories the way he does with Conrad's memory revisited:

> So there's that sense of sliding time and association, the way the mind works. It's that kind of more fragmented, but more real, way the mind works. They're movies of the mind. *Hiroshima mon amour* is a great example, or Tarkovsky's *The Mirror (1975)* – time and time again you get into the phenomenology of memory, like how the mind perceives the past and the present in a very jumbled way, which you can do in literature as well, but cinema has its own way of doing that.[31]

There are a few ways to understand what the director means by 'cinema's own way' here. But the ease with which film can make jumps back and forwards in time has perhaps made us take such moves for granted. It is inherent to cinema's way of telling stories that you can move seamlessly between different places in time and space. As put by Susannah Radstone:

> The cinema's long-standing and intimate relationship with memory is revealed in cinema language's adoption of terms associated with memory – the 'flashback' and the 'fade', for instance – to describe cinematic dissolves between a film narrative's present and its past. The routinized deployment of these terms has rendered them unremarkable, suggesting an apparently automatic, involuntary, and mechanical relationship between cinema and memory.[32]

But Trier exploits the inherent possibilities in his medium far beyond this. In his exploration of memory and how cinema can express what that is, what memories are, Neuman's term of 'intermingling' when talking about memories seems apt.[33] Trier employs different techniques to blend past and present in the different films.

We see this in *Reprise,* for example, when Kari and Phillip are strolling through Paris, talking about what they can recall: here images of the past and present intermingle. Or we get an intermingling of words and images, where the images we see and the words we hear are out of sync. When we hear Kari talking about what they did at one point, we see the estranged lovers sitting at a café table, in silence. When Conrad is in the classroom, the external words from the novel Melanie is reading intermingle with his own mental images, which in turn merge with and evolve into something else.

In Thomson's words 'his films stage an encounter with the temporal sublime and the undecidability of memory'.[34] This is not incorrect, but in a way the opposite occurs in Trier's films as well: he is able to capture the concreteness of memory. Memories can be vague and uncertain, but they can also adhere to us as fixed images that never let go. Like when geeky, lonely Conrad – on the very night he learns his mother took her own life – gets to take a drunk Melanie home.[35] In the midst of his loss and longing, he experiences a moment of intimacy, one that, though it does not give him any hope of getting to be with the most popular girl in school, becomes a crucial memory for him. Here, too, Trier makes an original move by letting Melanie have a voice-over over the shots of the two walking home in the dark:

> He could still, many years from now, recall the scene in odd detail, the lock of hair she carefully placed behind her ear, the way the washing label stuck out from the neck of her tank top, the streetlight that went out as they passed Kevin Anderson's house, that strangely familiar smell of damp earth he could not quite place.

The voice-over is both retrospective and contemporary. Melanie's voice is coming to us from a future of sorts, though she still sounds like a teenager, and as such, the timescale here is unclear. But the moment is fixed: the hair behind her ear, the lights coming off and the sun rising – those things are there to stay. Neuman writes about the 'mimesis of memory' when discussing literature's narrative forms and aesthetic techniques and claims that:

> literary texts stage and reflect the workings of memory. Rather than indicating a mimetic quality of literature, the term points to its productive quality: Novels do not imitate existing versions of memory, but produce, in the act of discourse, that very past which they purport to describe'.[36]

So it is also with Trier's films. They are not pure imitations or renderings of memories; they rather stage and reflect on the working of memory. Thus, they are both explorations of what memories are and of how cinema can capture or convey them. With Joachim Trier, cinema truly becomes an art of remembering. An aesthetics of memories can, as Trier's films demonstrate, be about both moments and movements. It is the frozen time and the unique moment captured, as well as the flow of time and the series of events that forms the past conveyed. When I say that memories and remembering are at the core of Trier's films, I am implicitly saying that his films are about time; and I will pursue this in this next chapter.

NOTES

1. Hillary Weston, 'The Art Form of Memory: A Conversation with Joachim Trier', The Criterion Collection, 8 April 2016, https://www.criterion.com/current/posts/4001-the-art-form-of-memory-a-conversation-with-joachim-trier.

2. Susannah Radstone, 'Cinema and Memory', in *Memory. Histories Theories, Debates*, ed. Susannah Radstone and Bill Schwarz (New York: Fordham University Press, 2010), 325–42, https://www.jstor.org/stable/j.ctt1c999bq.26. See also Chapter 7 below.
3. Radstone, 'Cinema and Memory', 326.
4. Throughout the book I will use the English subtitles from DVD editions to render the dialogue: when the subtitles fail to capture everything that I want to discuss, I will add information about this.
5. One of these clips is from the film *Remonstrance* (1972), made by Trier's grandfather, Erik Løchen. It is one of the most experimental works in Norwegian film history, and consists of three sections designed to be played in random order. The film is considered a classic today.
6. Son is a smaller place by the Oslofjord.
7. Bunad is a term for the Norwegian national costume, found in different regional variations, and often used in formal settings and celebrations.
8. This statement has been lightly edited for clarity. I have also added some quotations or words that were not included in the subtitles here.
9. Vegard Larsen, 'Joachim Trier', *Drivkraft*, 12 October 2021; Weston, 'The Art Form of Memory'. See also Epilogue.
10. Larsen, 'Joachim Trier'.
11. As pointed out by co-writer Eskil Vogt in the published version of the script (2011), except for his close friend Thomas, Anders never gets close to the people who actually mean something to him. His ex-girlfriend Iselin is not only on another continent, she never even picks up the phone. His parents are out of town, and his sister sends her girlfriend to meet him in her place. Breiteig, Bjarte, Eskil Vogt, and Joachim Trier 'Oslo, gjennom mørkt glass – Eskil Vogt og Joachim Trier i samtale med Bjarte Breiteig', In Eskil Vogt and Joachim Trier, *Osloo, 31 august*. Filmmanus. Oslo: Tiden Norsk Forlag, 2011, 177.
12. See, for instance, Radstone, 'Cinema and Memory'.
13. Benjamin Bigelow, 'Acts of Remembering, Acts of Forgetting: Architecture, Memory and Recovery in Oslo, August 31st', *Journal of Scandinavian Cinema* 10, no. 1 (1 March 2020): 7–24 at 13, https://doi.org/10.1386/jsca_00011_1, 13.
14. C. Claire Thomson, 'Louder Than Films: Memory, Affect and the "Sublime Image" in the Work of Joachim Trier', *Arts* 8, no. 2 (2019), https://doi.org/10.3390/arts8020055.
15. Birgit Neumann, 'The Literary Representation of Memory', in Astrid Erll and Ansgar Nünning (eds), *Cultural Memory Studies: An International and Interdisciplinary Handbook* (Berlin: De Gruyter, 2008), 333–43; at 340.
16. Svetlana Boym, *The Future of Nostalgia* (New York: Basic Books, 2001), 15.
17. See, for instance, Merriam Webster's definition: https://www.merriam-webster.com/dictionary/memory .
18. The scene with Julie in *The Worst Person in the World*, looking at the sunrise after walking the streets the night her ex-partner Aksel dies, seems also like an echo of this.
19. Linklater went on to also make the sequels *Before Sunset* (2004) and *Before Midnight* (2013) about Jesse and Celine and their reunion in the first sequel and their marriage in the last section of the trilogy.

20. Christer Bakke Andresen, *Norwegian Nightmares: The Horror Cinema of a Nordic Country* (Edinburgh University Press, 2022), 93.
21. See also Anders Lysne, 'Manifestations of Dread in Thelma', *Journal of Scandinavian Cinema* 9, no. 2 (1 June 2019): 235–9, https://doi.org/10.1386/jsca.9.2.235_1; Christer Bakke Andresen, 'Thelma: Empathic Engagement and the Norwegian Horror Cinema', *Journal of Scandinavian Cinema* 9, no. 2 (1 June 2019): 227–33, https://doi.org/10.1386/jsca.9.2.227_1; Bakke Andresen, *Norwegian Nightmares*.
22. Lysne, 'Manifestations of Dread in Thelma'; Bakke Andresen, 'Thelma'.
23. One take could be that these flashbacks did not happen at all, but that is not how I see it.
24. See Epilogue, 149.
25. See Eino Aleksander Kerr, *Minner og melankoli en auteurstudie av den norske filmskaperen Joachim Trier* (Trondheim, Institutt for kunst og medievitenskap, NTNU, 2013), for analyses of his advertising work.
26. Neumann, 'The Literary Representation of Memory', 336.
27. Audun Engelstad, 'The Concept of Time in Joachim Trier's Reprise', *Journal of Scandinavian Cinema* 9, no. 2 (1 June 2019): 197–202, https://doi.org/10.1386/jsca.9.2.197_1, 201.
28. This is a fictitious novel; the extract we hear was written by Eskil Vogt.
29. See also Dag Sødtholt, 'Louder Than Bombs: Joachim Trier's Play on Perspective', *Montages International Edition*, 16 January 2016, http://montagesmagazine.com/2016/01/louder-than-bombs-joachim-triers-play-on-perspective/.
30. See also Jørgen Bruhn and Anne Gjelsvik, *Cinema Between Media: An Intermediality Approach* (Edinburgh: University Press, 2018); Sødtholt, 'Louder Than Bombs'.
31. Weston, 'The Art Form of Memory.
32. Radstone, 'Cinema and Memory', 326.
33. Neumann, 'The Literary Representation of Memory'.
34. Thomson, 'Louder Than Films', 1.
35. See Sødtholt, 'Louder Than Bombs', for a Freudian reading of the relation between Melanie and Conrad's mother.
36. Neumann, 'The Literary Representation of Memory', 334.

CHAPTER 2

Fractured Narratives

The Oscar nomination for Best Original Screenplay that Trier, along with steady cowriter Eskil Vogt, received for *The Worst Person in the World* in 2021 was one of the highlights of his career to date. The Academy of Motion Picture Arts and Sciences rarely nominate scripts not written in English, and practically never scripts written in one of the Scandinavian languages. Ingmar Bergman (five nominations) and Ruben Östlund (nominated for *Triangle of Sadness* (2022) the year after Trier and Vogt) are the only other scriptwriters on that most exclusive list.[1] Upon his somewhat surprising nomination, Trier stated that he was proud of the work he and Vogt had done on the script and 'the intimacy that we achieved in the long dialogue scenes', but that he had also sought 'to counter it aesthetically with montage sequences, like the acid trip, and when Julie freezes time. This is cinema to me. It's to combine strange things that don't necessarily fit together.'[2]

As the various chapters of this book will show, it is just this mixing of different forms and styles – a realist focus on dialogue and believable characters; visually striking individual scenes and set pieces; the modernist exploration of cinematic language – that makes Joachim Trier stand out in Norwegian and international contemporary cinema. It is, accordingly, a little tricky to sum up his aesthetics in just a few words or features. The one shining exception is perhaps his creative iterations of the montage. These are incredibly important to Trier, as illustrated by the fact that the very first example I chose to discuss in this book was just one such montage – the prologue of *Oslo, August 31st*. A Trier film typically opens with a prologue, often one set outside the timeline of the film. Sometimes the prologue is itself a montage, sometimes it is immediately followed by one, typically of a fast-paced, innovative sort.

The melding of old images and new voices in *Oslo, August 31st* is, though original, far from the most radical example of a Trier montage. *Reprise, The Worst Person in the World*, and *Louder Than Bombs* all go much further with the technique, and these are the films I will be focusing on in this chapter. Trier's creative use of montage is founded on at least two important principles: his desire to explore and experiment with the relationship between film and time, and his interest in his medium's ability to depict people's inner realities. These concepts are both highly important in Trier's filmography, and of course closely related to his interest in memory, highlighted in the previous chapter.

This chapter will look at four examples of the Trier montage: the openings of *Reprise* and *The Worst Person in the World,* and two other central montages, one from *Louder Than Bombs* and another also from *The Worst Person in the World.* Trier's opening montages are effective tools for telling us not only what has happened before the film starts (as in *The Worst Person in the World*), but also for musing on what might happen in the future (as in *Reprise*). Montages are, in other words, a highly efficient form of narration, one that is able to depict or recount the events of longer stretches of time in a condensed way. But they may also be used for other narrative purposes, like painting a brief portrait of a character, telling the same story from multiple perspectives, establishing a tone or mood, or reflecting on a certain theme.

The latter two of these apply to the prologue in *Oslo, August 31st* – it is a tone-setting doorway into remembering, and into specific memories of Oslo. All of Trier's montages work almost as embedded mini narratives within the films and Trier has himself referred to them as 'micro-ballads'.[3] He has also repeatedly described how he conceives of the structure of a film like that of a hit album.[4] As an example: 'You know, I come from the hip hop world, I think my films are like an album – song after song, kind of dynamic; and sequences are songs, short elements that create the story'.[5] Trier's narrative montages characteristically also make elaborate use of different art forms (music, photography, cartoons, and so on) in combination with voice-overs. This also makes them an interesting tool for sharing the inner thoughts of his characters.

Here, I will look at Trier's innovative use of montage in context with his affinity for non-chronological structures, most developed in *Reprise* and *Louder Than Bombs*. As I touched on in the previous chapter, Trier is preoccupied with the ways in which the human perception of time is non-linear, and how 'the mind perceives the past and the present in a very jumbled way'.[6] This kind of exploration of how time can be expressed and represented in cinema is in line with Trier's modernist inspirations, and it is, as pointed out by others, at the very core of what distinguishes him as a filmmaker.[7] Trier's films, and *Louder Than Bombs* in particular, use an intricate blend of temporal layers in ways that are clearly indebted to modernist cinema. In my discussion here, I will focus on how these time shifts, together with the montages, create a mix of past, present, and future, a mix I call fractured narratives.

A film narrative can of course be constructed in countless ways, and the structure of a story will necessarily affect how we experience it. A reductive way of putting things might be to say that the classical narrative feature film (often called the Hollywood model) is plot-oriented, and has characters acting based on specific, clear motivations. It is structured clearly and linearly, often in three acts and with a chain of events leading to narrative closure. This kind of linear structure is often built on causality and chronology (though this is not an absolute rule). The film's relationship with time, both in terms of order and duration, can take several forms, but we will typically see the duration of the image correspond to the duration of the represented event – though this can be manipulated through the use of pauses, slow- or fast-motion.[8] How a film structures time in the sense of ordering the past, present, and future is more important. Breaking up a chronological narrative with something like a flashback is common enough, but audiences will generally have no trouble arranging the chain of events of a mainstream film in chronological time themselves.

Trier's most traditionally told and plot-driven film, *Thelma*, is a good example of a film that breaks with a strictly linear, chronological structure, but is still easy to follow. This film, too, opens with a prologue: a flashback to when Thelma was six years old and out hunting with her father in a Nordic winter landscape. They spot a deer; Thelma freezes and remains motionless, waiting for her father to take the shot. While she watches the deer, we see him, behind her, aim the rifle at her head. He changes his mind at the last second, sighs heavily and does not fire.

Following this prologue, we meet the now grown-up Thelma *in medias res* as a young woman who has left home to study in Oslo. We are soon made to understand that she suffers from some ailment causing what looks like epileptic seizures. The flashback prologue makes the viewer's first encounter with

Figure 2.1 Thelma's father considering shooting his own daughter.

this film a shocking one, the restricted narration creates a sense of suspense about what is up with Thelma (or indeed her father); what lies behind this dramatic scene? Christer Bakke Andresen describes this flashback as crucial to the audience's ability to develop empathy for a protagonist with potentially murderous supernatural abilities:

> This opening establishes a gut-level empathic connection with Thelma (no matter what a child has done, killing in retribution seems horrifically out of proportion), while at the same time putting the viewer out of alignment with her (she does not see what nearly happens, so we know more about her situation than she does).[9]

Part of the explanation for what makes Thelma special comes to us through two further flashes back to her childhood. In one of these, her infant brother somehow ends up trapped under a big, heavy sofa; in the other he ends up trapped under the ice covering a lake, and dies. Both scenes appear to be showing us things that actually happened, and that Thelma moved her brother into these perilous positions using only the power of her mind. These breaks in the general chronology of the story are easy to follow and grasp and are strategically placed so as to give us information about events in the past at the right time.

The first flashback occurs just under an hour into the film, when Thelma's new doctor informs her that her chart mentions she had some kind of breakdown when she was six years old, and was prescribed a strong antipsychotic. We are led into the flashback when the doctor suggests she ask her father, as he was her doctor at the time, to explain what happened to her back then. We then see Thelma at six, feeling rejected by a mother who is preoccupied with her new baby. As her brother lies shrieking in the next room, Thelma is shown, accompanied by intense, dramatic music, thinking hard and focusing intently on something. Suddenly, the crying stops. When she turns to look into the room where he just was, the baby is gone. Her mother suspects her of hiding him somewhere, demands heatedly to know 'where you've put him'. When she is pressed, Thelma's eyes to go the big sofa, and suddenly, the crying resumes. Her brother has inexplicably ended up underneath a piece of furniture too heavy even for an adult to move on their own. The scene ends with the two parents protectively cradling the infant they have just rescued, staring, in something like horror and disgust, at their daughter.

The next flashback happens when Thelma, deeply troubled by her romantic feelings for another girl, her seizures, and the thought that she might be at fault for Anja's disappearance, returns home to her parents. After her kiss with Anja, she prayed to God, begging him to 'remove it, make it go away'. And it came true, Anja mysteriously disappeared when Thelma, during a hospital examination, was instructed to think about something painful. The sum total of all these things makes Thelma break down. Back home, her parents sedate her, and her father tells her he must tell her something that will cause her a great deal of pain. This 'something' is a flashback, showing her mother leaving the room where she is giving Thelma's brother a bath, for just a moment. And then he disappears. Thelma is asleep when it happens, but when her father wakes her, she can point out exactly where the baby is. As Bakke Andresen shows, Trier's 'way of structuring the story' is crucial to our empathic engagement with Thelma here, engagement strong enough to have us cheering for her when she eventually kills her own father with pyrokinesis.[10]

Aside from these flashbacks, which have a clear, causal significance, *Thelma* features a couple of scenes that are more ambiguously anchored in time and space. These scenes relate to Thelma's grandmother, but this is not immediately clear to the viewer. They are also not realistic – featuring things like a snake slithering across the body of an elderly person – and can be read as dreams or fantasies. They serve to add emotional tension to the film and fit with the psychological horror genre it belongs to. *Thelma's* supernatural elements make us accept these scenes despite their lack of a clear function or immediate explanation. We understand them as mood-enforcing scenes that fit in this context. (We later learn that the elderly woman is Thelma's paternal grandmother, who also has supernatural abilities, and is currently being kept sedated by her own son; though this does not really explain the snake.)

Classical narrative films may also make use of relatively complex montage sequences. These can be used to speed up time, or to combine multiple plotlines by, for example, intercutting between events taking place in different places at the same time. A montage can be an efficient way of compressing the story-time into the film's discourse time. A classic example would be *Citizen Kane*, in which story-time covering Kane's seventy-five years of life is compressed into two hours of running time. The decline of Kane's marriage is, for example, famously compressed into a breakfast montage spanning two minutes.

Trier does something similar in the prologue of *The Worst Person in the World*, where he introduces us to Julie through a seven-and-a-half-minute montage. After an initial, brief scene in which we see her standing alone, smoking and scrolling on her phone, occasionally gazing out across the Oslo cityscape, the film opens with the title *The Worst Person in the World*, and then a title card reading 'A film in 12 chapters, a prologue and an epilogue'. The prologue offers a quick, playful montage covering several years of Julie's twenties, narrated in voice-over by a grown woman caustically remarking on the protagonist's feelings and choices. We see her, rapidly, jumping from medical school to a psychology degree to dropping out 'to become a photographer' – a change she finances with a student loan and a part-time job in a bookshop. Her time as a medical student takes up only two minutes of the montage, but includes a number of cuts: Julie with her classmates, in lectures, in study hall, at her desk in her bedsit, standing in the back of a class observing an autopsy. These clips are woven together with images of the feeds on her phone and computer that are pulling her attention away from her studies. The pace sometimes slows down a bit during conversations between Julie and her mother (Marianne Krogh), in which the mother is supportive when told of Julie's first planned career change, and a bit more apprehensive by the second. A change of scenery also means a change in lovers, and we see Julie break things off with one boyfriend in order to start seeing her psychology lecturer, who is followed by a model, during her photography phase, whom she in turn leaves for Aksel.

All these shifts are shown in different styles, each with its own mood, something that is also reflected in how Julie changes her hair, wardrobe, and personality along with each new 'her' she tries on. The changes in style are perhaps best described through the accompanying soundtrack. Over the course of these few minutes, we hear snippets of five different songs, all from different genres of music, including soft rock, Norwegian punk, and electronica, giving each of Julie's choices its own sound.[11] When Julie and Aksel meet, Christopher Cross's ballad 'Ride Like the Wind' is playing, and when they move in together, we hear Billie Holiday's 'The Way You Look Tonight'. The prologue ends as Holiday sings 'Someday when I'm awfully low / When the world is cold / I will feel a glow / Just thinking of you / And the way you look tonight'.

The montage has moved from a frustrated sense of indecision and uncertainty about choices to a feeling of established bliss as the image of the sleeping, infatuated couple fades out. Throughout it all, the sarcastic narrator offers comments on Julie's life and choices like 'This was wrong. This wasn't her', when she is a disheartened medical student, and 'Actually, she was a visual person', when she decides to try photography. The montage also features things like photos Julie has taken with her phone and comic strips drawn by Aksel; it comprises, in other words, a rich and varied mix of elements.

One of the most important features here – the voice-over narrator (Ine Jansen) speaking over a series of images – is taken even further in a later montage, in the chapter 'One's own family'. Julie is celebrating her thirtieth birthday at her mother's house, along with Aksel and her grandmother (Thea Stabell). Here, the montage is woven into a scene with the four of them together, having cake and talking. At first, the narrator pops in to point out that Julie's mother was a divorced single parent by the time she was thirty. At one point, Julie stares thoughtfully at her grandmother, and the narrator returns to continue a retrospective listing of her various foremothers: 'At thirty, Julie's grandmother had three children'. As the line, 'She played Rebecca West in *Rosmersholm* at the National Theatre' is spoken,[12] the camera pans up to the framed theatre poster on the wall, before moving on to a black-and-white photograph, presumably depicting Julie's great-grandmother Astrid. Astrid, the narrator says, was a widowed mother of four by the time she turned thirty. The parade of ancestors continues with a photograph of a great-great-grandmother and her husband, who, according to the narrator, had seven children. The montage speeds up, showing images of five new women in just ten seconds. Included here are drawings and a painted portrait, and the whole thing ends on a picture of an eighteenth-century headstone and a remark about how Julie's great-great-great-great-grandmother never even made it to thirty – 'the life expectancy for women at the time was thirty-five years'.

This montage also serves to compress time (three hundred years, in fact!), but it does a number of other things as well. By beginning with a close-up of Julie, it suggests to us that these are her thoughts, things that have been on her mind. And we have previously, in the first chapter, 'The Others', been shown how having children is a sore subject between her and Aksel: Should they or should they not have kids? The montage does as such connect to one of the core questions of the film: Is Aksel the right person for Julie, will they settle down together and make a family? But it also feels like a humorous digression from all of that, a half-satirical look at being a woman then and now. Which brings us back to another central theme in *The Worst Person in the World*: what sort of choices people have been able to make at different times, and the ways in which expectations of women have changed.

These montages have a very distinct style and sense of humour which are, to me, Trieresque. That said, there is a striking resemblance between Trier's montages and those of American director Mike Mills. Take, for instance, *Beginners* (2010). Mills's film (like several of Trier's) is about familial relationships and is structured around a present-time storyline and multiple flashes back to various points in the past. In the present, Oliver (Ewan McGregor) is pondering the life of his recently deceased father Hal (Christopher Plummer): the life Hal shared with Oliver's mother, the life he had after she passed, and his life when he, at seventy-five came out as a gay man. One of several montage sequences is as follows: We see a close-up of Oliver on a bed, staring at the ceiling, his voice-over stating, 'This is 2003'. Next follow pictures of the sky – morning skies and then night skies – and the lines 'This is what the sun looks like. And the stars.' We then, in quick succession, get a postcard with a landscape scene printed on it, a portrait of George W. Bush, and 'This is what the president looks like'. The pattern repeats: 'And this is the sun in 1955 (now in black and white), and the stars, and nature, and cars, and movies and the President.' The images and words change slightly, but only slightly. In a similar montage, Oliver describes the relationships he and girlfriend Anne (Melanie Laurent) had before they met each other, the way she tucks her hair behind her ears, her feet, and what it is like when she cries. The combination, here, of a somewhat stylised narrator and highly stylised images, is incredibly reminiscent of Trier's montages. A not insignificant difference, however, is how the non-diegetic voice-over in *Beginners* (and in Mills's *20th Century Women*) is a character in the film, whereas Trier tends to favour an external narrator.

It is no accident that these scenes appear so alike. Mills and Trier are mutually inspired by each other, and have each described this dynamic, and their friendship, in multiple interviews.[13] Trier has pointed to *Beginners* as one of his favourite films.[14] And Mills has described Trier as 'an important source of inspiration and assistance. He tends to watch my films at various stages and give his input'.[15] Olivier Bugge Coutté who has been Joachim Trier's regular editor since 2000, when they were students together, was brought in to edit *Beginners* after Mills saw *Reprise*.[16] Kasper Tuxen shot *Beginners* with Mills before he did *The Worst Person in the World* for Trier. The montages in *Beginners* could very well have directly inspired the ones in *The Worst Person in the World*, the style and tenor of which are similar to the American film. This was, however, not Trier's first time working with this type of stylised, distanced montage.

The technique was already present in *Reprise*, and already then clearly a deliberate aesthetic strategy for the first-time director. This can be seen in a conversation that was published along with the script of *Reprise*:

> I am interested in art that weaves all of this together. A film does not need to be this tightly drawn chain of cause and effect. It can just as well be a mosaic, each tile forming part of a greater whole. A whole that can emerge just when those analogies bounce off each other, when the different themes resonate together. If you have this, you can be less reliant on those narrative conventions.[17]

A montage functioning as an embedded narrative can be one such mosaic tile. The first one in *Reprise* (as in *The Worst Person in the World*) occurs only a minute into the film, before the title sequence. Before the montage kicks off, we have only been briefly introduced to a couple of anxious young men (Erik and Phillip) working up the courage to post their respective manuscripts, hoping to get published. *Reprise* and *The Worst Person in the World* both, in other words, start by quickly establishing a realistic, contemporary universe, before heading into more experimental territory. Unlike the montage contextualising Julie, *Reprise*'s opening montage is not about things that have happened before the present time of the film, but about what will happen in the future. Or, more accurately, it is a flash forward to an imaginary future of sorts. In the montage, both books are accepted for publication – in reality, or at least in the story the film sticks with following this sequence, only Phillip's is. The rest of the opening montage consists of a rapid succession of events tied to their book launches, press attention, challenges they face. All of this condensed into three minutes.

The montage is in black and white and has several other features to further distinguish it from the realistic world of the present that was just established. It appears, for instance, as if Phillip and Erik can both hear the external narrator speaking; Trier thus plays with the distinction between a diegetic and a non-diegetic universe. The montage can be described as a shared dream between the two and includes romanticised notions of a life of high drama – love and tragedy. But this, too, the visualisation of a shared dream, is a break with convention, and an impossibility. What sets *Reprise* apart from other Norwegian films, Gunnar Iversen argues, is how the different plotlines and the film as a whole are broken up by 'different moves that are in part satirising its own story and characters, making the narrative more complex, ambiguous, and secretive'.[18] The montages, of which there are several in *Reprise,* some of them retrospective too, are crucial to us experiencing the film in this way.

Figure 2.2 Erik and Phillip fantasising about future fame as authors.

When Erik at one point decides to break things off with his girlfriend Lillian (because his book has been accepted and he would like to live out a certain mythologised artist fantasy now), the action repeatedly pauses to bring up flashbacks to memories from his past: a derisive comment about girls from his friend Lars, an awkward moment with his mother, a painful incident of childhood bullying. With each thought he has, the frame freezes, the narrator appears, and the chain of events is further fragmented. In the end, Erik is unable to actually do what he intends, and ends up staying with Lillian (at least for a while). This montage, along with others, functions as meta-commentary on the film's plot and on Eric's character and state of mind, his relationships with women, his inability to own and stand by his own choices, his sense of guilt. But it is also commenting on cinematic conventions and traditional narration. It shifts between different places in time – now and then – and between realities – what is happening in the physical world (Erik is approaching Lillian in order to break up with her) and what is happening inside him (all the other things he is thinking about). The montage depicts a certain frame of mind, its rhythm set by the music.

Trier's montages also typically touch on the central themes of the films they appear in: most notably, perhaps, in *The Worst Person in the World* and *Reprise*. In the short scene preceding the opening montage, Phillip looks at his friend Erik, each of them with an envelope, ready to post, and says: 'This is when it all begins'. This brief moment, including Phillip's line, is repeated after the montage about what their future might hold. This repetition, or reprise, has Audun Engelstad interpreting the entire opening as a clear sign that this film is about time:

> This scene, and the sequence that follows, indicate in a sophisticated manner that time is key in this narrative. Narratively, we are at a 'now' that represents a momentary standstill, epitomised by the static camera shot. From this point – the point of 'now' – there will be movement – a development of action – caused by the 'it' that 'begins'.[19]

Engelstad further reflects on how this 'it' could refer to the posting of the manuscripts, setting off the chain of events taking the two young men to published authorhood, but also, from a meta-perspective, the film itself beginning: 'Within the realm of the story, it is an expression of his expectations about what might lie ahead; yet the remark is also a meta-reflexive comment about the story now put into motion'.[20]

This self-reflective tendency comes to Trier from modernist cinema, with films often drawing attention to the manner in which their stories are told by, for instance, fragmenting them. When Trier like, for example, French New Wave director Jean-Luc Godard before him, includes typed out chapter headings and numbers in *The Worst Person in the World*, he is underlining the episodic structure of his film. The chapters, each preceded by a title card (something also seen in the works of contemporary directors like Quentin Tarantino and Lars von Trier), contribute to the reflexive aspects of the film. This structure also allows for a storytelling mode in which not all scenes need a defined, narrative function, and it enables the director to be unusually free with his chronology. The latter point becomes particularly clear when reading Trier and Vogt's script for *The Worst Person in the World* (which has been published by Tiden, along with a conversation between the two and Norwegian novelist Mattis Øybø).[21] Trier was also inspired by Woody Allen's *Hannah and Her Sisters* (1986), which is also organised in chapters, and has himself pointed out how this framework allows him to 'liberate the structure and play around with different tonal shifts'.²² Between script and finished film, the order of the different chapters of Julie's life was changed up quite a lot. What Trier has ended up with is an almost chronological tale, told through the aforementioned prologue, twelve chapters, and an epilogue.

The continuous deconstruction of chronology in *Reprise* and the playful chapter structure of *The Worst Person in the World* both draw the audience's attention to the film as a constructed object.²³ Trier has no worries about this taking away from his viewers' experience or engagement; as he puts it, the audience know they are watching a film: 'I'm not afraid of a bit of *Verfremdung*, as they would say in the old Brechtian school. We're watching a movie! And I, as a filmmaker, am inviting you to play along with us'.²⁴

Narratively speaking, *Louder Than Bombs* is one of Trier's most complex works, perhaps the most complex of all. Norwegian film critic Dag Sødtholt has, in a rich and meticulous analysis, described it as a film with 'an intricate pattern' and 'a play on perspective'.²⁵ This description relates to the many motifs and thematic perspectives (human, ethical, material) of the film, but also its form. This family drama does, however, not feel distanced and meta-reflexive in the manner of, for instance, *Reprise*. The film's structure is complex and fragmented, but its subject matter and nuanced, believable characters make it, to my mind, more immersive. *Louder Than Bombs* contains a number of flashbacks, internal thoughts, dream sequences, and events shown from multiple perspectives, but the film is edited very seamlessly, giving the impression of a relatively straightforward story.²⁶ Put another way: it is far less insistent in the way it deconstructs its narrative, and the different perspectives come together to form a whole that ultimately feels closed.

This film also contains several radical montages. I have already mentioned how *Louder Than Bombs* depicts the internal thoughts and memories of fifteen-year-old Conrad, focused on his imaginings of his mother. The most striking montage sequence gives us direct access to his mind. It is radical in form, but securely anchored and elegantly explained in the story. This scene takes place after one in which the two brothers, Conrad and Jonah, have been bonding during a visit by the latter. Jonah catches Conrad, believing himself alone, dancing with abandon in his room. The two then just hang out, looking at old clips from their father's acting career, and Jonah gets to try gaming with his younger brother's VR headset. When Jonah bristles at Conrad's, to his mind, uncritical approach to shooter games ('You don't think these games are kind of stupid – you're aware that this is like a very one-dimensional representation of US Military intervention, right?'), Conrad abruptly shuts down the game and pulls up a document on his computer for Jonah to read.

It turns out to be a manuscript or journal of sorts, something the younger brother has written and presumably shares to demonstrate that he is more mature and contemplative than his grown-up brother might think. 'Did you write this?', Jonah asks. We see him in close-up, reading, curious, but hear Conrad's voice-over saying 'Am I crazy thinking about setting fire to Marion Wilkinson's hair?' In other words: Jonah is reading Conrad's text, but the audience gets access to it by way of Conrad himself reading it aloud in a voice-over, paired with intense, diverse visualisations of what he has written about. We cut from Jonah's face to the camera panning across the computer screen, barely giving us time to read the sentence we have just heard, before, suddenly, we are in a scene where Conrad sits in a high-school chemistry lab, safety goggles on, throwing matches towards the head of a girl with a great, red mane of hair sitting in front of him. As her locks catch fire, he says: 'hair that burns always smells very bad'. Next comes a collage of the faces of three babies, and the remark 'in 1993, three other boys with the name Conrad Reed were born'. This collage part, in particular, leads one's thoughts towards Mike Mills's montages in *Beginners*.

Following this, we get a procession of words and images in which Conrad is musing on how much toilet paper he consumes compared to other people (eight sheets, sometimes twelve), and how many possessions he has. Altogether, the text consists of an idiosyncratic and original mixture of dreams, reminiscences, dry facts, curious observations, and everyday occurrences. These are visualised through a stream of images from Conrad's own life, films, video games, and the internet (Wikipedia, YouTube, and so on). This creates an upbeat, visual stream of consciousness, comprising words, music and images, that is highly complex and yet easy to follow, and which provides a fascinating view inside the subjective life of Conrad. Many of his reflections are about his mother, but these are interwoven with bizarre contemplations about for instance the decomposition of corpses at different temperatures. The literary style is a paratactic first-person narration, where minute details (how many socks in his drawer) and existential issues (concerning death in particular) stand side by side. When Conrad provides the exact number of pairs of underwear he owns (fourteen), images of colourful underpants (at least ten) flicker by. Other things he will linger on a bit longer, like the fact that he swallowed a bullet he found in their home when he was nine years, and his complicated relationship with his father.

Some of these images stand out more than others, such as when Conrad mentions a lesson his mother taught him that had a 'profound effect' on him: that it is the framing (not the photographed object) that produces the full meaning of a given image. Here, we are presented with a series of famous photographs, initially cropped so as not to show the full picture. A woman holds a flower up before her face, but when the frame widens, we see soldiers pointing weapons at her. Women and children walk along a pavement, but as we zoom out, an IRA soldier, armed and masked, appears behind the corner they are approaching. A young child holds the hand of an adult – the hand turns out to be Hitler's.[27] The montage consists of several jumps and breaks, indicating that we do not get to share in everything Jonah is reading. One page from the manuscript flashes before us so briefly it would be impossible for a cinema audience to read. If you freeze the frame, it turns out to contain Conrad's thoughts about the 'Red Wedding' from *Game of Thrones*, and the titles of songs he has found on a playlist of his mother's. In other words, someone, most likely Trier himself, has taken the time to put together a playlist the audience will not actually see (a playlist that includes Glen Campbell, Talking Heads, Todd Rundgren, and Jay-Z, among others).[28]

The four-minute sequence is a literary mini-narrative steeped in, and inspired by, contemporary mediascapes to which it itself contributes. It beautifully captures an upbeat, intense, and formally rewarding version of a young man's attempt to make sense of his own life and the sometimes-incomprehensible world surrounding him. The most sophisticated aspect of this montage is perhaps the way it includes glances back on earlier moments in the film. We get a repeat of Conrad's father stalking him after school, and of Conrad unknowingly slaying his father's video game avatar. But in the montage, unlike in the previous iterations of these scenes, we see Conrad's versions of the events, from his perspective. I have called this text Conrad's journal, but that term is not a perfect fit, as the whole purpose of the work is for him to share it with his crush Melanie, so that Melanie might get to know and like him, maybe even fall in love with him when she can see him fully for who he is, in all this detail. When Jonah finishes reading, he exclaims: 'Dude, that is amazing!' My own reaction to this montage, the first time I saw it, was very similar. It is highly sophisticated, playful, and serious all at once. Jonah also calls it weird, but concludes his response to his little brother by stating that it is 'really weird, interesting and very good'.

It is obvious, not just from the frequency with which he employs them and the meticulous work and variation that goes into them, but also from statements made by Trier himself, that these montages are very important to him as a filmmaker. Of this video journal, for instance, he has said:

> In order to create and explore these very, very subjective portraits of individual characters, we thought a lot about literature where you can go into characters' minds, imaginations, memories, and dreams. The video games that the little brother plays are one representation of our fragmented perception of reality, which is obviously quite modern and natural for all of us now. I think the way images represent a portion of ourselves plays into our views on reality, and that should be mirrored in the way we tell stories in cinema. Cinema is the place where all these images come together. We can have a YouTube clip next to a war

photograph, both shot on 35mm film. I just like that it all ends up in the same big frame. I think something like that mirrors these characters' rather fragmented perception of Isabelle, not to mention the reality around them.[29]

The montage is a tool for capturing some of what film as a medium does best: movements and the passage of time. The montage is also a tool for Trier to capture what many have claimed cannot be captured on film: namely people's thoughts or inner worlds. When these things come together, the montages become a place for the director to test the boundaries of film convention, and to push these nearly to beyond what is possible. The world and our understanding of it are fragmented, Trier appears to say. And so our stories, too, must be fragmented: mosaics, moments, micro-ballads.

NOTES

1. Bergman's five nominations were for *Fanny and Alexander* (1983), *Autumn Sonata* (1978), *Cries and Whispers* (1973), *Through a Glass Darkly* (1961) and *Wild Strawberries* (1957).
2. Nick Chen, 'Director Joachim Trier Selects Ten of His All-Time Favourite Romcoms', *Dazed*, 2 March 2022, https://www.dazeddigital.com/film-tv/article/55580/1/joachim-trier-worst-person-in-the-world-ten-romcoms-top-ten. In this interview the scene is described as an acid-trip; however what they take is 'magic' mushrooms (*Psilocybe semilanceata*), which are illegal in Norway, but work as a hallucinogenic drug, sometimes compared with some of the effects of LSD.
3. Stephen Saito, 'Interview: Joachim Trier & Eskil Vogt on Finding Their Power in "Thelma"', The Moveable Fest, 4 December 2017, https://moveablefest.com/joachim-trier-eskil-vogt-thelma/.
4. Hillary Weston, 'The Art Form of Memory: A Conversation with Joachim Trier', The Criterion Collection, 8 April 2016, https://www.criterion.com/current/posts/4001-the-art-form-of-memory-a-conversation-with-joachim-trier; Eskil Vogt, Joachim Trier, and Mattis Øybø, 'Kunsten å oppnå sekvensiell nytelse', in *Verdens verste menneske. Filmmanus.* (Oslo: Tiden Norsk Forlag, 2021): 277–304. The latter of these interviews is also included in the collection of scripts published as *Oslo-trilogien* (*The Oslo trilogy*), as well as in the Norwegian publication *Vinduet*.
5. Victor Moreno, 'Joachim Trier in the Wheelhouse', *Metal Magazine*, 2015, https://metalmagazine.eu/en/post/interview/joachim-trier-in-the-wheelhouse-victor-moreno.
6. Weston, 'The Art Form of Memory'.
7. See for example, Audun Engelstad, 'The Concept of Time in Joachim Trier's Reprise', *Journal of Scandinavian Cinema* 9, no. 2 (1 June 2019): 197–202, https://doi.org/10.1386/jsca.9.2.197_1.
8. See also Chapter 3.

9. Christer Bakke Andresen, *Norwegian Nightmares: The Horror Cinema of a Nordic Country* (Edinburgh University Press, 2022), 95.
10. Ibid., 93.
11. All together, we hear excerpts from Daphni's 'Poly', Cobra Man's 'Bad Feeling', Amulet's 'Naked Eye', in addition to Christopher Cross and Billie Holiday. Included in the soundtrack, at a later stage, is also a song by Norwegian Big Band, whose leading man, Øystein Greni, is a longtime friend of Trier (see also an anecdote in the epilogue about their relationship).
12. *Rosmersholm* is an 1886 play by Norwegian playwright Henrik Ibsen.
13. Emil Mohr, 'Speed of Life: *The Worst Person in the World* Director Joachim Trier Interviewed by Mike Mills', *Filmmaker Magazine*, 18 January 2022, https://filmmakermagazine.com/112885-interview-mike-mills-joachim-trier-worst-person-in-the-world/; Emil Mohr, 'Mike Mills: – Jeg betrakter mammaer som mer avanserte vesener', *www.dn.no*, 7 April 2022, https://www.dn.no/d2/film/joaquin-phoenix/kino/joachim-trier/mike-mills-jeg-betrakter-mammaer-som-mer-avanserte-vesener/2-1-1165287; Aleksander Huser, 'Mike Mills og "C'mon C'mon": En fabel som imiterer livet', *Cinema*, 7 April 2022, https://cine.no/2022/04/08/mike-mills-og-cmon-cmon-en-fabel-som-imiterer-livet/.
14. Chen, 'Director Joachim Trier'.
15. Mohr, 'Mike Mills'.
16. Bugge Coutté has edited a number of Nordic films, such as the Icelandic *Virgin Mountain* (2015), Norwegian *The Congo Murders* (2018), Danish *Copenhagen Does Not Exist* (*København findes ikke*) (2022 – the latter with a script by Eskil Vogt); and television series, like *The Kingdom* (2022) and *Copenhagen Cowboy* (2023); Chen, 'Director Joachim Trier'.
17. Bjarte Breiteig, Eskil Vogt, and Joachim Trier, 'Overskudd og ambivalens. En samtale rundt tilblivelsen av *Reprise* mellom Bjarte Breiteig, Eskil Vogt og Joachim Trier', in Eskil Vogt and Joachim Trier, *Reprise. Et filmmanuskript* (Oslo: Tiden Norsk Forlag, 2007), 208–37, at 213.
18. Gunnar Iversen, 'Tiden leger ingen sår "Reprise"', in *Den norske filmbølgen: Fra Orions belte til Max Manus.* (Oslo: Universitetsforlaget, 2010), 315.
19. Engelstad, 'The Concept of Time', 198.
20. Ibid.
21. Vogt, Trier and Øybø, 'Kunsten å oppnå sekvensiell nytelse'.
22. Elissa Suh, 'A Stick, a Stone, the End of the Road: Joachim Trier Discusses "The Worst Person in the World"', MUBI, https://mubi.com/notebook/posts/a-stick-a-stone-the-end-of-the-road-joachim-trier-discusses-the-worst-person-in-the-world.
23. In a masterclass at the Department of Art and Media Studies, NTNU 2017, Trier described how he and then fellow student Olivier Bugge Coutté, were in continuous opposition to their teacher in film editing at NSFT, who always encouraged films that flowed without drawing attention to style.
24. Jackson McHenry, 'The Worst Person in the World Held Up Oslo for Its Freeze-Frame Sequence', *Vulture*, 17 February 2022, https://www.vulture.com/2022/02/behind-the-worst-person-in-the-worlds-freeze-frame-sequence.html.

25. Dag Sødtholt, 'Louder Than Bombs: Joachim Trier's Play on Perspective', *Montages International Edition*, 16 January 2016, http://montagesmagazine.com/2016/01/louder-than-bombs-joachim-triers-play-on-perspective/.
26. See also Jørgen Bruhn and Anne Gjelsvik, *Cinema Between Media: An Intermediality Approach* (Edinburgh: University Press, 2018).
27. The first photograph is Jan Rose Kasmir's *Woman with Flower at Pentagon* from 1967; the second is a picture from West Belfast, photographer unknown; the image of Hitler shows him with Joseph Goebbels' daughter, Helga Susanne.
28. See more on the different medial aspects of the montage in Bruhn and Gjelsvik, *Cinema Between Media*. See also Chapter 7 below.
29. Kee Chang, 'Q&A with Joachim Trier', *Anthem*, 21 May 2015, https://anthemmagazine.com/qa-with-joachim-trier/.

CHAPTER 3

Sculpting Time

Sometimes when we watch a film, certain scenes stand out. The ones 'everybody' is talking about on their way out of the cinema, or the ones that stay with you for years. Sometimes these are scenes that capture the very essence of the films they are in; other times, they are spectacular or highly unusual scenes that nearly outshine the movies themselves. Typical examples can be major action set pieces like the cable drop scene in the first *Mission Impossible* (1996 – where Tom Cruise's agent Ethan Hunt hacks into a high-security CIA vault while suspended in the air), the car chase from *The French Connection* (1971), or the bicycle scene in *E.T.* (1982).

The most iconic example of this phenomenon might be Gene Kelly's titular song and dance number from *Singin' in the Rain* (1952). To many people today, that scene epitomises the film. A number of factors make it memorable: the timing, the music, the choreography, and Kelly's charisma. Even in a feature filled with musical showstoppers, it stands out, because it is unexpected and because it is different. Bright, fantastical costumes have been exchanged for an umbrella, the stage for wet pavement, lights, colours, and glitter for puddles. The scene captures the 'glorious feeling' of being in love. More simplified, we could say that a combination of the visual work done by the filmmakers and the emotional payoff it offers the viewer is what makes this scene so special.

This musical number is a classic example of the set piece, which can be defined as 'an energetic, original, extended sequence that contains a big payoff for the audience'.[1] Such scenes often require extensive logistical planning. The term originally referred to scenes that were worth the expense and time a Hollywood studio (like musical specialists MGM) would need to spend constructing a whole new set for them (as opposed to repurposing existing stage dressing and structures). These scenes would not necessarily have a clear plot-related function; their value could just as well be aesthetic or emotional.

The so-called 'frozen time' scene in *The Worst Person in the World* is such a set piece, one that both stands out from and captures the very essence of the film as a whole. It is no coincidence that a still from this sequence was used for the film's main poster – it captures something essential about *The Worst Person in the World*. In the scene, or more accurately sequence, protagonist Julie runs through an Oslo in which all the other people have been frozen in place like statues. It is a grand, beautiful sequence, combining movement and stillness in a startling break with the otherwise realistic style of the film. It is a unique scene that, as I will show, has more than one thing in common with Kelly's pavement dance in *Singin' in the Rain*.

It is the kind of scene people end up talking about as they leave a screening. Let me provide a few examples of reactions:

> In one scene in the film, the world, quite literally stops so Julie can run through the city, unaccounted for. In this brief moment of euphoria, her life is completely her own. I and many others can only wish for a moment like this.[2]

In a more critical review, penned by Richard Brody in *The New Yorker*, what happens is described as Julie 'freezing the world for the sake of love'.[3] A more positive take on the film, but a more critical evaluation of its main character, is found in a long-form analysis in *Senses of Cinema*:

> Depending on the viewer's empathy or lack thereof for Julie, this scene can also be viewed as the sublimation of her self-centredness. She is so caught into her own mind games that the outside world stops existing. No one else matters. An anthem for the ages: I, me, mine; this is my truth and I'll make-believe that my actions have no consequences.[4]

I have called this sequence a 'time sculpture' elsewhere,[5] and I will argue that it is also a perfect example of how Joachim Trier thinks about cinema as an art form. He has, for instance, described how he likes to think of his films as 'hit albums'. Along with his script writing partner Eskil Vogt, he attempts to achieve what he calls 'sequential pleasure', meaning that the film should be a series of scenes that each, individually, have their own value outside of the plot. Trier and Vogt plan for scenes that are 'pleasant to spend time in': an album where every song is a hit.[6]

The frozen time sequence is an illuminating example of how Trier likes to play with cinematic possibilities and work with inspired set pieces. It is also a perfect example of how he engages with time in film. As already discussed in the two previous chapters, ideas about time – past, present, and future – are both central to Trier's films and closely related to the very concept of cinema as a time-based art form. I will continue later my more general discussion of how Trier, through playful use of the possibilities inherent in the medium, keeps exploring 'what cinema is', but here I will focus my analysis on this very specific example.

Trier has stated on multiple occasions that his love of play was an important factor in his desire to work in film, and is part of what he loves about directing: 'I always try to play around with form because I think we should push cinema to be more playful'.[7] His films therefore often contain one or more set pieces, memorable stand-out scenes like the café scene in *Oslo, August 31st*, Conrad's video diary in *Louder than Bombs*, or the scene where the doctor provokes a seizure in *Thelma*.

Trier is a filmmaker who believes film was meant for the cinema, and with *The Worst Person in the World*, he was particularly concerned with making a piece for the big screen. His specific desire to create a cinema experience was enhanced by the COVID-19 pandemic and all its restrictions on movie screenings and other social events, restrictions that were at their most rigid in Norway while he was shooting in 2020.[8] The end goal was a playful visual feast of great colour and emotion, a true 'big screen experience'.[9] This is also what leads him to shoot on 35mm film. All of Trier's feature films are shot on 35mm, a choice that becomes more unusual as the years go by. Analogue film outperforms digital in a number of areas – such as texture, light, and subtle details in colour and tone. The cinematographer on the film, Kasper Tuxen, also highlights celluloid's ability to capture the nuances of the human face, and its superiority, according to him, when it comes to the 'rendering of skin tones and the beauty of faces'.[10]

According to Tuxen, the choice of 35mm also had effects on more than the visual and aesthetic qualities of the film: 'One of the most important aspects of shooting this movie on 35mm was how it acted as an intensifier'.[11] When shooting on celluloid, the cost of pausing to correct something is significantly greater than with digital film. Tuxen compares the effect this has on the actors to the live nature of a stage play.[12] The increased pressure to get just the right take, without too many expensive starts and stops, injects a different sort of emotional energy and level of concentration into actors and crew alike. However, this also made the Danish cinematographer feel nervous ahead of shooting the frozen sequence, a scene requiring so much careful planning of everything from natural light to nearby traffic. Adding to the pressure was perhaps the fact that this was the first time Tuxen shot on 35mm.[13]

The sequence takes place in the middle of the film, in a chapter called 'Bad Timing', the fifth in Julie's story. It spans only about five minutes – somewhat in line with the hit songs Trier wishes for his scenes to emulate. Before it, we have gotten to know Julie through a montage about her life in her twenties, her drifting from one field of study, or boyfriend, to the next. We have seen her fall in love with successful cartoonist Aksel, fifteen years her senior, and move into his flat.[14] The fact that Julie and Aksel are at different stages of their lives is a constant source of tension between them, from the very beginning of their relationship. They go out with his friends, not hers; they discuss having children, something he wants and she does not. While he is passionate about, and successful in, his work, she is still figuring out 'what she wants to be' while 'temporarily' working in a bookshop.

On a day when this disparity weighs particularly heavily on Julie, she attends a launch party for Aksel's new graphic novel but feels terribly out of place. She ends up leaving early, on her own, and crashing a wedding reception she happens upon. She knows no one at this second party but slips in among the other guests and pretends to be someone else (as a matter of fact she pretends to be a doctor, which she might have been by then had she not dropped out of medical school). This is where she meets Eivind. The two are immediately attracted to each other; they flirt, test the limits of what it means to be (un)faithful, share intimate secrets. But a few hours later, they part ways at an intersection, without even telling each other their full names. As they both state, they do not wish to be unfaithful to their respective partners. This event takes place in the film's second chapter 'Cheating'.

We then accompany Julie in the time following this encounter, focusing particularly on her relationships with Aksel and her parents. Her thirtieth birthday celebration is a particularly emotional and ambivalent milestone. One day, Eivind randomly walks into the bookshop where she works, along with his girlfriend Sunniva (Maria Grazia di Meo). The attraction between Julie and Eivind is just as strong and immediate as before, and after initially leaving with Sunniva, he sneaks back into the shop to let Julie know he thinks a lot about her, but does not wish to disrupt her life if she is happy. 'Are you?' he asks. 'I don't know what to say', a blushing, smitten Julie responds. He says he would like to see her again, that she can find him in the café where he works if she wants that too. In the scenes following this coincidental, emotional reunion, Julie is pensive. Her mind wanders in the middle of conversations with Aksel and his friends, her nights are sleepless. As this brief synopsis shows, this chapter brings the film closer to the romantic comedy, particularly in how the plot is driven by chance encounters.[15] And it brings us into classic romance territory: a woman torn between two men – who will she choose?

This is where the sequence I am currently concerned with comes in. It plays out like this: Julie gets up in the morning, despondent. She looks like she has something to say. Aksel is in the kitchen, preparing breakfast; he does not notice her mood. She flips a light switch in their kitchen; the light comes on and hits her face. In that moment, Aksel freezes, right in the middle of pouring coffee into a mug. In the script, what happens next is described as follows 'Everything turns quiet. It is daylight, so the light does not change much, but time magically stops'.[16] The light switch appears to function as a kind of pause button, pausing everything (and everyone) but Julie. She stops to think for a moment, then turns her back on Aksel and exits the flat without a word. She runs through the streets of Oslo, looking for Eivind. As she speeds up, the camera is lifted high up on a crane, giving us an overview of the streets and people surrounding her. Her face is expectant, she is dressed casually in blue and white, clothes that, along with her hair, flow freely around her as she moves ever faster. Julie is the only person moving, all around her, school children, bikers, tourists, and suited commuters are immobile, frozen like statues. She finds Eivind, who, unlike everyone else, can also move, and he leans across the café counter to kiss her. They spend a few romantic hours together in a park (until next sunrise) before she runs back. On her way, she passes a young couple, frozen mid-kiss, and she runs back to place the girl's hand on the boy's bum. As she runs on, she faces the camera head-on for a moment and winks, almost in recognition of the way this scene breaks with the pattern of the rest of the film, as if to tell us this is all a game.

Figure 3.1 Aksel pouring his coffee as the world freezes in *The Worst Person in the World*.

Reality creeps into the pair's conversation as the sun is rising. In the script, this spell-breaking moment is compared to Cinderella's reality check at the royal ball: 'Suddenly she sees the sun climbing the horizon. She gets up and runs – just like Cinderella when midnight strikes'.[17] The two have now crossed the line they drew when they first met; now they have been unfaithful. He says

Figure 3.2 Julie running through the streets of Oslo while the rest of the world stands still.

'I don't know what we should do'. And yet infatuation, freedom, and joy are all that can be seen on Julie's face as she runs back.

As Julie returns, winded, to the kitchen, she takes a deep breath, flips the switch once more, and Aksel is put back into motion. The sound of coffee being poured replaces Marcel Ravel's 'Ma mère l'Oye', which has accompanied most of the sequence that just took place. Aksel hands her a mug and she says, 'Aksel, we need to talk.' We are immediately transported back to reality, the light of imagination turns off and the physical and emotional rules of the real world are reinstated. And then Julie, dramatically, breaks up with a dejected Aksel.

Vogt has described the scene as 'wrong on paper', something one cannot really choose to indulge in so far into a film that has otherwise been entirely realist.[18] Was it mere fantasy, or did what we just saw really happen? For all the other people in Oslo to freeze as Julie runs towards her new love is of course entirely unrealistic. The world does not revolve around a single person in this way. Aksel could not, truly, have stood motionless in his kitchen for twenty-four hours. This scene breaks with reality, as well as the realism the film has adhered to up to this point; it breaks with any realistic depiction of the passage of time. Here, time has simultaneously paused (for Aksel) and skipped ahead (for Julie), who emerges from the moment ready to break out of the relationship.[19]

The simplest explanation would be that this was just pure imagination, that what we are shown is what Julie dreams of doing. Another is that Julie is thinking of something that has already happened, that what we see as Aksel stands frozen is a flashback, an analepsis. The sequence taking place outside the kitchen could merely be her non-realistic memory of the time she went to see Eivind and spent a few, romantic hours with him, only to realise that she needed to leave Aksel. Or it could be prolepsis, an inner flash-forward: what we see is what will happen after she has told Aksel it is over. She will break it off with him, and then she can run towards Eivind. Whatever their rendezvous is, it cannot be purely dream or imagination, as, shortly after this, in 'A new chapter', the two move in together. For this to happen, Julie must have taken up Eivind's invitation to come find him.

However, one chooses to interpret it, this sequence bleeds into the remainder of the film. It also features more than courtship, kisses, and sunrises – it contains the very real concerns Eivind and Julie have about what to do, what the consequences of their choices will be, for both them and their partners. The scene provides sequential pleasure, yes, but it also holds repercussions for the remaining plot of the film, and it could be argued that it functions as characterisation for Julie, who is by nature a dreamer. Reviewer Salvador Carrasco writes that it is not a scene that freezes the world 'for the sake of love', but rather an example of how 'self-delusion leads to the kind of suspension of thought that culminates in betrayal'.[20] To his mind, Julie commits an act of betrayal here.

> During the loop, Julie has betrayed Aksel in thought, word, and most poignantly, deed, so whatever she says will feebly stand for an apology for why she did what she did. That is the dramatic significance of the time-freeze scene. What she saw as emancipating herself and felt so exhilarating actually doomed her relationship with Aksel forever.[21]

The sequence plays with the tension between the realistic rom-com about a contemporary young woman and the grand, cinematic depiction of great emotion. Though *The Worst Person in the World* is existential and melodramatic, it has characteristics, too, of both the romantic comedy and the musical. Out of Trier's films, it is the one in which the music means (and cost) the most; the soundtrack is extensive and prominent, mirroring Julie's character and moods throughout. The frozen time sequence also shares similarities with the song and dance numbers of classic musicals, where realism ceases to be a constricting factor and the world around the protagonist can suddenly just break into a song expressing just what he or she is feeling.[22] Though Julie does not break into song (or dance), her run through the streets has a similar effect. One of Trier's favourite films growing up, *Ferris Bueller's Day Off* (1986), has served as an inspiration here. In one scene, Matthew Broderick's Ferris sings and dances along to 'Twist and Shout' on a float in the middle of a parade in the streets of Chicago. Hundreds of people enthusiastically sing and dance along with him. For the crowd watching the parade to get caught up in the truant teenager's random performance in this way seems contrary to the realism of the rest of the film. But according to Trier himself, whether what is happening around

Ferris Bueller here is real or not is inconsequential. What matters is what sort of experience the scene offers the viewer, and how its playfulness and enthusiasm become contagious, even through the screen.[23]

Viewers feelings about or reactions to the scene might of course be mixed. One might dislike Julie's personality or her behaviour (sympathising, for instance, with Aksel), and still recognise and appreciate how the sequence captures the feeling of being in love. In my opinion, Julie's run through a frozen world is a genuinely romantic moment, one that takes the film to another level. Simultaneously, it also makes the viewer step out of the illusion and wonder how the filmmakers made it happen, not least because it was shot on film; the scene was not made using CGI. It was fully created on camera, with real people standing very still. Complex set piece that it is, it took meticulous planning and creativity to make its elements come together: from streams of coffee made of polymer clay, and blocks that could be used to keep a cyclist fixed in place, to the halting of all traffic in multiple central Oslo streets. At one point, Julie runs down a street where, normally, a tram will pass many times per hour. Shooting had to be coordinated around this. Some details, like the supporting blocks or cars moving in the background, were digitally removed in post-production, but the magic of the scene was otherwise made possible through traditional effects and a large group of extras. Prop master Hedda Virik made several of her own props for the takes, including fake dogs supported by rocks, and the aforementioned support blocks for bicycles.[24] Even the coffee Aksel is pouring is a traditional film prop, a sculpted replica the pouring liquid, supplemented with a small amount of actual coffee. Naturally, the choice to create the scene in this way elevates it: it looks better, and means more, than if it were created digitally.

Trier has posited that all directors seek to do their own take on 'what it is like to be in love'. With *The Worst Person in the World,* he wanted to make 'a show stopping scene of being in love'.[25] There are probably both film historical and psychological explanations for how his own 'Singin' in the Rain' number ended up taking the form it did. According to the director himself, he wanted to make a song-and-dance number, but was to 'too shy or too Scandinavian to pull that off quite yet'.[26] Musical numbers were an important source of inspiration for him, but so probably were other frozen time moments from other genres. Examples like the intense bullet-stop scene in *The Matrix* (1999), or the hilarious moment in Wes Anderson's *The French Dispatch* (2021) where the actors freeze and only the camera moves, show the range of what is possible with this sort of effect.[27] One common feature, however, is that it tends to be applied to moments of great emotion or tension. As such, its use is reflective of well-established psychological phenomena: one will often remember particularly dramatic or impactful events as moments frozen in time. Recalling exactly where one stood when something major happened, or exactly what music played when an important piece of news came in. The way we experience time can also change when we are in love; we can feel like time stands still or moves slower, or we wish to press pause on life, to just remain in a joyful moment.

But human life is more than what happens to us externally, we contain inner worlds as well. In the behind-the-scenes feature included on the Criterion Collection DVD edition of *The Worst Person in the World*, Trier explains how he was inspired by a book by British psychoanalyst and writer Adam Phillips: *Missing Out* (2013).[28] In this, Phillips writes about how our lives have two components: the experiences we have, and the ones we don't. He argues that our unlived lives, all the things we thought or hoped would or could happen but that never did, are just as formative as the experiences we actually lived.[29] As Trier puts it: if someone were to write your biography, they would not include such things, but they are nonetheless part of what makes up your life.[30] Julie not becoming a doctor is such an element. With this inspiration – the contrast between a lived life and a shadow life – as a backdrop, the scene clearly seems to be intended as a depiction of imagination, to be meant to capture what life did not contain, what was dreamed of. As the script describes it: a Cinderella moment. In other words: a fairy tale. In my opinion however, it does not matter, upon watching it, whether one interprets it as a dream or as a real event. In the moment, as this marvellous scene unfolds, you experience it as entirely real. It sublimely captures a sense of frozen time, of that moment where only a single thought or emotion matters, and everything else becomes set dressing.

Trier has stated that he wished for *The Worst Person in the World* to be 'a consoling, yet truthful film about the fact that time is limited'.[31] Not even the lightest, most playful of his works gets around the deeper, more existential questions. On the whole, the film is more typically Trier than classically rom-com. This despite how Trier will happily namedrop a number of classics within the genre when discussing his inspirations – films like *The Philadelphia Story* (1940) and *Notting Hill* (1999).[32] Critic Sarah O'Malley takes stock of this in the following way:

> *The Worst Person in the World* clearly has rom-com blood running through its veins – *Annie Hall* woven into its DNA helix – but there is a dark and existential strain present, an uneasy awareness of mortality and of time passing, that spills out beyond the confines of the genre.[33]

Others have described this as Trier's desire to explore an ongoing negotiation between our imagined lives, what we had in mind when we were young, and the reality of existence is illustrative of his approach to the romantic comedy. 'In reality', he says, 'we don't have a lot of time ahead of us.'[34] And this is painfully experienced by Julie towards the end of the film, when her ex-boyfriend Aksel is suddenly struck by cancer. This dichotomy, between what happens and what we wish would happen, is also explored in *Reprise*, where there are several points of ambiguity about whether what we see is objective reality or Erik and Phillip's thoughts and fantasies.

Last but not least, the frozen time sequence fits squarely into Trier's interest in exploring the cinematic medium's relationship with time. Put another way: the film is not merely about the time we humans have at our disposal, but also how cinema can render and depict time as a concept. Trier has stated that what he wanted to explore was the feeling of being able to freeze time.[35]

This wording appears to echo one of Trier's sources of inspiration, Russian master director Andrei Tarkovsky: 'Unlike all other art forms, film is able to seize and render the passage of time, to stop it, almost to possess it in infinity. Film is the sculpting of time.'[36] This term became the title of his book on art and cinema and inspired the title of this chapter.[37] Cinema can 'take an impression of time', as Tarkovsky put it, and in his view, film's relationship with time is exactly what makes it appeal to the audience:

> I think that what a person normally goes to the cinema for is *time*: time lost or spent or not yet had. He goes there for living experience; for cinema, like no other art, widens, enhances and concentrates a person's experience – and not only enhances it but makes it longer, significantly longer. That is the power of cinema.[38]

Artists within different forms and traditions all work with different materials and media: the painter with paints, the composer with sounds, the sculptor with clay or marble. Trier and Tarkovsky have both claimed time as the matter from which they craft their works. The sequence thus functions as a sort of meta-commentary on what film is, and what it can do as a medium and art form. Cinema can, for instance, freeze time.

NOTES

1. Joachim Trier, 'Masterclass with Joachim Trier in Conversation with Anne Gjelsvik'. Department of Art and Media Studies, NTNU, 18 September 2017.
2. Kaiya Shunyata, 'The Worst Person In The World Perfectly Captures the Rawness of Young-Adulthood', *Obscur* (blog), 10 March 2022, https://obscurmagazine.co.uk/the-worst-person-in-the-world-the-rawness-of-young-adulthood/.
3. Richard Brody, '"The Worst Person in the World" is a Sham, Except for Its Lead Performance', *The New Yorker*, 7 February 2022, https://www.newyorker.com/culture/the-front-row/the-worst-person-in-the-world-is-a-sham-except-for-its-lead-performance.
4. Salvador Carrasco, 'Anatomy of a Breakup or Her Life to Fix: The Worst Person in the World', *Senses of Cinema*, 2022, http://www.sensesofcinema.com/2022/feature-articles/anatomy-of-a-breakup-or-her-life-to-fix-the-worst-person-in-the-world/.

5. Anne Gjelsvik, 'Sculpting Time: Joachim Trier's The Worst Person in the World', *Montages International Edition*, 17 December 2021, https://montagesmagazine.com/2021/12/sculpting-time-the-worst-person-in-the-world/.
6. Eskil Vogt, Joachim Trier, and Mattis Øybø, 'Kunsten å oppnå sekvensiell nytelse', in *Verdens verste menneske. Filmmanus.* (Oslo: Tiden Norsk Forlag, 2021), 277–304, at 282.
7. Joachim Trier, *Behind the Scenes Criterion Collection*, DVD, 2021; Jackson Wald, 'Joachim Trier's Cinema of Intimacy', *Interview Magazine*, 7 February 2022, https://www.interviewmagazine.com/film/joachim-trier-cinema-of-intimacy.
8. In 2020, the shooting of *The Worst Person in the World* had to be put on hold during the first phase of the pandemic. When it could resume a few months later, heavy COVID restrictions were in place on set.
9. Ben Croll, 'Joachim Trier on Rounding Out His Oslo Trilogy With "The Worst Person in the World"', *Variety*, 9 July 2021, https://variety.com/2021/film/news/joachim-trier-on-rounding-out-his-oslo-trilogy-with-the-worst-person-in-the-world-1235012245/.
10. Francois Reumont, 'Kasper Tuxen, DFF, discusses the shooting of "The Worst Person in the World", by Joachim Trier', Afcinema, 15 August 2021, https://www.afcinema.com/Kasper-Tuxen-DFF-discusses-the-shooting-of-The-Worst-Person-in-the-World-by-Joachim-Trier.html. This was Trier's first collaboration with Tuxen, and it came about because his regular cinematographer, Jakob Ihre, was not available. Trier knew Tuxen's work from years back through Mike Mills, but they had not met. As inspiration for their collaboration, they used the work of cinematographer Nestor Almendros, known for his collaborations with Eric Rohmer, Francois Truffaut and Terrence Malick.
11. Kodak, 'DP Kasper Tuxen DFF Lenses a Modern-Day Love Story on 35mm for Joachim Trier's 2021 Cannes Contender "The Worst Person in the World"', Kodak, 8 July 2021, https://www.kodak.com/en/motion/blog-post/the-worst-person-in-the-world.
12. Kodak 'DP Kasper Tuxen'; Reumont, 'Kasper Tuxen'.
13. Lindsay Pugh, 'An Interview with Kasper Tuxen', in *Existential Detours: Joachim Trier's Cinema of Indecisions and Revisions* (Toronto: Seventh Row, 2024).
14. The age gap between the two characters (along with age and aging in general) is made an explicit part of what the film explores, unlike in film classics where, for instance, Audrey Hepburn would be paired up with men played by actors twenty to thirty years older than her (like Humphrey Bogart in *Sabrina* [1954]). See also Woody Allen's filmography for consistently big yet often unaddressed age gaps between the male and female leads.
15. Audun Engelstad, *Film og fortelling*, 2nd edn (Bergen: Fagbokforlaget, 2022), 42.
16. Eskil Vogt and Joachim Trier, *Verdens verste menneske: filmmanus* (Oslo: Tiden Norsk Forlag, 2021), 126.
17. Ibid., 129.
18. Ibid., 286.
19. Engelstad, *Film og fortelling*, 161.
20. Carrasco, 'Anatomy of a Breakup'.
21. Ibid.

22. Music plays a large part in this film, as in every Trier film. See, for instance, his long-time collaboration with Ola Fløttum and Torgny Amdam. In this film, more money than ever before was used on the soundtrack, which includes songs by Harry Nilsson, Art Garfunkel, Todd Rundgren and Amerie among others.
23. Jackson McHenry, 'The Worst Person in the World Held Up Oslo for Its Freeze-Frame Sequence', *Vulture*, 17 February 2022, https://www.vulture.com/2022/02/behind-the-worst-person-in-the-worlds-freeze-frame-sequence.html.
24. Hedda Virik shares her work in a YouTube video made by Insider. 'How Frozen-In-Time Scenes Are Shot For Movies And TV', *Movies Insider: Insider*, 2022, https://www.youtube.com/watch?v=OrgbZD2sRnU. See also Trier, *Behind the Scenes*.
25. Trier, *Behind the Scenes*.
26. McHenry, 'The Worst Person'.
27. Wes Anderson is also frequently mentioned by Trier as an inspiration.
28. Trier, *Behind the Scenes*.
29. Sheila Heti, 'Second Selves', *The New York Times*, 18 January 2013, https://www.nytimes.com/2013/01/20/books/review/missing-out-by-adam-phillips.html.
30. Trier, *Behind the Scenes*.
31. Ibid.
32. Tara Brady, 'Making The Worst Person in the World, an Oscar-Nominated "Unromantic Comedy"', *The Irish Times*, 19 March 2022, https://www.irishtimes.com/culture/film/making-the-worst-person-in-the-world-an-oscar-nominated-unromantic-comedy-1.4824526.
33. Sheila O'Malley, 'The Worst Person in the World: Lost and Found', The Criterion Collection, 2022, https://www.criterion.com/current/posts/7844-the-worst-person-in-the-world-lost-and-found.
34. Álex Vicente, 'Joachim Trier: "The Monogamous Are the Real Romantic Heroes of Our Time"', *El País* English, 17 March 2022, https://english.elpais.com/culture/2022-03-17/joachim-trier-the-monogamous-are-the-real-romantic-heroes-of-our-time.html.
35. Mekado Murphy, 'Watch Time Stand Still in "The Worst Person in the World"', *The New York Times*, 4 February 2022, https://www.nytimes.com/2022/02/04/movies/worst-person-in-the-world-clip.html.
36. Andrei Tarkovsky, *Andrei Tarkovsky: Interviews*, Conversations with Film Makers Series (Jackson: University of Mississippi Press, 2006).
37. Andrei Tarkovsky, *Sculpting in Time: Reflections on the Cinema* (London: The Bodley Head, 1986).
38. Ibid.

CHAPTER 4

Oslo

The very first frame of *The Worst Person in the World* shows an elegant young woman in a formal dark dress, smoking a cigarette in the evening sun. Behind her a very Norwegian landscape opens up: a fjord, a city, forests and hills. Julie is on the terrace of the Ekeberg restaurant, situated in the hills above the Oslo fjord, having a break from a party where she feels out of place. A jazzy piano tune drifts by, briefly drowned out by the sound of a motorcycle somewhere in the streets below. Julie turns to look out over the city, takes a few puffs of her cigarette and sighs. She spends some time scrolling on her phone before the camera moves in and shows her in profile, bathed in the summer

Figure 4.1 Julie overlooking Oslo from Ekebergåsen.

light. As the picture fades to black, she turns away from us, to face the city once more.

Inhabitants of the city would describe Julie's view from this vantage point as the very essence of Oslo. The Norwegian capital is a relatively small, compact city, with both fjord and forest in close proximity; a modern, urban space where nature, wilderness, is still nearby. It is bisected by a river, Akerselva, often seen as the border between the working-class east and the more well-to-do *vestkanten*, or westside. Julie is looking down upon a part of town that encapsulates both old and new Oslo. Though its history as a town spans a thousand years, as a capital it is young – having been established as such in 1814, when Norway gained independence from Denmark, after four hundred years of Copenhagen rule. Close to where Julie stands lies Bjørvika, a former container port recently redeveloped. The fjord has been filled in and made home to several cultural institutions (the Oslo Opera House (2008), the Munch Museum (2021), the Deichman Library (2020)), office buildings, and expensive residences. The areas surrounding these towering new structures have been made available and accessible to walkers and swimmers, and include a number of floating saunas sprinkled around the fjord. Just a little further up lies the part of Oslo that was first constructed, now called Gamlebyen (The Old Town).[1] On the furthest side of the next hill over, the ski jump at Holmenkollen, can be seen – one of Norway's most popular tourist attractions and a cultural icon in a skiing nation. Though Renate Reinsve's Julie is in focus, these images of Oslo are important parts of both this opening scene and the film itself. As described by critic Ella Kemp: 'Trier's film beautifully paints the city that played such a huge part in sculpting its characters'.[2]

This description could be applied to a number of Trier's films. Four of them are set (and were for the most part shot) in Oslo (*Louder Than Bombs* being the only exception), and three of these, *Reprise* (2006), *Oslo, August 31st* (2011) and *The Worst Person in the World* (2021), constitute a series referred to as the 'Oslo trilogy'. Focusing mainly on these three, this chapter will discuss different aspects of Trier's use of Oslo and specific places. The city encountered in these works is both similar to and unlike Oslo as it exists in the real world; it is a cinematic space with its own character identity, one we can call Trier's Oslo.[3] Shot over a period of fifteen years, the films form a sort of portrait of the city's development in the twenty-first century; and I will touch on what this portrait can tell us about contemporary urban culture within the European upper middle class in general.

The three films were never planned as a trilogy; this designation only emerged when Anders Danielsen Lie, who stars in all of them, read the final script.[4] Now the scripts and DVDs are sold in 'Oslo trilogy' box sets, though the plots and characters of each film are unique and not connected. Rather than a narrative series, the continuation here is more thematic, emotional or visual in nature. As such, the term 'triptych', though originating in and often associated with religious and devotional art, might be just as appropriate as 'trilogy', with the setting and the visual style as the common denominator. The three films form a whole, but each part stands on its own. Applying the term trilogy has, however, been a good strategy for highlighting Trier and his back-catalogue, following the international success of *The Worst Person in the World*.

Aside from Anders Danielsen Lie, Oslo and its depiction is indeed the most important feature shared by all three films. Each of them makes active and extensive use of different parts of the city, with a large number of outdoor shots. Though *Thelma* is set there too, it comes across as less of an Oslo-centric piece, not least because so many of its central scenes are set in non-specific indoor spaces like doctor's offices, hospital rooms, study halls, or swimming pools – spaces that could be anywhere. There are exceptions to this: there are important scenes set on the Blindern university campus, at the Opera House, and in the Enerhaugen residential area, all recognisable Oslo settings. The mood and stage are, however, set by Oslo in an entirely different way in the trilogy. Trier's American colleague and friend Mike Mills (*Beginners*, 2010, *C'mon, C'mon*, 2021) has called the feel of these films 'Os-loneliness', capturing perfectly how these films are all about people feeling lonely and alienated in a city that is familiar, that should feel like home.[5] The degree to which these characters truly belong in Oslo varies, however, and I shall elaborate on this.

It was not a given that the two budding filmmakers who left their native city and country to study in England (Trier) and France (Vogt) would one day return to make films in and about Oslo.[6] 'You know what, we need to get out of this country', brash Phillip tells Erik in the opening of *Reprise*. Just as the two authors-to-be have dropped their respective manuscripts into the mail box, they are surrounded by hordes of Norwegians celebrating the 17th May, Constitution Day, with all that entails: flags, inebriation, national costumes and the expectation that they march along with the others.[7] The scene is a clear visualisation of how these surroundings are too cramped for two young men of artistic ambition. In this film, Oslo is a city far too small for the future Phillip and Erik envision. Like one of the anonymous voice-overs says in the prologue of *Oslo, August 31st*: she found that Oslo offered freedom, until she discovered how small the city really was.

Anders in *Oslo, August 31st* expresses a need to escape a city that feels oppressive too: 'I have to get away from Oslo', he says in a message left for his ex-girlfriend Iselin.[8] Before his time to record it runs out, he somewhat aimlessly and unrealistically suggests coming to New York. Iselin has stopped taking his calls, but he says he wants to go to the big city to start over, to be with her, perhaps to study. Shortly before this, he has said that, at thirty-four, he cannot imagine starting all over, and that the academic life his friend Thomas leads seems entirely pointless to him. In these first two films, finding new opportunities is, in other words, synonymous with metropolises like Paris and New York. The concept is particularly well-developed in *Reprise,* where friendships, careers, and love lives that have stagnated in Oslo can all be reignited in Paris, at least in one's imagination.

To Julie in *The Worst Person in the World,* however, Oslo is a city filled with opportunity, with things to study, careers to pursue, and attractive and interesting men. When medical school feels wrong, she drops out and enrols in psychology, which she subsequently abandons for photography. The 2021 film version of Oslo is no longer characterised by barriers and limitation. If anything, Julie's problem is being faced with too many choices, and the accompanying sense of pressure and expectation. As put by critic Carlos Aguilar: The film addresses 'the ticking clock of society-imposed for one to succeed professionally, settle down romantically, or reproduce'.[9]

Oslo, like any community, has its conventions and demands, and Trier's characters struggle to abide by or satisfy these, whether they be imposed on them by their families, their friends, or society at large (or indeed by the characters themselves). All of Trier's privileged, young protagonists wish not only to fit in, but also to stand out, to be unique and set apart from everyone else. Phillip and Erik desire a place among Oslo's cultural elite, the people who attend parties at Kunstnernes Hus (an art centre) and get their names in the papers. Anders speaks derisively of the others at the treatment centre who would be content to find a warehouse job and have a baby with 'some former raver'. Julie considers herself different from, and more than, 'those teacher's pets in psychology'.

Evidently, feeling at home in Oslo means different things to the different characters. Erik and Phillip chum around with other young men who share their tastes and ideals. Though this camaraderie is to some extent built on illusions, they still move between parties and venues where they seem to be very much in their element. Anders in *Oslo, August 31st* on the other hand, navigates a city that has changed, one where his friends have moved on from him (to new partners, new families, new lives). Here, Oslo is regarded with a bit more distance.[10] In *The Worst Person in the World*, on the other hand, Julie is constantly changing, having to adapt to new milieus in the city. Joachim Trier and Eskil Vogt have spent a lot of time talking about why the backdrop for the films they ended up writing together had to be Oslo.

Ella Kemp points out how their characters are shaped by their environment, just as the writers were shaped by the city they grew up and spent most of their lives in.[11] As such, what Trier and Vogt offer up in their scripts is not a sociological portrait of Oslo, but a subjective rendering of a city whose streets and codes they are intimately familiar with: 'We portray the city in our own palette, letting our temperament influence each choice, down to jargon and fashion sense', Trier said of making *Reprise*.[12] This aspect is most notable in the debut feature, with all its specific references to a particular young male subculture, at a specific time and place, but it can be found in all three films of the trilogy. The scripts, which have all been published, are littered with precise location directions, making it clear that scenes were written with certain places in mind. Trier and Vogt are also very concerned with geographical continuity, meaning that when Anders moves towards his friend Thomas's house, he is actually walking down the appropriate Oslo streets, in the right direction. Similarly, when Julie ends up at a party in the Old Town, the scene is shot in just the spot one would pass if walking towards the city centre from the Ekeberg restaurant. Along the way she walks past scenery famously found in the background of Edvard Munch's iconic painting *The Scream*.

Trier has repeatedly described his own films as personal, and so it seems natural that they be set in settings he knows.[13] He places a great deal of importance on the ability of *mise-en-scène* to communicate certain moods, often moods connected to specific memories. One example of this is the documentary footage of the demolition of the Philips building, seen in the prologue of *Oslo, August 31st*. To the outsider, these clips may seem far-removed from the context of the film, but they represent an event that looms large for many Oslo citizens, including the director himself. The building was a modernist landmark in the Majorstua area, and at the time of its construction (1958) the tallest building in Oslo. It was, however – spectacularly, and in front of a crowd – brought down in a controlled demolition in 2000; and thus a structure that had shaped the urban environment Trier grew up with simply vanished.[14] Trier has also spoken about French director Alain Resnais's preoccupation with the relationship between places and memories, his particular way of creating moods through the use of specific spots and buildings that had inspired him.[15]

> Alain Resnais's way of using the camera as a gaze, sliding across buildings, and then engaging in that notion as a memory – we all have cities and streets that we walked through on that joyful day, on that sad night, in the winter and the summer. The layers of memories that places inhabit for us, is the most fundamental, existential experience that cinema can show us, that spaces carry us, and they will remain when we're gone.[16]

Hiroshima mon amour is a film in which cities and their (tragic) histories have such an effect on two lovers that they call each other by the names of the places they are from – 'Hiroshima' and 'Nevers'. Trier and Vogt also base themselves in places they know intimately, though they do have a stated goal of finding something that will be applicable to people who have not lived or spent much time in Oslo.[17] Indeed, a lot of the response to Trier's work seems to suggest that his films strike at a certain contemporary, urban culture that is based as much in age and social class as any particular nationality.

Out of the three films, *Oslo, August 31st* received the most praise for the way it captured the city, and this topic was a major focus in Norwegian reviews. Oslo-based critics interpreted the film as a portrait of the city, and more than that, as both an homage and love letter to it, as can be seen in the following examples: 'He celebrates Oslo in an unprecedented way', '*Oslo, August 31st* is Joachim Trier's caustic, yet genuine declaration of love for the capital', and 'One of the most beautiful and melancholy homages to Oslo ever captured on film'.[18] Another Norwegian review described it as 'an observant and elegiac portrait of a city and a generation', and held that the city alternated between being the background and the foreground of the film.[19]

The look and significance of the place were not lost on international critics either, though. American David Thomson opened his glowing review by pointing out the particular feel of a far-north summer: 'Late in June, in the depth of summer, the sun sets in Oslo at 10:40 p.m. And then its light lingers, so that the sun can rise again just before 4 a.m.' But his brief, emotional text also questions whether such bright nights are entirely a good thing: 'Are five hours of pale dark enough if you need to dream, to hide or contemplate dying?'.[20] Danish reviewer Eva Novrup Redvall touches upon something similar in her encounter with the film: 'Cinematographer Jakob Ihre has lyrically captured the light and the sense of a season in which one knows that, though the weather still is fair, it can only get worse going forward'.[21] The light in *Oslo, August 31st* is at times an obscuring curtain, but, as I have suggested before, there is a duality and ambivalence at play in this portrait of Oslo.

To Anders, Oslo is both a city in the throes of great change and an old, familiar place. A place filled with summery nostalgia (parks and bars) and traumatic memories of lost opportunity, of confinement (crowded streets, scaffolded pavements, courtyards). One example is the scene where Anders and his friends sneak into the outdoor pool complex Frognerbadet for an illicit night swim. The others are swimming, playing, and kissing in the bright, blue water, and the sun is rising above the park, but Anders remains seated in shadow. Eventually he just walks away, to end his life, in the bright summer night. The ambivalent mixture of brightness and darkness here is similar to the one we get when Julie is wandering the streets of Oslo, all night long, as Aksel lays dying. She is grieving, but the sunrise bathes her face in beautiful light.

Trier and his team were also on the hunt for a particular sort of duality, one found in several of his films, a space where poetry and realism meet. As he puts it when talking about writing the script for *Oslo, August 31st*:

> We want conserve the poetic, but also to acknowledge the city as it is. During the writing process we talked a lot about where in Oslo the specific scenes might take place. What is it like to bike down Kirkeveien at early twilight, when it's all empty of cars? What does it look like when

the sun rises on the Frogner park on a summer morning? What can one observe over the course of an hour at Åpent Bakeri in Parkveien? We wanted to show the space in a way that was sensuous and emotional, without straying from the logical.[22]

An aspect of *Oslo, August 31st* that greatly contributes to the realist, nearly documentary impression it leaves of Oslo is the sound. What can be heard in the film *is* the sound of Oslo. Gisle Tveito, one of Norway's most prolific and famous sound designers, has worked with Trier on all his films, and for this film decided that all recordings would be made in actual Oslo environments.[23] In an interview, Tveito has stated that the aim of these recordings was to contribute to a portrait of Oslo, a city he describes as an organism. A city that has its bustling, hectic spaces, yes, but also places of, and for, quiet.[24] Oslo is a city brimming with parks and green spaces, with places to find refuge from the noise. Tveito and Trier collaborated closely to find the right sounds, to figure out both what belonged in their cinematic universe, and what did not.

Music is, for instance, used very sparingly in this film. Ola Fløttum's score is carefully introduced in the prologue, and Norwegian pop band a-ha's 'I've been Losing You' hits us as Anders heads towards the city in a taxi. But aside from this, there is no music for the first forty-nine minutes of the film. In the same interview, Tveito also discusses the importance of letting the conversations between Anders and Thomas be naked and honest. This is why things like birdsong, the wind in the trees, children playing, and snippets of conversations can be heard, along with aeroplanes, sirens, and urban soundscapes – but no music. The central thing is this conversation, between two friends who used to be close but have drifted apart. This conversation needs no music to be affecting. The spaces and sounds of the city are merely the backdrop to their attempt to reconnect, to find the intimacy they have lost.

As a contrast, the sound very much takes centre stage in another important scene – the one where Anders listens to the conversations of strangers in a café. Here, a unique, acoustic space is constructed, one in which the sounds of other people are in focus, and Anders himself remains entirely quiet. The intention behind the sound design was to evoke the sense that the viewers themselves are there, listening in on the conversations in this room, as one (perhaps) does when alone in such places.[25] The scene was carefully planned, while the dialogues were more improvised. By coincidence some girls hired as extras started to talk about Kurt Cobain's suicide while sitting in the café, and this was incorporated in the film.[26] By letting other people's conversations play the dominant part, Trier offers us insight into Anders and his frame of mind (we are listening along with him, as Gunnar Iversen puts it in his analysis of the sound in this film), but also a realistic representation of what navigating an urban landscape is like.[27] This is what it is like to share a large, somewhat anonymising space with other people. One can suddenly and unexpectedly be pulled into someone else's intimations, thoughts and dreams, things they never meant for anyone else to hear. And then, just as abruptly, the moment passes; you will never hear any more about this person's life again. Perhaps another sound caught your attention and focus. In this highly original scene, one of Trier's best, the sounds of Oslo have been carefully selected, curated to say something about both the city and him. They function as something external and concrete (they are the sounds made by the city around him), but they simultaneously grant us access to Anders's inner, subjective reality (they are the sounds he picks up, focuses on). The sound of Oslo is not just a realistic, aural setting, it is something that can draw our attention and evoke specific moods.[28]

Figure 4.2 Anders at Åpent Bakeri.

The café seen in this scene, Åpent Bakeri, no longer exists. Seeing older films from familiar places can often strike one with a sense of what time does to a place. Just like the footage of the demolition of the Philips building, the Oslo trilogy itself functions as documentation and a reminder of the evolution Oslo underwent over the fifteen years that passed between the filming of *Reprise* and *The Worst Person in the World*.

The trilogy also shares a common feature with the French New Wave films they (particularly the first two) were inspired by: the French directors of the 1950s and 60s were known to head into the city streets for their shoots. Eskil Vogt has highlighted the documentary qualities of these French films, their ability to 'make the background come alive and capture some of life surrounding the stories'.[29] Vogt also compares cinema to painted still lifes; an artist painting fresh, gleaming fruit to remind the viewer of the fleetingness of life. 'It's powerful to think that people will be able to watch *Oslo, August 31st* and those cafés will be gone, the people in the streets as close to ghosts as you can get'.[30]

Nothing is more illustrative of the change that has taken place in Oslo than the fact that when *Reprise* was made in 2005, none of the buildings in Bjørvika that Julie can see from the hills existed. It was a container terminal and a junction. Now, traffic moves through a tunnel beneath the fjord. The Opera House, where Thelma has her powerful, emotional experience, was finished in 2008, and construction barely underway at the time of Trier's debut film. The first image of 2010 Oslo shown in *Oslo, August 31st* (following the retrospective prologue) shows just what I have described here: a city that is changing, that is under construction.[31] When Anders leaves the treatment centre and enters the city, he emerges through a tunnel to a view of a Bjørvika that is dominated by cranes and construction. Behind them, Oslo's new and (from a Norwegian perspective) towering skyline rises. This particular stretch of buildings was named Barcode for the image it strikes from a distance. And so, when *The Worst Person in the World* was shot, Anders's 2010 café had closed down, but a new branch of the same chain had opened in one of the new structures, and this is where Eivind works as a barista, a decade on.

Trier's films thus document the shifting of the city centre, the repurposing of the waterfront, and the gentrification of an old part of town. Oslo is a city that, in Benjamin Bigelow's words, has been 'excavated, renovated and reshaped' in the fifteen years gone by between films one and three.[32] Such processes carry tensions too, between the city Oslo was and the one it might become. In his analysis of *Oslo, August 31st*, Bigelow writes about how the city holds many kinds of memories, personal as well as collective: 'Constantly subject to change, expansion, development, building and renovation, cities like Oslo are simultaneously sites for the objectivation and preservation of cultural memory in a modern society.'[33]

When Eivind and Julie, during their first, flirtatious encounter, decide to share something they have never dared tell anyone else with each other, his first secret is: 'I was going to say I like the Barcode project. It looks pretty from the bridge when I go to work'. When Julie, who has just shared something intimate about her sexual preferences exclaims 'Why the hell haven't you dared tell anyone that?'[34] he says it's 'Because everyone thinks it's ugly'. And indeed, the development down by the fjord has been heavily, though perhaps not unanimously, criticised. In an article about Trier's Oslo, magazine and film editor Karsten Meinich uses Eivind's very word, ugly, to describe the skyline: 'Different sizes of cubes, and kind of modern architecture, but also quite ugly'. He goes on to discuss how its construction was perceived as a (negative) contrast to the new opera house, which was immediately lauded as beautiful:

'We just built the opera house, it was so expensive and beautiful. And then the next thing coming up is ugly.'[35]

Eivind's line about enjoying Barcode is also a means of demonstrating that he does not have the correct cultural capital, the currency so crucial to so many of Trier's characters, not least Phillip and Erik and their circle in *Reprise*. It seems doubtful that Julie's boyfriend Aksel, whose new graphic novel was just launched at a party with the city's cultural elite, and his friends would share Eivind's appreciation for the new structures. Because while Trier's films and characters move through a number of streets and neighbourhoods in Oslo, they mostly belong on the westside, and come from homes filled with both literal and cultural capital, with social and financial stability. Phillip, a young man with no steady source of income, lives alone in a lofty apartment, with plenty of space for his well-stocked bookshelves. Anders's parents own a villa on the westside of town, with at least three fireplaces, a grand piano, and rare artworks on the walls. Julie's family are of a more ordinary Norwegian middle class, but her grandmother played iconic parts at the National Theatre (Nationaltheatret), and her mother works in the publishing industry. Julie also came from paintings and pianos, and she has the financial freedom to enrol in and drop out of several degree programmes without much in the way of consequences. Thelma, on the other hand, came from out of town and lives in an Enerhaugen bedsit. Eivind's flat is in the same part of town, and neither of them belongs in a social environment where it is all about knowing the right people, the right authors, the right places. With his two latest films, Trier has widened his scope, considered additional sides of the city. As Julie puts it after switching social scenes: 'Oslo had become an entirely different city, new places, new faces'.

Trier's Oslo remains chiefly the Oslo of the white middle class, however, and his films do not venture out into the suburbs where towers blocks and immigrants are the majority.[36] I described 2021 Oslo as a city of endless opportunity above, but while this may be true for Julie, it is not necessarily so for the citizens not belonging to the upper or middle classes. Oslo can be a party where many feel out of place. Norway ranks among the countries in the world with the highest standard of living, but it is not immune to rising social inequality. While Oslo saw a great population increase between *Reprise* and *The Worst Person in the World*, this growth has since died down. One reason is a high cost of living; the difficulty of buying a home on a teacher's or nurse's salary has become a recurrent story in the media (a shocking development in a country where owning one's home has more or less been the norm).

The depiction of different places around Oslo is largely shaped by the characters' movements and actions.[37] Trier once described Anders's journey through Oslo as a road movie.[38] But Trier's characters never drive, and rarely use public transport. Just like the director prefers to do, they tend to walk the streets of the city. Trier's Oslo could as such be the product not only of his upbringing, of familiarity and local knowledge, but also of inspiration from film history, of deliberate aesthetic choices. James Tweedle wrote that to the French New Wave directors, 'the act of walking in the city emerged as one of the most revelatory of cinematic actions' and stated that this would become an important feature of all the most iconic films from this movement.[39] In Tweedle's words, the New Wave films combine the corporeal and the concrete, allowing us to experience the cities at these young walkers' pace (rather than the speed of the train or the car). His description, however, could just as well be applied to Trier's work:

> These characters both move and linger in space ... This figure in motion also becomes a support for the eyes and ears that absorb and process a welter of information present in the streets, architecture, and crowds. Like a camera travelling carefully through the city, the body serves as a device for recording the goings-on throughout town. The city is imagined as an extension of the body in motion and the body as an extension of cinema.[40]

One of the many aspects of the French New Wave to inspire Trier was the way directors like Jean-Luc Godard, Francois Truffaut and Agnes Varda used the city, and images of it, in their films. One of his chief inspirations in this regard was of course Louis Malle's *The Fire Within* (*Le feu follet*, 1963), based on Pierre le Rochelle Drieus's novel of the same name. This film, too, was shot on location in Paris. Trier was struck by this work, which he considers a masterpiece, but in his own version, the Place de la Concorde, Latin Quarter, Café de Flore, the Seine, and the Luxembourg gardens have been replaced with the Vigeland park, the Frogner baths, Åpent bakeri, and Kirkeveien in Oslo.[41] The Norwegian director was captivated by the universal and existential in Malles's story, but also certain that his own take would have to be personal, and as such, time- and place-specific.

> I knew that would mean the film would exist in a certain bubble of time and that it would age. But I think people should keep making versions of this film every ten or twenty years, in different cities and with different characters, and maybe it will be a mirror of society at a certain time.[42]

While *Oslo, August 31st* is more directly about Oslo than any of Trier's other films, the city also functions as a character in the other two parts of the trilogy. It is a means of explaining and understanding the (other) characters, but those characters also shape our perception of the city. As A. O. Scott wrote about *The Worst Person in the World* in *The New York Times*: 'The cliché that the city is a character in its own right seems woefully insufficient. The Norwegian capital is what gives the film its character and explains its characters. It's a clean, well-lighted metropolis with a broken heart'.[43]

Scott also situates Trier within a tradition along with Edvard Munch, Karl Ove Knausgård, and August Strindberg, where the melancholy is never far away, even when the sun is shining: 'A mood of somber rumination falls over the fun like a slant of winter light. Somebody's tears are always on the horizon, and mortality lurks around every corner'.[44] While there are elements of truth to this description of his films, Trier's Oslo is above all a city of summer. While real-world Oslo can, quite literally, be dark and cold, Trier's films are always bathed in a light that seems to suggest a sun that never sets.

NOTES

1. The Old Town is the oldest urban area in Oslo. It used to be the town centre, but when the capital was moved slightly away from this site and named Kristiania (between 1624 and 1924), the area kept the name Oslo and existed as a suburb. 'Old Town' came into use when the capital as a whole was again named Oslo in 1925 and reabsorbed this part of town into the city proper.
2. Ella Kemp, 'Cool World: Norway's Capital Through the Eyes of the Oslo Trilogy', *Journal: A Letterboxd Magazine*, 28 March 2022, https://letterboxd.com/journal/cool-world-oslo-norway-capital-trier-vogt/.
3. See also Sigrid Haugros, 'Triers Oslo', *Z Filmtidsskrift*, no. 2 (2012): 64–75.
4. Kemp, 'Cool World'.
5. Carlos Aguilar, 'How Joachim Trier's Unplanned Oslo Trilogy Became a Cinematic Masterpiece in Three Distinct Parts', *IndieWire*, 1 February 2022, https://www.indiewire.com/2022/02/joachim-trier-oslo-trilogy-interview-1234695516/.
6. Vogt's two feature films as director, *Blind* (2014) and *The Innocents* (2021) are also set in Oslo.
7. Norway's Constitution Day is celebrated on 17th May, and a noteworthy aspect of the celebrations is the children's parade. In an interview from 2008, the then young director talks about the footage from the actual parade and describing it as: 'an embarrassing parade': 'We needed documentary footage, and that's reality for you in Norway, this little country that has this forced national day parade, which is kind of funny and a little bit embarrassing. My Danish editor saw the rushes for that, and he said, "My God, this looks like Austria in the 30s". It's like ridiculous, all costumes and flags.' Chris Tinkham, 'Joachim Trier. Co-Writer and Director of Reprise', Under the Radar, 2 May 2008, https://www.undertheradarmag.com/interviews/joachim_trier_interview_052008..
8. The full sentence is not reflected in the subtitles, so I have expanded a bit.
9. Aguilar, 'How Joachim Trier's Unplanned Oslo Trilogy'.
10. See also Haugros, 'Triers Oslo'.
11. Kemp, 'Cool World'.
12. Bjarte Breiteig, Eskil Vogt, and Joachim Trier, 'Overskudd og ambivalens. En samtale rundt tilblivelsen av Reprise mellom Bjarte Breiteig, Eskil Vogt og

Joachim Trier'. In Breiteig, Vogt, and Trier, *Reprise. Et filmmanuskript*. Oslo: Tiden Norsk Forlag, 2007, 208–37, at 223.
13. See, for instance, Hillary Weston, 'The Art Form of Memory: A Conversation with Joachim Trier', The Criterion Collection, 8 April 2016, https://www.criterion.com/current/posts/4001-the-art-form-of-memory-a-conversation-with-joachim-trier.
14. See Aguilar, 'How Joachim Trier's Unplanned Oslo Trilogy'.
15. The interview is about films that have inspired him, and he will often point to *Hiroshima mon amour* (1959) as a major inspiration.
16. Nick Chen, 'Director Joachim Trier Selects Ten of His All-Time Favourite Romcoms', *Dazed*, 2 March 2022, https://www.dazeddigital.com/film-tv/article/55580/1/joachim-trier-worst-person-in-the-world-ten-romcoms-top-ten.
17. Breiteig, Vogt, and Trier, 'Overskudd og ambivalens', 228.
18. Mode Steinkjer, 'Triers lavmælte triumf', *Dagsavisen*, 31 August 2011. Ulrik Eriksen, 'En storbysymfoni', *Morgenbladet*, 26 August 2011, https://morgenbladet.no/kultur/2011/en_storbysymfoni; Kjetil Lismoen, 'Et svært sterkt skuespillerløft', 19 May 2011, https://www.aftenposten.no/oslo/byliv/i/GnVV/et-svaert-sterkt-skuespillerloeft.
19. Inger Merethe Hobbelstad, 'Bevegende bysommer', *Dagbladet*, 18 May 2011, https://www.dagbladet.no/kultur/bevegende-bysommer/63687380.
20. David Thomson, 'A Small Norwegian Film and the Critic Who Praised It', *The New Republic*, 12 September 2012, https://newrepublic.com/article/107141/thomson-oslo.
21. Eva Novrup Redvall, 'Sidste omgang i Oslo', *Information*, 26 October 2011, https://www.information.dk/kultur/anmeldelse/2011/10/sidste-omgang-oslo.
22. Bjarte Breiteig, Eskil Vogt, and Joachim Trier, 'Oslo gjennom mørkt glass – Eskil Vogt og Joachim Trier i samtale med Bjarte Breiteig', in *Oslo, 31. August. Filmmanus.* (Oslo: Tiden Norsk Forlag, 2011), 178.
23. Svenn Jakobsen, 'Lyden av Oslo, 31. August', *Rushprint*, 19 March 2012, https://rushprint.no/2012/03/lyden-av-oslo-31-august/.
24. Ibid.
25. Jakobsen, 'Lyden av Oslo, 31. August'.
26. Joachim Trier, 'Masterclass with Joachim Trier in Conversation with Anne Gjelsvik'. Department of Art and Media Studies, NTNU, 18 September 2017.
27. Gunnar Iversen, 'Lyden av Oslo, 31 August', in Gunnar Iversen and Asbjørn Tiller *Lydbilder: Mediene Og Det Akustiske* (Universitetsforlaget, 2014), 101–17.
28. Ibid.
29. Breiteig, Vogt, and Trier, 'Oslo gjennom mørkt glass', 180.
30. Ibid., 181.
31. See also Haugros, 'Triers Oslo'; Benjamin Bigelow, 'Acts of Remembering, Acts of Forgetting: Architecture, Memory and Recovery in Oslo, August 31st', *Journal of Scandinavian Cinema* 10, no. 1 (1 March 2020): 7–24, https://doi.org/10.1386/jsca_00011_1; Iversen, 'Lyden av Oslo, 31. August'.
32. Bigelow, 'Acts of Remembering', 13.
33. Ibid., 14.

34. In the subtitles this is translated as: 'Why is that a secret?', which does not really capture the exclamation.
35. Keith Phipps, 'An Insider's Guide to the Oslo of "The Worst Person in the World"', Substack newsletter, *The Reveal* (blog), 15 February 2022, https://thereveal.substack.com/p/an-insiders-guide-to-the-oslo-of.
36. Whereas Vogt's *Innocents* is shot in the suburb Romsås.
37. Haugros, 'Triers Oslo', 67.
38. Hillary Weston, 'Everyday Magic: Joachim Trier on Reimagining Louis Malle', The Criterion Collection, 17 December 2017, https://www.criterion.com/current/posts/5039-everyday-magic-joachim-trier-on-reimagining-louis-malle.
39. James Tweedie, 'The *Mise-En-Scène* of Modernity: The French New Wave, Paris, and the Global 1960s', in *The Age of New Waves: Art Cinema and the Staging of Globalization*, ed. James Tweedie (Oxford University Press, 2013), 63, https://doi.org/10.1093/acprof:oso/9780199858286.003.0002.
40. Ibid., 64
41. See Jon Inge Faldalen, 'Utfor vestkanten', *Vinduet* 2, 2011, 92–101 for a methodical comparison between the novel and Malle's film.
42. Weston, 'Everyday Magic'.
43. A. O. Scott, '"The Worst Person in the World" Review: Oslo, Her Way', *The New York Times*, 3 February 2022, sec. Movies, https://www.nytimes.com/2022/02/03/movies/the-worst-person-in-the-world-review.html.
44. Ibid.

CHAPTER 5

Closures and Openings

Towards the end of *Oslo, August 31st*, there is a short scene set in the Vigeland Park, a sprawling sculpture park on Oslo's westside.[1] In the bright summer night, thirty-four-year-old Anders, fresh out of treatment for drug addiction, walks through the park with a distant friend and two younger women he just met at a party. Anders and his friend have each been flirting with one of the girls, and while the other couple circle them on a bike, Anders leads 'his' girl towards an open spot in the park. 'The echo-point?' his friend casually asks as he passes. 'Yes, yes – it's a classic Oslo spot,' Anders says, 'we have to share it with the newcomers'. He gently positions the girl in the middle of a circle in an area paved with stones and asks her to stomp the ground, hard. The sound of her foot echoes around them as Anders leans into the circle and barks a short 'hi'. Her back to him, the girl continues shouting different 'ah-s' and 'oh-s'. Outside the circle, the other couple still looping joyfully around, Anders closes his eyes and, for a short moment, retreats into his own melancholy self. The camera closes in on him, and although the girl continues to send him teasing glances and smiles over her shoulder as she shouts her way through every vowel in the alphabet, it becomes increasingly evident that he is beyond reach.

As has already been established in previous chapters, Joachim Trier is known for his nuanced treatment of weighty, existential subject matter. In his own words, his films have 'got to be about something existential' to be worth making.[2] Like several of the modernist filmmakers that inspired him – Michelangelo Antonioni and Ingmar Bergman among others – his wish is to make films about what it is to be human. And so, *my* claim, that Trier's films are about people seeking to understand themselves, should not be controversial. This theme is perhaps most overt in *The Worst Person in the World*, but I would argue that it features prominently in all of them.

However, I posit that Trier's films also dig deeper than these typical descriptors of modernist existentialism might indicate, primarily because mental health and mental illness are at the core of several of them.[3] Trier himself has at times sought to tone down this perspective, stating in one interview that he is somewhat wary of the definition of 'mental illness' as a topic in his films.[4] However, I do not see any conflict between acknowledging that Trier's films are open to a range of interpretations and also their specific value as works that shed light on an important issue. On the contrary, focusing on this topic can underscore the richness and depth of his films, and I will argue that several of them offer insight into what it means to struggle with mental illness – in fact, *The Worst Person in the World* is the only one in which this is not the case.

I am not the only person to draw attention to Trier's preoccupation with mental health, but as the opening paragraph of this chapter is intended to show, here I am also interested in how the relationship between the main characters and their visual environment is used to portray mental illness.[5] I argue that Trier uses different spaces or settings to give insight into mental states, as exemplified by the setting in the Vigeland Park scene. The main focus in this chapter will be on *Oslo, August 31st* and *Thelma*, two films that are more closely connected than they may appear at first glance, in which space is used to create a sense of mental imbalance or struggle.

Mental health is, however, also of vital importance in two of his other films, and so I shall briefly look at these first, to establish how important this subject is to Trier. In *Reprise* (2006), we follow the two aspiring writers, Erik and Phillip, and witness how they both must deal with Phillip's mental breakdown, his hospitalisation following a psychotic incident, and his struggle for recovery. The film centres on the two friends' writing ambitions, and the consequences of Phillip's psychosis for his work and his relationships with Erik, his other friends, and his girlfriend Kari. *Reprise* can be described as a film balancing light and darkness, satire, and solemnity, and as an anti-psychological narrative. This because we get no psychological background for Erik and Phillips's stories, nor any explanation for Phillip's psychotic break.[6] While direct causes can be difficult to establish, psychotic symptoms and episodes can often be the result of non-psychological issues like somatic medical conditions, drug and alcohol use, genetics, hormonal or brain-chemical factors, or external stressors. As Tarja Laine foregrounds in her reading of the film, psychosis is a disoriented state that leads to an inability to act in the world. Laine, like me, also highlights the film's setting, and sees Oslo as representing the world as it is, while Paris functions as a utopian realm where Phillip can once again act and take control of his reality.[7]

In *Louder Than Bombs* (2015), three family members try to process their trauma and loss after the mother's sudden death. The psychological challenges in *Louder Than Bombs*, are less extreme than those found *Reprise*, its exploration of the experience of bereavement making it perhaps more relatable to a wider audience. The two sons, Jonah and Conrad, and husband, Gene, must cope with their grief, memories, and deceptions following the death of Isabelle, mother and wife, which occurred two years before the events of the film. Her death is described as a suicide, and though we never know for certain, the film indicates that it could have been the result of post-traumatic stress and depression following her work as a war photographer. Among other things, she experienced a bombing, which could have claimed her life and left her with physical, and perhaps mental scars.

Both her husband Gene, and her oldest son Jonah, are haunted by guilt over their lack of action when (they knew) Isabelle was struggling, and Conrad appears especially affected by what happened to his mother. He is a lonely boy, friendless at school and non-communicative with his father. Here, the teenage bedroom, with its permanently closed door, and the desire to hide away in a virtual reality or within the bubble of a pair of headphones, functions as a space to mirror Conrad's mental state. Places, spaces, or settings are, however, not the most important means of depicting such things in this film. In *Louder Than Bombs*, the emotional challenges faced by the wounded family are primarily depicted through the complex narration, with different points of view and a fractured chronology with flashbacks, memories, and dreams. At the core of this film are the communicative hurdles the members of the family struggle to get past.[8]

Oslo, August 31st and *Thelma* stand out from Trier's other stories in how they emphasise the connection between place and psychological states to a much greater degree. In *Oslo, August 31st*, we follow a depressed drug addict through his final twenty-four hours in the Norwegian capital, which will end with his suicide. The eponymous Thelma struggles with emancipation while simultaneously suffering from strange, unexplained seizures, potentially either supernatural or psychological in nature. In the following, I will look closer at how Trier uses the significance of place and the construction of space to create emotion in these two films. This is something Trier has himself foregrounded in several interviews, stating, for instance, that he is 'interested in the movements of things and how to treat space, and how space can somehow carry emotion'.[9]

Place is of particular importance in Trier's second feature film, as signified by its title, *Oslo, August 31st*. As discussed earlier the significance of Oslo was also underscored in the film's opening sequence: the very first images shown are old aerial shots of an Oslo cityscape, followed by archival footage and private film clips from different streets and parts of town. Norwegian newspaper *Dagbladet*'s reviewer, Inger Merete Hobbelstad, made a subtle connection between the existential crises in Trier's film and that of the anonymous narrator in Knut Hamsun's modernist masterpiece *Sult* (*Hunger*, 1890) when she closed her review by paraphrasing the novel's famous opening: 'But those who approach this strange film with sincerity and candour will not leave it until it has left its mark on them'.[10] In Hamsun's words: 'All of this happened while I was walking around starving in Kristiania – that strange city that no one escapes from until it has left its mark on him'.[11] This connection makes a lot of sense: both works describe a young man at a threshold in his life, feeling isolated and alienated from the city and people around him. But this alienation hits these two characters rather differently: while *Hunger*'s narrator ends up nourishing a strong, desperate hope for a better future, Anders in *Oslo, August 31st* feels little aside from hopelessness and a sense of things coming to a close.

The opening sequence of *Oslo, August 31st* ends as mentioned, with the controlled demolition of a large commercial building in Oslo (the Philips building) in 2000, almost as a forewarning of our main character's self-inflicted death. These images, though the building's collapse is planned and controlled, are evocative of images from the 9/11 terrorist attacks. The opening thus sets a melancholy tone, capturing the same tension between a nostalgic sense of longing for a safe and happy place and a feeling of loneliness and lack of belonging as the film as a whole. As a side note, the nostalgia evoked by the film was enhanced for the local audience by the fact that Oslo was hit by two brutal terrorist attacks on 22 July 2011, a mere month before it premiered in Norway.[12]

Trier has himself described Anders as a strong, intelligent character with integrity and lofty aims and ideals, but without the ability to achieve the goals he sets for himself.[13] Reflecting on Anders's situation when we meet him, following years of drug abuse and a subsequent long rehabilitation stay, film blogger Hillary Weston comments, 'but when you feel as though you've failed yourself, as if your life can go nowhere even with all the incredible things living inside you, the necessity of breathing begins to slip away'.[14] This is the exact mood the film captures as it follows Anders down various Oslo streets. Unlike many other films where a protagonist moves through a landscape, Anders's journey is almost entirely aimless.

Anders is an addict with a long history of betrayal. He has let down his former girlfriend Iselin, his friends, his family. But none of these things, not his background, not his betrayals, nor his addiction, are the focus of the film, which instead deals mainly with his state of mind. The specificity of time and place – Oslo, the last day of summer – is naturally of importance here. Co-scriptwriter Vogt has said that it was 'this raw state he'd be in on the eve of his return that we wished to tackle', and further that a therapist he and Trier consulted had compared the process of returning to society after addiction treatment to letting a little child out in the world on her own for the first time.[15]

It is in this especially vulnerable situation that Anders's suicidal state becomes fatal. Thus, while the film starts with a specific place, Oslo, it moves on to be about space in a more general sense, about how Anders engages with the world, or rather is unable to engage with it.

Depressive disorders can be long-term or recurrent and impair the suffering person's ability to cope with their daily life. Most people will experience periods of depression at some point, but it is when these negative emotions become intense enough to dominate the sufferer's life, making them unable to cope with normal situations and daily mechanisms, that they are diagnosed as part of a mood disorder.[16] Depressive disorders are the most common mental disorders, afflicting millions of people on different scales. The term is often used to describe a state of unhappiness or persistent sadness, a lack of energy and the loss of enjoyment of activities that would ordinarily be pleasurable. According to the World Health Organization's definition, depression is 'a common mental disorder, characterized by sadness, loss of interest or pleasure, feelings of guilt or low self-worth, disturbed sleep or appetite, feelings of tiredness and poor concentration'.[17] Julia Kristeva has termed depression (or melancholia) a non-communicable grief and, based on her own experiences, describes it as an inescapable abyss that makes people 'lose all interest in words, actions and even life itself'.[18]

In *Oslo, August 31st*, many of these symptoms are evident. During the final twenty-four hours of his life, Anders appears to lack purpose, motivation, and self-worth. In the scene described at the start of this chapter, he has experienced a bright summer night with a girl he is attracted to, and is about to regain his freedom from the institution where he has been a patient, but this is not enough to make him feel that life has value. Following the opening sequence and then the title of the film in white letters set against a black background, we meet Anders sitting quietly on a bed in the dark. He is framed in a close-up, with a young woman lying on the bed behind him. Distant sounds of traffic can be heard. The change in mood from the bittersweet nostalgia of the opening sequence, with young people reminiscing about memorable things, is unsettling, almost harsh. Later, Anders will describe this erotic rendezvous with Malin, something he had been looking forward to for a long time, as ultimately pretty empty for him. Even through the dark, Anders's face and body language convey how he experiences a closed-off darkness inside, and the fact of this is also visualised through the contrast between the window opening out into the brightness of the world, and the darkness of the room he is in. While Malin is in the shower, he gets up and pulls back the curtains, letting daylight into the room, but he soon steps back into the dark and takes his leave, seemingly without saying goodbye. But even out in the brightness of day, he is visually framed by constricting features, like bridges and fences.

Figure 5.1 Anders framed in his own darkness.

After this unsatisfying encounter, we see Anders trying and failing to drown himself in a lake in the woods. All his actions after this can be seen as one last attempt at finding some meaning in life, or at least to connect with people. He seeks out his former best friend Thomas, an academic with a wife and two small children, with whom he has a long, emotional, and existential talk while walking through, and pausing to sit down in, various Oslo parks. He then attends a mandatory job interview that goes wrong. He walks around the city, sits alone in a café before a frustrating meeting with his sister's girlfriend, who shows up to the appointment because the sister refuses to meet him. He crashes an old girlfriend's birthday party and steals money from her guests, money he subsequently uses to buy a large dose of heroin. He joins three other guests to go out clubbing, and, after the walk in the park described at the beginning of this chapter, leaves them by the outdoor swimming pool before retreating to his parents' home to die.

But before closing the curtains in his childhood bedroom, effectively closing himself in in much the same way as when we found him at the start of the film, Anders moves through Oslo, through a series of beautiful, open spaces – like when he spends time with Thomas in various, bright parks, or when he is on a bicycle, zipping down an empty street at night. In his conversation with Thomas, Anders tells his friend that he cannot face the situation he is in, exclaiming that he will not be able to start over. While his first suicide attempt at the beginning of the film – drowning himself by putting stones in his pockets – feels like something on a whim and maybe not a serious attempt, his conversation with Thomas is truly devastating. Anders tells Thomas that if it ends, Thomas should know that this was his own choice. Seen in an unsentimental way, Anders argues, nobody needs him. This is evidently an important confession and very hard to say, but also to hear. And Thomas exclaims that it is impossible for him to relate to the fact that Anders tells him that he will kill himself. Thomas argues that Anders has had hellish suicidal thoughts before and been able to overcome them. At this Anders smiles through tears and asserts that, 'It'll get better. It'll work out'.[19] As his smile fades and he looks, for a long time, at Thomas, he concludes sorrowfully, 'Except, it doesn't'. Blogger Hillary Weston describes the effect of this scene, shot in close-ups and beautiful summer light as

> It's a sentiment that feels refreshing to see portrayed. Usually we sense that the character feels this way, yes, but to have him verbalize that is heartbreaking to see, and Lie does a beautiful job of conveying this raw pain. . . He's stubborn and resolute in his fatalism.[20]

In a phenomenological take on Trier and Vogt's films, critic Benjamin Yazdan has described how Anders's feelings of meaninglessness are the clear focal point of *Oslo, August 31st*, and that the spectator is pulled between feeling close to and separated from him. It is the contrast between what we/the camera perceive and how Anders perceives the same reality that makes the film so overwhelming.[21] A night-time bike ride, Anders on the back behind the girl he has just met, might seem a sweet moment, full of vivacity, to us spectating, but it is not so for him.

Scriptwriter Eskil Vogt has said the following about what they were looking to do when writing out the relationship between Anders and Oslo:

> Our goal was to capture Anders's state of mind through his encounter with the city. And it's not like things are exclusively dark and hideous for him. He sees the beauty too. Summer at its peak, but already about to disappear. There's sunshine, there are cute girls, life is there, and he sees it, but there's no comfort in that, because it's not for him.[22]

This is why a film ending with a suicide can be described as a love letter to Oslo, one that leaves the viewer feeling that the city is beautiful and life valuable, even if Anders can no longer feel these things. In other words: the concrete place is beautiful, but Anders's experience of the space he is in is not.

The film mostly does not show any open roads ahead but depicts Anders as someone whose life has become closed off; he is caught on a threshold, unable to walk out into the real world.[23] This threshold is visualised as a near-invisible barrier between Anders and his surroundings through the extensive use of windows. We see this in the opening bedroom scene, where he faces the busy road outside, but also when he is sitting alone in his room at the rehab facility, while the other residents are having fun outdoors. His planned meeting with his sister takes place in a restaurant filled with large windows, allowing him to see that his sister has sent her girlfriend as a proxy long before she enters the room.

Having performed terribly at his job interview, Anders sits alone in a café, surrounded by people sharing thoughts and experiences with their friends. This scene is one of the film's emotional cruxes, a chief example of how Anders can share a space with a lot of other people and yet feel excluded. Of particular interest here is the way the space is used to inform us about Anders's feelings. His aural and visual attention is pulled between people on the inside and outside of the large glass windows, and twice we follow passers-by visually, a young woman and a young man. These narrative detours show these unnamed people going about their days, but both end with them appearing distressed when alone. Their apparent emotions could just be Anders projecting his own depressed state of mind, but they could also be genuine reflections of their lives out of other people's sight. Distress is often only allowed to surface when people feel secure within their own personal spaces.

While we do not know for sure if the restaurant and the café have any special significance to Anders (unlike for instance *Reprise*, *Oslo, August 31st* does not use flashbacks to give us insight into the character's background), many of the other places he visits do. The different relationships he has with the people in his life are reflected in the sites where he connects, or fails to connect, with them. His talk with Thomas takes place in the open, bright setting of a park, and it is with his old friend that Anders comes closest to finding understanding and sympathy, though the literary scholar also offers meaningless phrases like 'Proust is Proust' in response to Anders's confession about his depressive state of mind. All his efforts to connect with his former girlfriend Iselin, on the other hand, take place over the phone and in darkness: the first time in a dim passage in the city centre, the second in a dark bedroom at the party, and one final time in his childhood home, on its way to being sold, where he is surrounded by old memorabilia. Here, having made his final decision, he draws the curtains, stopping the summer light getting through, before he sits with his back to the window. Half the frame is shimmering with morning light, but Anders remains stuck in the dark. In fact, his greatest obstacle is his own inner darkness.

Anders's inability to connect with anyone or anything is rendered narratively, but also subtly visualised through setting and cinematography. Throughout the film he is constantly out of focus or only visible in a small part of the frame.[24] Filmcritic Sødtholt describes him almost like a ghost, little and without any purpose, almost erased as a person. The camera follows behind him as he walks through passageways, before he enters his old bedroom and closes the curtains one last time. When the camera closes in on where he lies, he is not in the centre of frame; the pivot point is the light streaming through the small gap between the curtains.

The sense of an ending – or closure – is present from the start of the film. The opening sequence tells the story of a city that has changed but that people still remember. In the end, in an emotional, moving epilogue, the city is still there, but Anders is gone, leaving behind an empty space worth remembering. This epilogue consists of a series of shots, in reversed chronological order, of some of the places he went during his final twenty-four hours, but in each, the space occupied before is now left blank.

In *Thelma*, Trier explores the topic of mental health further, again featuring Oslo as an emotionally significant setting. Overall, the urban space is a place of loneliness, both out in the light and the open, and in the closed and dark areas of town. *Thelma*, being a psychological thriller heavily influenced by horror movies like *Carrie* (1976) and *Rosemary's Baby* (1968) and the works of Alfred Hitchcock, among others, displays a more striking use of *mise-en-scène*. The film represents a change in Trier's film style; it contains 200 shots featuring CGI, and was filmed in Cinemascope, a format that creates tension between open-space scenes and intimate close-ups, both of which the film explores.[25]

Thelma was Trier's first film to feature a female protagonist, and tells the story of a young, inexperienced girl who moves from the countryside to the capital city to attend university. While already struggling under several intersecting stressors – finding her place as a Fresher biology student, freeing herself from her pious parents, falling in love with a girl for the first time – Thelma experiences several unexplained seizures (see Chapter 1 for more plot detail). The film can be described as the story of a young woman moving towards finding her own identity, breaking away from barriers imposed by patriarchal, medical, and religious authorities along the way. As such, it fits with recurring themes in Trier's filmography. Thelma's obstacles are personified most importantly by her father, Trond, who is also a doctor, and deeply, conservatively religious. A similar role is played by the authoritarian doctor she encounters at the hospital. Although *Thelma* in many ways, particularly because of the thriller aspect, is Trier's 'lightest' film, it also delves deeply into some darker ideas. The plot can be read as conventional in the context of the supernatural genre movie, but also as a philosophical exploration of quantum physics, as per Gabriella Beckhurst: 'Crucially, what is at stake is not just a cross-formation of identity (faith, gender, sexuality): *Thelma* is an ambitious undertaking in radically undoing concepts of being and identity'.[26]

Just like Anders, Thelma can be described as a vulnerable person released into a landscape she is ill-equipped to traverse. The university campus setting enables Trier to explore the stress a new student in an unfamiliar environment can experience; he uses the Blindern to create different emotional spaces. (Blindern is the main campus of the University of Oslo: also the place where

Thelma is studying.) We are introduced to Thelma through an extreme bird's-eye shot of her crossing the main square on campus – one small, lonely human being in a vast, almost inhuman environment.

Trier has stated in an interview that he believes 'that certain spaces combined with certain life situations will elicit very particular emotions'.[27] *Thelma* visualises the emptiness and loneliness of a student flat and study halls at night, as well as the self-aware awkwardness of entering a lecture theatre or a library and feeling everybody's eyes on you or being lost in a new place. Anxiety is often triggered by overwhelming situations, and unfamiliar spaces can create stress for students.[28]

This backdrop was not a major focus in the initial reception of *Thelma*, which was more concerned with Harboe's acting, how Trier twists horror tropes and mixes them with art cinema, the feminist potential in an original take on the coming-of-age plot, and the lesbian love story. There are exceptions, of course. Psycho-drama was a word that appeared in several reviews, and in *Film Journal*, the aspect of psychological stress was foregrounded: 'But the film's most distinguished achievement lies in recognizing what most films about adolescence prefer to tackle lightly: Coming of age is bloodcurdling stuff'.[29] There are few direct references to mental illness in the reception of *Thelma*, but a reviewer in the Norwegian edition of *Le Monde Diplomatique* commented that it was rare that anxiety, depression and a psychiatric diagnosis were at the core of a Norwegian film.[30]

By focusing on one scene in particular, I will now argue that *Thelma* can give insight into what it feels like to suffer from stress and anxiety. However, the film (like all of Trier's films) is open to different interpretations, and whether Thelma is in fact ill, or exhibiting some kind of supernatural power (or both), remains a somewhat open question; although the film's epilepsy specialist defines her illness as psychogenic non-epileptic seizures. These are fits that look like epileptic seizures, but are not caused by abnormal electrical discharges, and do not have any neurological explanation. It is a real diagnosis, but outside the cinematic realm it is a controversial one. I will not pursue this further, but merely note that the term psychogenic indicates that the fits are psychologically or psycho-socially caused. Thelma also learns that there might be a secret history of mental illness in her family. She tracks down her paternal grandmother, someone she had been told had died many years ago, and finds her sedated in an institution, per Thelma's father's instructions. Thelma's fits are at the core of the plot, and central to her development,[31] but I will focus on one episode that has broader significance than merely for the specific diagnosis in the film, and that stands out as a cinematic depiction of symptoms of mental illness.

Thelma is strongly attracted to Anja, but although they quickly connect and develop an intimacy, there are obstacles: Thelma, with her conservative religious upbringing, cannot permit herself to act on erotic feelings for a person of the same sex. When Thelma is invited to The Norwegian Opera and Ballet Opera and Ballet with Anja and her mother, the grandeur of the opera house makes a strong impression on her; she is even further outside her comfort zone than usual.[32] Sitting in the large auditorium, Anja confides that she has broken up with her boyfriend, and gently takes Thelma's hand in hers. Thelma's breathing intensifies, and when Anja's hand brushes against her bare leg, she starts trembling and shaking. Her eyes dart about in time with the music, which is building. In an attempt avoid falling into another fit, she grips her own hand tightly. But it is not only her body that shakes: above her, the large chandelier vibrates violently, to the extent that it looks like it is about to fall down on the audience.[33] The intimate, erotic situation between the two girls develops into a scene where the great auditorium at the opera house, the spectacular performance, and Thelma's own body all rise into a horrifying, uncontrolled cinematic seizure of sound and images.

Within the film's narrative, the shaking of the chandelier could be the result of Thelma's supernatural powers, but it is also possible to read the scene as a depiction of Thelma's emotional state, the physical room as a representation of Thelma's inner turmoil. In other words: it merely feels to Thelma as if it is moving and threatening to fall down and kill her. I argue that what we experience in this scene resembles a full-blown panic attack. Despite having a psychological cause, a panic attack is very much a physical experience, and a full-blown attack is intense and can be extremely frightening. Among the symptoms are an accelerated heart rate, trembling and shaking, shortness of breath, derealisation, and a fear of 'going crazy or dying'.[34] Losing control of your body and your surroundings and feeling as if you might die are common descriptions of panic attacks, and in this scene, the distinction between what is happening with Thelma's body and with her surroundings is blurred.

Figure 5.2 The performance at The Norwegian National Opera & Ballet, where Thelma has a panic attack.

Figure 5.3 Thelma recovering from her panic attack at the opera house. Copyright: Motlys.

However, Thelma is able to get her reaction in check. She does not have a fit, and manages to leave the room, distressed but in control. She rests up against a wall in the hallway and regains her breath. Anja follows her and finds her in tears in the cloakroom. When she kisses Thelma, it is evident that Thelma wants this just as much as Anja, or even more, and their kisses grow increasingly passionate, but in the end, Thelma runs away, distressed and disgusted. She looks like she might be sick in front of Anja, and feeling nauseated is a common bodily reaction to a panic attack. She crosses the open space outside the opera house (the vastness of the space and the spectacular architecture echoing the opening scene) in haste and tears, and in her flat she sits, her head against the wall, and chants: 'Dear Lord, remove this from me. Save me from these thoughts. Please, I beg you, take it away'.

After this, Thelma's condition worsens. During her medical evaluation at the hospital, she is forced to think about matters that are troubling her (a common method for treating anxiety disorders is exposure therapy). In this process, she is in fact able to 'remove Anja'. During a violent seizure, provoked by the doctor, the chant, 'remove it, remove it', is repeated as part of a dramatic montage that includes images of Anja at the university (in the study hall, the lecture theatre, and at the library), blinking lights, Thelma's eyes, and heavy breathing. In the end, we witness Anja dramatically disappearing from her own flat in a blast of shattered glass, and Thelma calms. We then get three shots of places where we have seen Anja before, but this time we see them without her in them. Unlike the subtle use of this technique in *Oslo, August 31st*, where it seems almost a melancholy afterthought, here, the camera zooms in on the empty spaces left behind, creating a more disturbing dramatic effect.

After Anja is gone, Thelma experiences both a sense of emptiness and of being even more trapped within herself and her isolation. At the swimming pool (somewhere she also encountered Anja before), she has another seizure, and as she sinks down into the water, it appears unnaturally deep and dark, but she also becomes disorientated and mistakes down for up. In this desperate scene, she attempts to break her way through the bottom of the pool. When she finally breaks free from her father (seemingly by psychokinetically setting him on fire), she walks out into the lake by her childhood home and swims towards the deep, but then resurfaces in the pool again. This is the scene where the Thelma's entrapment is visualised most dramatically. By literally breaking through a physical barrier, the surface of the water, she can find Anja again. The film can be read as an emancipation story, one in which challenging one's own limits and other imposed limitations mean succeeding in breaking down the walls mental illness can put up. Simultaneously, one could also argue that this conclusion, very much in line with Thelma's doctor's advice to just delve into her emotions, is a rather gross oversimplification of how to recover from mental illness.[35] In the end, it is through facing her greatest fears that Thelma gets well. She brings Anja back, and in the final scene they cross the open space on campus together, this time in harmony and sunlight. In sum, I argue that the thriller, or psychological horror film, *Thelma* is not only about supernatural powers, but also offers insight into the subjective experience of anxiety.

Joachim Trier's films are both rich and subtle in their treatment of the human condition, and open to a wide range of interpretations as I will pursue further in the next chapter. My aim here has not been to reduce this openness and richness, but rather to suggest new ways of approaching their portrayal of the emotional impact of living with mental health issues. I argue that these films treat complicated emotional conditions with subtlety and much-needed understanding.[36]

Despite their differences – *Oslo, August 31st* being a realistic, understated story about a young addict with no particular strengths, and *Thelma* a supernatural genre movie about a young girl with special powers – the two films share important similarities. *Oslo, August 31st* is *about* a state of mind in which meaninglessness and the impossibility of change create both emptiness and closure. *Thelma* is not about fear and anxiety in the same way *Oslo, August 31st* is about depression, but rather about change and openings. By positioning their protagonists in cinematic spaces that foreground their mental states and emotions, both films shed light on what it feels like to live with mental illness, depression, and anxiety, whether this means being trapped in closed spaces or lost out in the open. As Trier himself has said about the topics of his films: 'honestly, I think all my characters have been in a place of vulnerability. More than anything, I think that comes from my curiosities about that human space of vulnerability, both in male and female characters.'[37]

According to film blogger Hillary Weston, *Oslo, August 31st* is 'like a shot in the arm of melancholy' that leaves viewers examining our own condition and finding touches of beauty that make people want to carry on.[38] This may be the case, even for viewers struggling with depression themselves, but the film's primary achievement is that it manages to provide insight into Anders's state of mind without condoning or supporting his decision. *Thelma*, on the other hand, shows that it is possible to overcome obstacles in your life, including anxiety, by facing them rather than banishing them. This way Thelma is able to transform an unsafe space into a secure place where she can be who she is. Whereas *Oslo, August 31st* is about depression and suicidal ideation, *Thelma* can be seen as a story about recovery from trauma. Or, to put it differently: *Oslo, August 31st* is about an ending and *Thelma* a beginning.

NOTES

1. The Vigeland Park, the world's largest sculpture park made by a single artist, was created between 1939 and 1949 and displays two hundred sculptures by famous Norwegian artist Gustav Vigeland. 51-69
2. Quoted from Epilogue interview, see 149.
3. This chapter is based on my previously published article (Anne Gjelsvik, 'Openings and Closures: Mental Health in Joachim Trier's Cinematic Universe', *Journal of Scandinavian Cinema* 9, no. 1 (1 March 2019): 75–88, https://doi.org/10.1386/jsca.9.1.75_1), but has been heavily rewritten.
4. Jeffrey Bloomer, 'Director Joachim Trier on the Problem With His Movies and Louder Than Bombs' Curious Ending', *Slate*, 8 April 2016, http://www.slate.com/blogs/browbeat/2016/04/08/louder_than_bombs_interview_with_joachim_trier_on_the_movie_s_ending_and.html.
5. See, for instance, Hillary Weston, 'The Quiet Allure of Joachim Trier's "Oslo, August 31st"', 1 February 2013. http://hillaryweston.squarespace.com/new-page-17/; Tarja Laine, 'Trauma, Queer Sexuality and Symbolic Storytelling in Joachim Trier's Thelma', *Journal of Scandinavian Cinema* 12, no. 3 (1 September 2022): 291–305, https://doi.org/10.1386/jsca_00077_1; Bloomer, 'Director Joachim Trier'.
6. See, for instance, Gunnar Iversen, 'Tiden leger ingen sår "Reprise"', in *Den norske filmbølgen: Fra Orions belte til Max Manus*. (Oslo: Universitetsforlaget, 2010).
7. Tarja Laine, *Feeling Cinema: Emotional Dynamics in Film Studies* (New York: Continuum, 2011).
8. See also Jørgen Bruhn and Anne Gjelsvik, *Cinema Between Media: An Intermediality Approach* (Edinburgh: University Press, 2018); Dag Sødtholt, 'Louder Than Bombs: Joachim Trier's Play on Perspective', *Montages International Edition*, 16 January 2016, http://montagesmagazine.com/2016/01/louder-than-bombs-joachim-triers-play-on-perspective/.
9. Sophie Blum, 'Interview: Joachim Trier, Director of Oslo, August 31st', *Film Comment*, 23 May 2012, https://www.filmcomment.com/blog/interview-joachim-trier-director-of-oslo-august-31st/.

10. Inger Merethe Hobbelstad, 'Bevegende bysommer', *Dagbladet*, 18 May 2011, https://www.dagbladet.no/kultur/bevegende-bysommer/63687380.
11. Knut Hamsun, *Hunger* (trans. Robert Bly). New York: Farrar, Straus and Giroux, 1967): 16. Before 1924, Oslo was named Kristiania.
12. On 22 July 2011, Norway experienced the worst events in its recent history. Far-right extremist Anders Behring Brcivik detonated a car bomb at the Government quarter complex, killing eight people and wounding approximately two hundred. Two hours later, he continued his attacks by methodically shooting participants at the Workers Youth League (AUF) summer camp on the small island Utøya. There he killed a further sixty-nine people and wounded thirty-three, most of them teenagers, making his attack the deadliest to occur in Norway since the Second World War. Interestingly, the proximity in time to this tragedy was not a major theme in the reception of *Oslo, August 31st* upon its release, but for a couple of examples see, for instance Christian Mongaard, 'Fortællingen om den dobbelte skam', *Information*, 26 October 2011, https://www.information.dk/kultur/2011/10/fortaellingen-dobbelte-skam; Terje Eidsvåg, 'Glødende om fortvilelse', *Adresseavisen*, 31 August 2011, https://www.adressa.no/kultur/i/KzyPb4/glodende-om-fortvilelse..
13. Don Simpson, 'Joachim Trier (Oslo, August 31st). Interview', *Smells Like Screen Spirit*, 21 May 2012, http://smellslikescreenspirit.com/2012/05/joachim-trier-oslo-august-31st-interview/.
14. Weston, 'Quiet Allure'.
15. Bjarte Breiteig, Eskil Vogt, and Joachim Trier, 'Oslo Gjennom mørkt glass – Eskil Vogt og Joachim Trier i samtale med Bjarte Breiteig', in *Oslo, 31. August. Filmmanus.* (Oslo: Tiden Norsk Forlag, 2011), 166.
16. Danny Wedding and Ryan Niemiec *Movies and Mental Illness: Using Films to Understand Psychopathology*, 4th edn (Boston: Hogrefe Publishing, 2014), 44.
17. WHO, 'Data and Resources. Prevalence of Mental Disorders', 28 May 2018, http://www.euro.who.int/en/health-topics/noncommunicable-diseases/mental-health/data-and-resources.
18. Julia Kristeva, *Black Sun: Depression and Melancholia, European Perspectives* (New York: Columbia University Press, 1989), 3.
19. These lines are not included in the subtitles.
20. Weston, 'Quiet Allure'.
21. Benjamin Yazdan, 'Å se med og på – det fenomenologiske blikket i Joachim Trier og Eskil Vogts filmer', *Montages*, 2014, http://montages.no/2014/03/a-se-med-og-pa-det-fenomenologiske-blikket-i-joachim-trier-og-eskil-vogts-filmer/.
22. Breiteig, Vogt, and Trier, 'Oslo Gjennom mørkt glass', 179.
23. In her Masters thesis discussing *Oslo, August 31st* as an adaptation of Pierre Drieu Le Rochelle's novel, *Le feu follet* (*Will O' the Wisp*, 1931), Guro Johansen uses Mikhail Bakhtin's concept of the chronotope to describe this; Johansen, 'Sted og selvrefleksivitet'.
24. Dag Sødtholt, 'Alt skal glemmes, men ikke Oslo, 31. August', *Montages*, 21 September 2011, http://montages.no/2011/09/alt-skal-glemmes-men-ikke-oslo-31-august/;
25. Emily Buder, '"Thelma": Joachim Trier on Shooting the Norwegian "Carrie" on Cinemascope', No Film School, 14 November 2017, https://nofilmschool.

com/2017/10/joachim-trier-thelma-interview; Tasha Robinson, 'Joachim Trier on His Dreamy Gay Coming-of-Age Superhero Story', *The Verge*, 10 November 2017, https://www.theverge.com/2017/11/10/16635068/joachim-trier-thelma-interview-behind-the-scenes-academy-award-submission.

26. Gabriella Beckhurst, '"Intra-Active" Desire in Joachim Trier's "Thelma"', *Another Gaze: A Feminist Film Journal*, 18 January 2019, https://www.anothergaze.com/intra-active-desire-joachim-trier-thelma-feminist-lesbian/.
27. Don Simpson, 'Joachim Trier'.
28. According to recent surveys on mental health among Norwegian students more than 20% of female students report multiple serious symptoms of mental illness. Anxiety and depression are the most common disorders. One explanation is that being young usually means multiple periods of transition and major changes, something that causes vulnerability. Marit Knapstad, Ove Heradstveit, and Børge Sivertsen, 'Studentenes helse- og trivselsundersøkelse 2018 [Students' Health and Wellbeing Study 2018]'. (Oslo: Studentsamskipnaden i Oslo og Akershus, 2018).
29. Tomris Laffy, 'Film Review: "Thelma": Film Journal International', *Filmjournal* 11, 2017, http://www.filmjournal.com/reviews/film-review-thelma.
30. Arnstein Bjørkly, 'Psykogen bedehusmagi', *Le Monde diplomatique*, 7 September 2017, https://www.lmd.no/2017/09/psykogens-bedehusmagi/.
31. Dag Sødtholt, 'Joachim Trier's Thelma, Part III: The Epilepsy Test', 9 December 2017, http://montagesmagazine.com/2017/12/joachim-triers-thelma-part-iii-the-epilepsy-test/.
32. The ballet is Sleight of Hand by Sol Leòn and Paul Lightfoot, music by Philip Glass.
33. The chandelier, the largest found in Norway, is a work of art in itself. It has a diameter of seven metres, weighs more than eight tonnes, and is made up of 8,000 light emitting diodes and 5,800 handmade crystals. It also functions as an acoustic reflector. It was designed by Snøhetta, the firm to design the Oslo Opera House itself, and made by Hadeland Glassverk.
34. ADAA [no date], 'Symptoms: Anxiety and Depression Association of America, ADAA', no date, https://adaa.org/understanding-anxiety/panic-disorder-agoraphobia/symptoms.
35. See Kym McDaniel *Why Can't I Be Who I Am: A Queer Disabled Analysis of Joachim Trier's 'Thelma'* (School of Professional Studies, City University of New York), 2021 for a critical reading of the way *Thelma* depicts disability.
36. Other examples of this approach are *Silver Linings Playbook* (Russell 2012), *Infinitely Polar Bear* (Forbes 2014) and *Deux jours, une nuit* (*Two Days, One Night*) (Dardenne and Dardenne 2014).
37. Robinson, 'Joachim Trier'.
38. Weston, 'Quiet Allure'.

CHAPTER 6

The Human Condition

In the first chapter of *The Worst Person in the World*, protagonist Julie and her boyfriend Aksel are spending time in a cabin with some friends and family of his, two other couples and their children. To the viewer, and to Julie – younger, childless, and the newest addition to the group – the bright summer days in the modernist summer house seem, at times, like a holiday from hell. This vignette perfectly captures so much of what is awkward and uncomfortable about forced intimacy with people you do not know well: the invasive questions they feel entitled to asking, the private arguments you are not supposed to overhear, the

Figure 6.1 The awkwardness of invasive questions from strangers.

ins and outs of parenting laid bare for all to see. One alcohol-steeped evening, the adults dance, prompted by Julie who has pulled up Amerie's 'I Thing' from a playlist. As viewers, we are placed right there with her, in the middle of the dance floor, as she lets go and is present in the moment. Suddenly, the scene is broken, the sound is dimmed, and we are pulled back to a more distanced voyeur's position, watching through the great, lit windows. For a short moment, we watch them all, from the outside, dancing within.

It is strange, perhaps, that when encountering a film that is otherwise so memorable for its grander, more magical set pieces, I was so struck by this particular scene. This binary, from-within-and-yet-from-without perspective suits Julie, who in many ways is a spectator to her own life (as she herself puts it at one point: 'I feel like a spectator in my own life. Like I'm playing a supporting role in my own life'). But in my view, this scene is also characteristic of Joachim Trier as a director. One of his finest qualities as a filmmaker is this certain way he has of observing human nature and behaviour, and putting what he has seen into a kind of cinematic expression that creates a real sense of presence. His films often also feature some reflexive aspect, a form of commentary on their own narrative that makes us step back and become aware of our position as observers to the lives of others.

This ability to provide intimate portraits of human relationships that simultaneously function as a sort of meta-commentary on human behaviour is essential, I think, to Trier as a filmmaker. A recurring theme in his work is the notion that we, as people, constantly view and define ourselves in relation to others: our partners, prospective partners, parents, friends, random people encountered at parties. The way we perceive ourselves as being perceived by others informs our perception of ourselves, as does our assessment of our own performance in the different roles we inhabit: am I a good partner, writer, friend, or father? How am I defined by the words that are said about me, or how other people see me? Am I the worst person in the world? When asked, in an interview, to characterise his collaborator Trier's interests as a filmmaker, Eskil Vogt homed in on similar questions: 'What do we do, as people? Why do we treat each other like that? Why can't we be happy? Why do we make such stupid choices?' He continued, 'Investigating that has always been an interest of Joachim's, but it is increasingly seeping into the films, more and more'.[1]

Trier's film work is therefore often given labels such as 'ambitious, existential drama' and 'existential rom-com', or described as featuring 'deep psychological insight and empathy'.[2] On one hand, his films are time- and place-specific portraits of people from a handful of particular social or cultural circles in certain urban environments in the western world, set in the present or near past. He is able to capture a sense of the zeitgeist, particular ways of thinking or acting for a particular time or place. For instance, a young Norwegian woman of today might find herself having so many opportunities that she finds herself unable to choose either a man or a career path. On the other hand, Trier is also exploring universal, existential questions that have been central to many artistic forms and movements across hundreds of years – not least the modernist films and novels of the twentieth century. When challenged about the cultural specificity of his work, the director himself always insists that these universal themes (transcending things like gender and class) are his driving interest. The relational, existential drama descriptor is used both in praise and in derision of Trier. Eskil Vogt once referenced an Iraqi filmmaker who said he liked Scandinavian cinema because the films were never about anything. Vogt initially interpreted this line as criticism, but eventually came to understand it to mean that a lack of specific content makes more room for the exploration of the medium as an art form.[3]

With the exception of *Thelma*, Trier's films are not plot driven. The characters – who they are, what they do, what they do not do – are the core of his work. Often, they find themselves unable to make choices; all his films are about characters facing existential decisions of some kind: careers, partners, how to approach or deal with secrets or lies. These are all commonplace challenges that a majority of people will have faced in their own lives, and find themselves able to relate to. The same is true of how his work particularly centres on transformative periods in a person's life. Several of his films have coming-of-age elements, be they transformations that occur in one's teens (Conrad in *Louder Than Bombs*) or early twenties (Phillip and Erik in *Reprise* and Thelma), or on the cusp of one's thirties (Julie). As such, the films demonstrate how maturing into one's role(s) and self is not necessarily something that happens only in adolescence (which is what we more usually see in film and literature). As one critic put it:

> The transition from childhood to teendom is painful, yes, but nothing compares to the fragmentedness of adulthood. With *The Worst Person in the World*, Joachim Trier makes it clear that he is fully aware of this, and the messiness of your late 20s need not . . . be loathed, but perhaps celebrated.[4]

The films also show characters negotiating the people they will be and the roles they will inhabit even later in life than this. After Aksel (*The Worst Person in the World*) becomes terminally ill, he claims that he has long ceased to seek out new things. He describes his forties as a time for reliving old experiences, rehearing old music and rewatching old films. Isabelle and Gene in *Louder Than Bombs* are continuously negotiating the balance between their work-selves, their parent-selves, and themselves as a couple. When Isabelle dies, Gene must rediscover himself as a father.

One thing captured perfectly by Trier is the way common human behaviours often result from us attempting to portray ourselves as someone other than who we are. Erik, for instance, pretends to have written a short story in a single night, in a bid to make Phillip think he is a more gifted writer. Julie, upon meeting Aksel for the first time, pretends to have read the underground comic strip *Gaupe*, wanting him to think her cooler and more with-it than she really is. One interviewer chose 'Representations of Self' as the title for his portrait of Trier, and this was no accident.[5] Trier's work is always about identity, about how it is created and constructed through transformations and negotiations with others. Though his films vary in terms of form and genre, they are all, arguably, existential dramas exploring relational challenges and conflicts. More specifically, we might say that his different films focus on different kinds of interpersonal relationships: *Reprise* is a film about friendship, *Louder Than Bombs* a film about family, and *The Worst Person in the World* about romantic relationships. In this chapter, I wish to examine how Trier's films can be considered investigations of the human condition in contemporary society, with a focus on family, friendship, and romantic relationships. Singling out one core kind of relationship for each of the films is, however, reductive: infatuation, love, friendship, and friendlessness are all features in all of Trier's work.

Familial relationships are a major, sensitive, theme that features, to some extent, in all of Trier's films. Anders in *Oslo, August 31st* has let down and betrayed his family to the point where they no longer wish to see him. Both of the young men in *Reprise* have somewhat strained relationships with their mothers, who they find invasive and overbearing. When Phillip is in hospital, his mother enters his flat to remove all pictures of his ex-girlfriend Kari, for whom he still has strong feelings. Phillip reacts with anger and confiscates her key. Erik's relationship with his single mother is comically portrayed through a retrospective scene in which she discovers that he has been accessing porn on the family computer. The mother's reaction is a mixture of understanding of a young teen's curiosity and gently mocking feminist critique. The awkwardness peaks when she confronts him with one of the images she has found and says, 'What if this girl was me?' This scene functions as a sort of explanation for how Erik ended up the somewhat evasive young man he is, unable to break up with his girlfriend, stand up for his friends, or own his personal beliefs.

Julie's parents are also divorced. Here, too, the parent–child relationship is rendered with poignancy and humour. Her father drops out of her thirtieth birthday celebration at the last minute, for 'health reasons'. Julie lambasts him to her boyfriend Aksel, but, typically, comes to his defence when her mother attempts to do the same. When Julie and Aksel instead go to him for a private celebration, they discover that, on the actual day, he had gone to watch his youngest daughter play handball. His present for Julie is a piece of sportswear not at all in her style, and identical to one her little sister is already wearing. Following the awkward visit – during which her father is mostly preoccupied with his new family and his own issues, be they parking or prostate related – Aksel concludes: 'You have to make your own family'. With a bit of distance from it all, the pair can laugh a bit at the misery together, but in her father's house, his behaviour sparks tension between the two of them too. Aksel wants to poke at all of her father's betrayals, while she prefers to smooth things over. These scenes are comical illustrations of the strange patterns that might form within families, old and new. They shed a revealing light on parents focused only on themselves. It is typical of Trier's somewhat distanced style that he treats such sensitive, primal subject matter – feeling neglected and rejected by a parent – with equal parts humour and gravity.

While Julie's father is uninterested in anything she does or says, Thelma's parents pay too close attention to her life and behaviour. She has left her hometown and strict, religious family to study biology at the university in Oslo. One day she fails to pick up the phone when they call, and when questioned by her mother about what she has been doing, where she has been, she lies and pretends she was in a lecture. This leads to an awkward moment when Thelma discovers her parents have been looking up her class schedule on the internet – 'Daddy showed me how to keep track of everything online.' They know exactly what her calendar looks like, even from a distance. Thelma's strong emotional responses in this scene, as well as her palpable desire to break free from her parents' stifling control, are believable enough to spark recognition in a wide audience. But in line with horror film convention, her parents' controlling behaviour has been dialled up a few notches, and horror-film scholar Christer Bakke Andresen describes the emotional abuse her parents, and particularly her patriarchal father, subject their daughter to as unparalleled in the history of Norwegian cinema.[6] At one point, Thelma describes how her father would make her hold her hand above a burning flame when she was a child, so that she might remember what it would feel like end up in hell.

As it turns out, her parents may have good reason to keep an extra watchful eye on Thelma's comings and goings, to control her and her state of mind: assuming, of course, that we accept that she has some supernatural ability that puts her and others at risk. The horror premise this film is built upon is that she, as a child, caused her infant brother's death. In a psychoanalysis-informed reading of the film, scholar Tarja Laine argues that Thelma's traumatic memories of killing her own brother are not real, but the result of false memories implanted in her by her father. *Thelma* opens with a scene in which father and daughter are out hunting in a snow- and ice-clad landscape, the father looking sombre. When they spot a deer, he lifts his rifle as if to take aim, but then turns to point the weapon at six-year-old Thelma instead. It is a chilling moment. Her father takes a deep breath and does not shoot. Laine interprets this scene as not actually a diegetic event, but an allegorical and symbolic representation of

> the toxic relationship between the protagonist and her father. Rather than literally killing Thelma, her father 'kills' her (sexual) identity by

suffocating it with medicine and a strict religious upbringing, which in my interpretation is the true source of her trauma.[7]

I consider the death of her brother as factual events in the story, but this does not mean that these events cannot be read allegorically as well. As Laine demonstrates in her article, Trier's films are often filled with allusions to Sigmund Freud, and in *Thelma*, his theories on both dream interpretation and the Oedipus complex are referenced. 'In the Oedipal narrative, the father as the principal authority figure must be "killed" so that the offspring can assume the subject role in their own right' – just as Thelma (seemingly) kills her father by pyrokinesis, in order do subsequently live a free life with a partner of her own choosing.[8]

As it is in *Thelma*, the parent–child relationship is a central theme in *Louder Than Bombs*. Conrad, too, has a controlling father who keeps track of him both at school and online. That is, Gene tracks his son both in the real world and in a virtual one. In a desperate attempt to get closer to his quiet, closed-off kid, he learns how to play *The Elder Scrolls Online*. Gene is excited to meet his son in the virtual reality he seems to prefer, but after lengthy preparation only manages to be instantly decapitated by his son, who is oblivious to the fact that the avatar he slays is his father's. Here, Trier allows himself a playful and humorous approach to the Oedipus myth, in a film that also suggests an amount of erotic attraction between older brother Jonah and the mother Isabelle. Both sons could as such be seen as suffering from some form of an Oedipus complex. This also comes into play when new father Jonah struggles to accept his own paternal role. He leaves his home and is unfaithful with an old girlfriend while his wife cares for their newborn daughter alone. The parent–child relationship, and the contrast between freedom and protection, is approached with a mixture of playful levity and melancholy solemnity.

One of the stalking incidents in *Louder Than Bombs* is shown from two different perspectives – the father's and the son's respectively. In the first version, we see how Gene, who works at the high school Conrad attends, follows him after school and watches his withdrawn loneliness with concern. We see Conrad lying on the phone with Gene, claiming to be with friends, while his father on the other end is actually watching him sit alone in a playground. In the second version, we see Conrad discovering that his father has been stalking him, and feeling limited by that in what he is able to do. In his video journal, he describes this as 'Dad is everywhere. When I turn around, he is there'. In an attempt to show Gene he is doing something meaningful, he lets his father follow him to the cemetery where his mother is buried, but when he fails to find the right grave, he simply throws himself down before a random one. His father, unaware that Conrad has found him out, watches on, shocked at his son's bizarre behaviour.

From a meta-perspective, it seems significant that the headstone Conrad chooses, seemingly at random, reads 'Carlos Valdes'. This is a reference to

Alfred Hitchcock's *Vertigo* (1958), a playful nod from Trier to the cinephile viewer in the know. In *Vertigo,* Carlotta Valdes is a mysterious, deceased woman only heard about and seen depicted in a portrait. Her likeness is used in an intricate game designed to deceive traumatised police officer Scotty (James Stewart). Madeleine (Kim Novak) is seen admiring the painting in a museum, while Scotty, hired as a private detective to follow her, is spying on her. *Vertigo* is arguably one of film history's most significant films about loss, truth and identity. And so this reference is more than an homage from one nerdy director to another. It introduces certain connotations, a suggestion that things may not always be as they appear to the person looking on from behind a tree. Though the situations that arise in these complicated family relationships may be comical, the characters are portrayed in such a way that we are able to understand and empathise with parent and child both. As put by film scholar Søren Birkvad, it is typical of Trier's approach that he 'considers all sides of a matter' and treats all of his characters with thoughtfulness and respect.[9] The audience get to feel irritated at both the hovering parent(s) and the unresponsive child.

The family can be a lonely place in Trier's films. Not necessarily because the parents are unsympathetic, unfeeling or evil (with the possible exception of Thelma's father) – they are often doing their best. That being said, families are also places for secrets and lies: Thelma's father tells lies about her grandmother being dead, and Conrad's father lies about his mother's death, or at least keeps things secret. The main problem is that, rather than being deliberately evil, the characters lack the ability to see or communicate with each other.[10] They hurt each other because they misunderstand each other. Isabelle is, for instance, portrayed as a wise, loving, and emotionally present mother, but simultaneously one who, frequently and for long stretches of time, leaves her children at home as she goes off to practise her dangerous trade as a war photographer. Gene, too, is a present and well-meaning parent, but does not always make the wisest choices. Birkvad has described the parents in Trier's films as antagonists, though not (again except for *Thelma*) in the classical sense known from the typical genre film. They are people exercising a form of soft power. Birkvad founds this in how Trier (and Vogt):

> represent an art cinema ideal that stresses ambiguity and epistemological uncertainty as a basic condition in life, but also as an artistic virtue: an ability to psychologically dissect fictional characters while at the same time sustaining a fundamental respect for their integrity and complexity as humans.[11]

Louder Than Bombs is, accordingly, not a film about parents who have let their children down. It takes its place within a tradition of American family dramas in which *Ordinary People* (1980) and *The Ice Storm* (1997) are important forebears, but stands apart from them in its reluctance to assign any blame. It is also a far lighter, more optimistic film than these two, or other films one might compare it to, like *The Sweet Hereafter* (1997) or *Manchester by the Sea* (2016). It is not weighed down by its subject matter of grief, in part because we enter the story not as tragedy strikes, but at a later stage in the mourning process. In the end, Conrad and Gene come together in an emotional, reconciliatory, if awkward embrace. In general, this is a film in which physical displays of affection between family members often appear awkward or half-hearted.[12] After this resolution, of sorts, for the relationship between Gene and his youngest, he goes to his older son Jonah and says, 'It's time to go home'. The film ends with Gene taking Jonah home to his wife and new-born daughter Isabelle. The final scene shows father and sons together in the car, not speaking. Jonah, who is in the passenger seat, meets his father's gaze and they smile at each other. In the backseat, Conrad finds the eyes of his imaginary mother, and they share a smile, before he puts his head down on her shoulder to sleep soundly.

Figure 6.2 Conrad resting on the memory of his mother.

Romantic love is a tricky thing as well, and perhaps this is why it, too, is such an important recurring theme in all of Trier's work. Across the five feature films Trier has made to date, we find romantic relationships in a wide range of forms and phases. We get the first crush – the one that is only experienced from a distance and never requited – when quiet Conrad dreams of the most popular girl in class. We see the first infatuation that turns into a first important relationship when Thelma meets Anja and they, despite major challenges, become a couple by the film's end. There is the first great love that

Phillip has with Kari, before losing her, and then maybe finding his way back together with her again. And there is the troubled relationship that falls apart when Anders loses Iselin to his addiction, and she moves far away and starts dodging his calls. There is Julie's serial monogamy (and borderline infidelity), a string of relationships ranging from unimportant to life-changing (Aksel and Eivind), though none of them last. We have the new marriage that turns Jonah into a young father, and the mature one, between Gene and Isabelle, that lasted until death, but consisted of lies and secrets as well as parenthood and communion. Trier's focus tends to be on the complicated, difficult sides of all types of relationships no matter what phase they are in.

The explicitly erotic is rarely centred in these relationships, Trier tends to depict love and infatuation more as romantic and sensual attraction than direct sexual desire. Norwegian film scholar Anne Marit Myrstad has studied some of Trier's female characters (with a particular focus on girlfriends) and argues that a clear inspiration from the French New Wave can be seen here too. In line with the ideals of the male French directors of the 1950s and 60s, Myrstad says, Trier's portrayals of female attractiveness tend to be in the form of 'non-threatening, low-key sexual attraction', as opposed to Hollywood's sex bombs and femmes fatales.[13] When the camera rests on the face of a beautiful young woman in a Trier film (of which there are plenty), it tends to focus more on a natural face, or her hair, than provocative clothing or a sexualised body. Myrstad describes the eroticism of his female portraits as 'a cinematically created ideal of beauty', expressed 'through close-ups of hair and skin, the curve of a neck, hair spread over a pillow or a gentle and secretive face touched by time'.[14]

In an auteur-inspired close reading of Trier's first four films, critic Dag Søtholdt also points to close-ups of hair, necks, and hands as arguable hallmarks of his aesthetics, in particular as a way of depicting femininity.[15] In his richly illustrated study, Søtholdt demonstrates how a focus on hair, among other things, recurs throughout the filmography. In *Reprise*, Phillip's girlfriend Kari is introduced through a strand of hair he finds on his jumper, months after their last encounter. We then cut directly from the close-up of the hair in his hand to one of Kari's neck, her own hand running through her own hair. After Anja spends the night at Thelma's, Thelma finds some of her friend's hair on the pillow she slept on. She picks it up, and then puts it back in her bed. When they lie down next to each other, she must restrain herself from running her hand across her sleeping friend's tresses. She only lets it hover above her head. These scenes speak to Trier's general love of close-ups, but also a certain attention to minute details, like particular hand movements or other physical peculiarities.

All this being said, *Thelma* and *The Worst Person in the World* do feature some (more) explicit sex scenes. These are quite different from each other, in part due to different genre conventions. While Trier's first three films can all be described as different takes on the existential drama, inspired by European icons and American family dramas, *The Worst Person in the World* and *Thelma* are built on the traditional features of the romantic comedy and the supernatural thriller respectively. Thelma dares not give in to her desire for Anja. The fact that the object of said desire is another girl does not make things easier, given her inexperience and conservative upbringing. This is why Thelma rejects Anja's touches and kiss at the opera house. Not because she does not want Anja – if anything, it is because she wants her too much.

Following this event, Thelma keeps her distance from Anja as best she can, but at a party they both attend, she is persuaded to smoke what she believes to be cannabis. We see her lose touch with the room around her and start kissing Anja ferociously. What unfolds breaks both with Thelma's usual demeanour and the film's generally realist style. As the scene goes on, it feels increasingly symbolic and dreamlike, until it appears as if the two girls are alone, floating together in a black void. Their caresses become more erotically charged, Anja fondles Thelma's breasts beneath her clothes. As Thelma lets her head fall back, submits fully to her desire and allows Anja to reach inside her underwear, a snake appears, slithering out around her neck. It coils itself around, tightly, before its head penetrates her mouth and enters her throat. This is when another party guest rouses Thelma from her hallucination, stopping her from masturbating in front of Anja and the others. It is a voyeuristic, uncomfortable scene that ends with Thelma throwing up and leaving in tears. Trier has himself described this as a scene about shame, but he has also been questioned about what it means for him as a straight adult male director to stage a queer sex scene between two young women in this way.[16]

There are hints of cliché and an objectifying perspective on female sexuality here, but it is also one of several examples of Trier attempting to visually represent a character's subconscious (see also the magic mushroom trip in

Figure 6.3 Thelma and Anja.

The Worst Person in The World and Conrad's dream about his mother having a new baby who is an old man).[17] In a Norwegian context, this scene stands out not just because of its stylised eroticism, but because *Thelma* is one of very few Norwegian films to feature a queer protagonist at all, let alone a queer female one.[18] When challenged on whether or not he is the right person to tell such stories, Trier tends to refer back to his own interest in the universal, the pan-human, and say that the gender perspective is less important to him. He took the same stance when asked whether he and Vogt were the right people to write a character like Julie:

> I have to say that I've written men and women before – old and young people who are quite different from me – but I believe as an artist that's my duty: to try to be truthful and, from myself, try and find a way to understand someone that is not myself, which is the character.[19]

Although this can in part come across as the male director not really catching the relevance of such criticism, it is equally apparent that Trier does attempt to adjust to some of the feedback he has been getting about his portrayals of women. In *The Worst Person in the World*, he lets protagonist Julie be the carrier of 'the gaze'.[20] Julie is the kind of girl who turns to look when a pretty boy passes her by, who keeps risqué pictures of her male lecturer on her phone, and whose relationships all start with sex. When she encounters Eivind at a party, their forward flirtation is entirely built on a mutual understanding that she wants him. In the scene where we find out that they are moving in

Figure 6.4 Julie, a woman with the gaze.

together, she is the hungry, active party, the one to practically tear his clothes off as they enter their flat. Just as she was earlier, in an almost identical scene, with Aksel – actively initiating sex when he was ready to break up with her. And when she eventually leaves him, that, too, ends in an intense sex scene. The breakup scene in *The Worst Person in the World* is a display of all the emotion the dissolution of a relationship can bring about in both parties. We see grief and rage and also sex in a heady mixture. And here, too, we get ambivalence – it is both sad and right for Julie to break up with Aksel. As Julie puts it herself, 'Yes, I do love you. And I don't love you.' And the way it happens is both sad and amusing, in part because of the distancing effect of the narrator. As Julie leaves, Aksel remains, in a moment the script describes as follows: 'In a full shot he stands in the middle of the sitting room, naked from the waist down, a t-shirt on up top. It would be funny were it not also so sad. Half-naked and abandoned.'[21]

The final kind of relationship in Trier's filmography that I have chosen to highlight is friendship. A recurring criticism of *The Worst Person in the World* is that Julie is a woman without any close female friends.[22] Critical voices have pointed out that this aligns the film with a general trend in modern cinema, in which female characters are portrayed chiefly or exclusively through their relationships with men. This feminist critique is most clearly expressed through the so-called Bechdel test.[23] This 'test' was inspired by a strip called 'The Rule' in American cartoonist Alison Bechdel's comic book *Dykes to Watch Out For* (1986), in which two female friends debate going to the cinema. One of them says she will only watch films that fulfil three basic requirements: 'One, it has to have at least two women in it. Two, they have to talk to each other. Three, about something besides a man'. When the Bechdel test is applied today, a fourth criterion stating that the female characters must be named – meaning they cannot just be random passers-by or anonymous shop employees, they must be full characters – is often added.[24]

My own view of the Bechdel test is that, through its straightforward simplicity, it functions as an ideal illustration of a democratic problem within the film industry. Women speak less on film than men do, and their range of roles is much narrower. By setting the bar so low, the test can be a useful eye-opener. A shocking number of films do not pass. The test is, however, best suited as a general illustration when applied to a large number of films, collectively. Applying it rigidly to individual features is less useful. A film like *Gravity* (2013), for instance, notable exactly for its so-called strong female protagonist, does not pass. Protagonist Dr Ryan Stone (played by Sandra Bullock) spends a majority of the film alone in space, where she does not speak to anyone. Similarly, criticising a film like *Oslo, August 31st* for not featuring two women speaking together, is, to my mind, a little narrow-minded and beside the point of this kind of awareness campaign.

But when discussing films like *Reprise* and *The Worst Person in the World*, set in realistic contemporary environments and featuring a great number of characters, this type of perspective becomes more relevant. Seen in context with comparable contemporaries, *The Worst Person in the World* is just one of many films whose protagonists lack female friends. Seen as an individual case, however, Julie's general lack of close friends can be seen as just part of her character. She is inherently capricious, always changing course and moving from one environment, one circle, to the next. A dearth of lasting friendships can be seen as a symptom of her constant degree- and career-hopping. The (published) script did have a couple of scenes in which Julie discussed topics like abortion and the meaning of life with her childhood friend Ingvild, but these did not make it into the final film.[25] Both scenes make clear that Ingvild, who has a daughter, feels that Julie has ceased to include her in her seemingly exciting life.

No Trier film has received more feminist criticism than *Reprise*, whose female characters have been described as stereotypical, dull, and without agency in a film all about cool boys.[26] Critics are, however, not quite in agreement about how the film's depiction of an arguably misogynist, laddish culture is to be understood. Norwegian film historian Gunnar Iversen writes that '*Reprise* is a boy's film, by and about boys, and paints an unflattering portrait of the Westside lads' view of the opposite sex'.[27] He calls the film's only meaningful female character Kari 'weak', and believes the film depicts girls as 'best when they are cute and quiet'.[28]

Anne Marit Myrstad has a different take, believing the boys' view of girls and the film's view of women to be discordant. She experiences the film as more critical of the culture it depicts: '*Reprise* repeatedly reveals and implicitly criticises the perception of women as both inferior and threatening, evident both in psychiatry and in contemporary young men's talk'.[29] She also rejects the notion of Kari as a character without any will, strength, or agency of her own, writing that 'Kari's acts are in keeping with the traditionally "feminine" qualities of caring and compassion, though she does not ignore her own feelings and needs'.[30] Kari is given a lot of space, and represents a positive force in the film, and in Phillip's life according to Myrstad. However, one can clearly argue that Kari functions as a girlfriend first and foremost in the film. But as Myrstad points out, Kari does get the last word. As her voice says 'stop', the film stops. Myrstad describes the power she finds in Trier's women as a 'soft strength'.

The fact that different scholars read this film so differently is perhaps down to the film's own ambiguity. When Johanne (Rebekka Karijord) meets the group of guys for the first time, and confronts them about how they tease and talk behind each other's backs, it is hard not to agree with her. And yet by the end of the film, she ends up marrying the guy to tells her she is 'so adorable when she's angry'. It is conspicuous, too, how when minor female characters and extras are mentioned in Trier's and Vogt's script, they are described as 'A strikingly beautiful French girl sits by the window of a spacious apartment', 'A pretty girl who is sunbathing looks for Erik', 'Morten is nearby, talking to a very pretty girl in her early twenties', and so on.[31] I do, however follow Myrstad in interpreting the film's depiction of the rough humour and lack of care and consideration in the friend group as inherently critical. It is hard to argue against *Reprise* being a young men's film, though, or that Trier is better at depicting male than female friendship.[32]

Still, it is often the nuances and challenges of such friendships that he does best; not least because the dialogue in the films is often so affecting and piercing. Friends and friendships are shown as important in his films, but also as status markers. Friends show up for parties, but not always for crises. In both *Reprise* and *Oslo, August 31st*, friendship falls short when one friend must battle illness or addiction. As Anders so poignantly puts it, his parents never prepared him for 'how most friendships dissolve. Until you are strangers, friends in name only'. Trier's interest in what a friendship can be was one thing that drew him to the idea of adapting Louis Malle's *The Fire Within* (1963). He describes Malle's film as a powerful experience for him personally, exactly because of how it depicts friendship, or more precisely, conversations between friends:

> At the heart of it is an honest conversation between two friends about the most difficult thing in the world: one of them doesn't know if he wants to live anymore. It's an impossible conversation, but in art you can talk in an intimate way about something that serious'.[33]

To me, the dialogue between two friends who have drifted apart in *Oslo, August 31st* is a highlight of Trier's filmography. Few others could make a conversation covering Proust, teething, and parents playing Battlefield, simultaneously so hilarious and deeply melancholy, or direct the actors in ways that make the dialogue come across as so genuinely realistic and true.

Trier's films have been described as 'melancholy meditations concerned with existential questions of love, ambition, memory, and identity'.[34] But it is in the combining of these subjects and a playful cinematic language that Trier's particular mix happens. When Julie leaves Aksel's launch party at the high-end restaurant in the hills, she at one point stops to gaze out across Oslo and the fjord landscape. As the camera circles her, her mood shifts. From absorbing and admiring the view, we see her gaze, and her thoughts, turning inward, as she represses perhaps not a scream, but at the very least a tear. She stands almost exactly at the viewpoint Edvard Munch was inspired by when he painted his masterpiece *The Scream* (1893). This painting has been considered both an icon of existential crisis and an expressionist symbol of the human condition. Shortly after this moment, however, Julie slips into the role of fake wedding guest, and sneaks into a party to dance and flirt. Trier positions himself in a landscape in which the romantic can be combined with the existential, the comical with the tragic.

Another way to describe this mix is to say that Trier's films combine depictions of the human experience (often tragic) and human behaviour (often comical). The subject matter may be both grand and grave, but he uses levity and lightness to conceal the fact that they are literally about life and death. Children are born in his films, and in most of them, people die. The passage of time, the beginnings and ends of lives, the meaning of life – Trier's concern is with the big questions. But the small, intimate moments that fill the spaces inbetween are his, too. A conversation with a friend, a shared experience of intoxication, splitting a cigarette, waiting as the girl you are crushing on pees behind a parked car, a gentle brush of fingers over a tattoo, the letting go of existential worries to dance with abandon.

NOTES

1. Kåre Bulie, '– Av å se film lærer man mye om det å være menneske og om hverandre', *www.dn.no*, 14 October 2021, https://www.dn.no/d2/film/joachim-trier/eskil-vogt/filmfestivalen-i-cannes/-av-a-se-film-larer-man-mye-om-det-a-vare-menneske-og-om-hverandre/2-1-1076331.
2. Hillary Weston, 'The Art Form of Memory: A Conversation with Joachim Trier', The Criterion Collection, 8 April 2016, https://www.criterion.com/current/posts/4001-the-art-form-of-memory-a-conversation-with-joachim-trier; Wendy Mitchell, 'Joachim Trier on his Existential Romantic Comedy "The Worst Person in the World"', 9 July 2021, *Screen Daily*, https://www.screendaily.com/features/joachim-trier-on-his-existential-romantic-comedy-the-worst-person-in-the-world/5161391.article; Alex Heeney, 'With *Thelma*, Joachim Trier continues to develop his "dirty formalism"', *Seventh Row*, 25 November 2017, https://seventh-row.com/2017/11/25/thelma-dirty-formalism/.
3. Bulie, '– Av å se film lærer'.
4. Kaiya Shunyata, 'The Worst Person In The World Perfectly Captures the Rawness of Young-Adulthood', *Obscur* (blog), 10 March 2022, https://obscurmagazine.co.uk/the-worst-person-in-the-world-the-rawness-of-young-adulthood/.
5. Daniel Kasman, 'Representation of Self: Discussing "Louder Than Bombs" with Joachim Trier', MUBI, 29 May 2015. https://mubi.com/notebook/posts/representation-of-self-discussing-louder-than-bombs-with-joachim-trier.
6. Christer Bakke Andresen, 'Thelma: Empathic Engagement and the Norwegian Horror Cinema', *Journal of Scandinavian Cinema* 9, no. 2 (1 June 2019): 227–33, https://doi.org/10.1386/jsca.9.2.227_1.
7. Tarja Laine, 'Trauma, Queer Sexuality and Symbolic Storytelling in Joachim Trier's Thelma', *Journal of Scandinavian Cinema* 12, no. 3 (1 September 2022): 291–305, https://doi.org/10.1386/jsca_00077_1, 298.

8. Ibid., 295.
9. Søren Birkvad, 'In Search of the Antagonist: On Inner Struggles and Soft Parental Power in Joachim Trier's Films', *Journal of Scandinavian Cinema* 9, no. 2 (1 June 2019): 203, https://doi.org/10.1386/jsca.9.2.203_1.
10. Jeffrey Bloomer, 'Director Joachim Trier on the Problem With His Movies and Louder Than Bombs' Curious Ending', *Slate*, 8 April 2016, http://www.slate.com/blogs/browbeat/2016/04/08/louder_than_bombs_interview_with_joachim_trier_on_the_movie_s_ending_and.html; Jørgen Bruhn and Anne Gjelsvik, *Cinema Between Media: An Intermediality Approach* (Edinburgh: University Press, 2018), 51–69.
11. Birkvad, 'In Search of the Antagonist', 204.
12. See also Dag Sødtholt, 'Louder Than Bombs: Joachim Trier's Play on Perspective', *Montages International Edition*, 16 January 2016, http://montagesmagazine.com/2016/01/louder-than-bombs-joachim-triers-play-on-perspective/.
13. Anne Marit Myrstad, 'Soft Strength, Mild Mystery: Female Characters in the Films of Joachim Trier', *Journal of Scandinavian Cinema* 9, no. 2 (1 June 2019): 211–18, https://doi.org/10.1386/jsca.9.2.211_1.
14. Myrstad, 'Soft Strength', 216.
15. Dag Sødtholt, 'Touchstones – a Guide to Joachim Trier's Cinematic Universe', *Montages International Edition*, 7 December 2021, https://montagesmagazine.com/2021/12/touchstones-a-guide-to-joachim-triers-cinematic-universe/;
16. Casper Hindse, 'Ordleg med Joachim Trier', *Filmmagasinet Ekko*, 30 November 2017, https://www.ekkofilm.dk/artikler/joachim-trier-/.
17. See Laine, 'Trauma', for more on the symbolism of the snake.
18. Between 2013 and 2020 Thelma was the only main character without a heteronormative sexuality, according to a report made for the Norwegian Film Institute in 2021.
19. Andrew Bundy, 'Joachim Trier Talks The Inspiration For "The Worst Person In The World", His Love Of Graphic Novels & More', *The Playlist*, 2 February 2022, https://theplaylist.net/joachim-trier-talks-the-inspiration-for-the-worst-person-in-the-world-interview-20220202/.
20. See Laura Mulvey, 'Visual Pleasure and Narrative Cinema', *Screen* 16, no. 3 (Autumn 1975): 6–18, on the male gaze.
21. Eskil Vogt and Joachim Trier, *Verdens verste menneske: filmmanus* (Oslo: Tiden Norsk Forlag, 2021), 140.
22. Anne Lise With, 'Det levende og det fryste: Noen betraktninger omkring "Verdens verste menneske"', *Montages*, 6 January 2022, https://montages.no/2022/01/det-levende-og-det-fryste-noen-betraktninger-omkring-verdens-verste-menneske/; Hannah Bull Thorvik, 'Hun kjeder meg voldsomt', *Dagbladet*, 25 October 2021, https://www.dagbladet.no/kultur/hun-kjeder-meg-voldsomt/74450358.
23. Alison Bechdel prefers her friend Wallace to also be credited, as the idea was originally hers, and the term 'Bechdel-Wallace test' is accordingly sometimes used. I will stick to using the more common 'Bechdel test' here.
24. See, for instance, bechdeltest.com. The test also inspired a Swedish campaign (initiated by Rio Cinema, and now spread to multiple countries) which issues films that pass the test a so-called A certificate. See also http://www.a-listfilm.com/

25. Vogt and Trier, *Verdens verste menneske*. One of these deleted scenes features on Criterion's DVD edition of the film.
26. See, for instance, Oda Bahr, 'Ti år som kjedet kvinnen', *Rushprint*, 1 January 2010.
27. Gunnar Iversen, 'Tiden leger ingen sår "Reprise"', in *Den norske filmbølgen: Fra Orions belte til Max Manus.* (Oslo: Universitetsforlaget, 2010), 280.
28. Ibid., 282.
29. Myrstad, 'Soft Strength, Mild Mystery', 216.
30. Ibid., 214.
31. Vogt and Trier *Verdens verste menneske*, 16, 124, 203.
32. See also Chapter 8 about the relationship between Anders and Thomas.
33. Hillary Weston, 'Everyday Magic: Joachim Trier on Reimagining Louis Malle', The Criterion Collection, 17 December 2017, https://www.criterion.com/current/posts/5039-everyday-magic-joachim-trier-on-reimagining-louis-malle.
34. Weston, 'The Art Form of Memory'.

CHAPTER 7

A Good Picture

The importance and value of art is a thread running through all of Joachim Trier's work, taking different turns and coming to expression in a number of ways. Several of his characters are artists themselves: Erik and Phillip in *Reprise* dream of, and achieve, authorship, Aksel in *The Worst Person in the World* is a successful cartoonist, Isabelle in *Louder Than Bombs* a renowned war photographer, and Julie, also in *The Worst Person in the World*, seeks to become – and becomes – a photographer. The people populating his films live in homes filled with paintings, theatre posters and books; they dance and attend concerts; computer games, exhibitions and literary references are consistently integrated into their stories. Art is part of what shapes their identities, how they see and understand themselves in relation to others.

Erik and Phillip dream of a future in which life and prose, for better or worse, are woven into one tapestry; and when Aksel looks back upon his life, his memories of items like comic books, record stores, and VHS tapes of European art films are the things he finds to have shaped him as a person: 'That's all I have. That's what I've spent my life on. Collecting all these experiences, be they albums or books . . .' Interviews with Joachim Trier himself are often overflowing with references to the filmmakers that have formed him, and it is clear his own sense of identity, of self, is closely tied to different forms of artistic expression: 'Like Aksel, I built my identity on what bands I liked, what films I associate myself with'.[1] Also a DJ, Trier has compared his approach to filmmaking to that of making music: 'I always imagine a movie is a record with different songs on it, and I want it to only be hits'.[2] Trier comes from a family of jazz musicians, artists and film workers. He still works as a DJ from time to time, and his interest in the arts shapes his thinking about both himself and his chosen medium.

His films are not just shaped by art, though, they are also largely about art: they explore what art is, what it can do, and what its different forms can do differently. How photography, for instance, can show a person's true face, or how literature can capture our inner realities. Above all, Trier is exploring the distinct characteristics, possibilities, and limitations of cinematic art, but he does this partly through a parallel exploration of other art forms – literature, photography, and music in particular. Along with his regular co-writer Eskil Vogt, he has developed stories more closely aligned with the form of the modern novel than the classical, plot-driven tale championed by Hollywood and screenwriting instructors like Robert McKee and Syd Field. The two co-authors consider themselves filmmakers more than storytellers. When they integrate things like photographs and literary devices into their work, as they do in *Louder Than Bombs*, these are means, I will argue, of investigating the formal properties of both the film medium and other art forms.

I will discuss some of the recurring techniques and elements in Trier's work that have, by some, been described as 'literary' – voice-overs, lengthy dialogues, stream of consciousness – in Chapter 8. In this chapter, I will be looking mostly at how different, non-cinematic visual art forms are explored in his films. My main focus is visual media, and specifically photography as it is employed and explored in *Louder Than Bombs*, but I will start with *The Worst Person in the World*.

The depiction of Aksel and his work as a cartoonist in *The Worst Person in the World* is a great example of the dedication and attention to detail with which Trier makes space for art in his movies. The cartoonist sees great success with his underground comic strip *Gaupe*, and the choice of the comic book as Aksel's medium stems from Trier's own interest in, and passion for, the form. He has proclaimed Chris Ware 'one of the most important contemporary artists in any field' and pointed to other cartoonists, like Robert Crumb and Dave Sim as important sources of inspiration.[3] His hiring of Norwegian illustrator Bendik Kaltenborn to create posters for the film, one of which also became the cover art for the Criterion Collection's DVD edition, is also emblematic of his enthusiasm for comics and comic art.

Gaupe was inspired by real-life Swedish comic strip Arne Anka, drawn by Charlie Christensen. The eponymous Arne in this strip, who is visually very similar to Donald Duck, is a failed poet who spends his days in the pub, philosophising with his friend Krille Crocodile. Christensen himself was hired to draw *Gaupe* as it appears in *The Worst Person in the World*, and produced illustrations of the strip's wildcat protagonist, three covers, and a handful of actual strips. The word '*Gaupe*' means 'lynx' in Norwegian, and the lynx is the only wild feline found in Norway – just as *Gaupe* the character is described as wildcat in a world of domesticated specimens. Both comic and character are depicted as somewhat sexist and out of touch. The comic strip made for the

Figure 7.1 The comic *Gaupe* in *The Worst Person in the World*.

film is itself filled with other cultural and intertextual references: *Gaupe* is for instance a fan of the fictional band Kommune ('kommune' is the Norwegain word for municipality), who feature in *Reprise*, and one panel features one of Trier's favourite real-life Norwegian authors, Tor Ulven, fittingly depicted as a wolf ('ulv' means 'wolf' in Norwegian). Ulven's works were also referenced in *Reprise*, where character Sten Erik Dahl – revered by the film's two protagonists – was clearly inspired by him.

Over the course of *The Worst Person in the World*, Aksel evolves as an artist, and eventually publishes two autobiographical works called *Childhood* and *Youth* that are more mature in tone and style than the strips that made him famous. Charlie Christensen produced several pages of the latter of these titles as well, work that can only be seen for a few seconds in the film, displayed on a wall in the background of the launch party scene. The story in this strip is, according to Christensen, based on an embarrassing moment from Joachim Trier's own life, in which, aged fourteen or fifteen, he attempted to impress a girl he fancied by explaining which of the nudes in the Vigeland Sculpture Park he most identified with.[4] The creation of these comic strips that can barely even be seen in the film demonstrates the amount of work that goes into constructing a fully formed cinematic universe featuring complete, believable characters, but the anecdote behind this story from *Youth* also – at least if Christensen is to be believed – highlights how far back this connection between art and identity goes for Trier.

The clearest example of this relationship between artistic expression and the self is, however, perhaps found in the utilisation and exploration of photography in *Louder Than Bombs*. Trier's American family drama is, to my mind, not merely an investigation of complex familial relationships, communication issues, grief, and pain, but also a sophisticated cinematic exploration of the role of media in our lives – be that computer games, online and communication media, literature, or photography.⁵

Let me begin my analysis of *Louder Than Bombs* by looking at a scene that very explicitly explores what a photograph can do and mean. Young academic and new father Jonah has returned to his parents' home to help his father Gene sift through the archives of his deceased mother, renowned press photographer Isabelle Reed, ahead of an upcoming memorial exhibition. To the family, and perhaps to Jonah in particular, it is important that the exhibition's curators not be the ones to sort through his mother's private collection. Ahead of this scene, we have been told that Isabelle took her own life three years earlier, and that though youngest son Conrad has not been informed of this 'truth', as it is called, her colleague Richard (David Strathairn) intends to include it in an article about her. This scene, filled with some of the bright, anticipatory energy of a brief visit home after a long time away, breaks with the melancholy tenor of the rest of the film. There is a mixture of familial closeness and distance here, rushed attempts at turning absence into presence, into communion. In his mother's darkroom, Conrad finds an old photo, a headshot of his father as a young actor, which he laughingly shows his older brother. Jonah points to this picture as evidence that the archive must remain private, and exclaims, mirthfully: 'We wouldn't want this to fall in the wrong hands, would we?' and 'What *are* we even looking at here?'

Figure 7.2 A picture of Gene: 'She thought that was a very good picture of me'.

Jonah then playacts an imaginary casting agent filling a role based on this particular photo: 'Yes, we would like him.' Jonah, Conrad, and even Gene laugh until Gene shows the boys the back of the photo, with a signature and professional photographer's stamp. The headshot was done by Isabelle Joubert (their mother's maiden name), and the suggestion is that this was how their parents met – her the photographer, him her object. 'She kept it, because she thought it was a very good photo of me', Gene says.

Were I to attempt to encapsulate *Louder Than Bombs* in a single sentence, I would do so by asking just this question: What is, or makes, a good photo, or picture, of a person? Beneath the intricate emotional and existential familial knots being tied and untied, this scene, like the film itself, investigates what images and photographs do in our lives, and what an image is. It explores the ways in which photographs shape how we see ourselves and others.[6]

Photographic images are ubiquitous, present throughout the lives of most people alive today, and we mostly see and use them without ever thinking about the specific characteristics of the photography medium. And yet it is intimately connected with our private and public identities. We use photographs when we identify ourselves, with our passports or driver's licenses, and we share images meant to portray our best selves on platforms like Instagram, TikTok, or Facebook. Do the images we post online really represent our true selves? Can we trust the images we encounter to give a true impression of the people they depict? Such questions about photographs lead us directly to the universal, existential questions typical of all of Trier's films as discussed earlier: can a person truly be known? What is the truth about someone? Are you defined by what you yourself can see and remember, or by what is seen and remembered by another?

This question of how we perceive ourselves and each other runs through the introduction of each central character in *Louder Than Bombs*. Jonah is shown in the very first image of the film. He sits staring at his new-born daughter, something we, the viewers, can see through close-ups of what he sees: his own, massive finger in the infant's little hand; his face as he looks at her. Conrad is introduced as we, and then his father, peer at him through a classroom window. Isabelle is presented through a retrospective documentary about her career, produced by the gallery, and Gene's introduction is an extreme close-up of his teary eye as he watches this film. *Louder Than Bombs* is, in many ways, a subtle exploration of how we as fellow human beings *see* each other – both literally and figuratively. And as it explores these concepts, the film repeatedly focuses on the use of photography as a means of portraying a person, of capturing the truth, and of remembering.

The film most obviously demonstrates the importance of photography through Isabelle's work as a photographer specialising in war and conflict. In 2015, when the film was made, journalists and photographers would cover

Afghanistan and Syria – today it might have been Ukraine or Gaza. Her job is to say something about other people, about who they are and how they are doing, through the camera of a press photographer. Isabelle herself, who is already dead at the film's beginning, as mentioned is shown to us through a sort of documentary collage set to be part of a memorial exhibition. This cinematic portrait of her is evocative of how Orson Welles introduces his dead main character through a newsreel in the beginning of *Citizen Kane* (1941).

The short documentary portrait of Isabelle is in itself a complex mixture of different components: audio recordings and both still and moving images. The first thing we hear is her own recorded voice, speaking about her work – explaining its challenges and why she chooses to do it – shots ringing out in the background all the while. This is followed by video recordings of her at work, her own photographs, and a recording of her colleague Richard describing her as a photographer, set against more images from war zones. There are clips from an awards show, a televised interview with Isabelle (also featuring several of her photographs), and a news report about the car accident that led to her death. Finally, there is a black-and-white portrait of her with the words 'Isabelle Reed 1954–2011' superimposed. The newsreader's voice tells us that she was not just a photographer, but also a spouse and a mother. This depiction of her consists, in other words, of different medial modes of expression: fictional scenes with actors Isabelle Huppert and David Strathairn blur into clips from real-life talk show *Charlie Rose*, and are interspersed with a number of authentic warzone photographs, taken by press photographers like Alexandra Boulat. This sequence is a typical example of how Trier employs speedy, narrative montages, a technique also seen in both *Reprise* and *The Worst Person in the World*. This style of narration allows him to say a lot about a character in a very short amount of time. The collage is a portrait and a memorial, but also an imperfect attempt at capturing the truth about its subject. Isabelle's death was, as we are about to learn, most likely not an accident, and she was not (merely) the successful photographer known to the public. She was a woman with struggles and secrets.

The montage is, however, not only a portrait of Isabelle, but also a crash course in several of the central questions that have occupied theorists of the photographic medium, like Susan Sontag and Roland Barthes. Photo theorists, like many film theorists, have largely been pursuing the very essence of the medium, exploring the relationships between photographic images and reality, or a camera's objectivity and a photographer's point of view, and the span between proximity and distance. And said theorists have debated the ethical challenges inherent in documenting acts of evil and brutality, and the different positions held by the photograph, in society, at different times. All these themes are present in the collage, either directly – through words spoken by Isabelle or Richard – or indirectly – through the images chosen for it.

Photography has often been described as the medium of memories. As such, an interest in photography is hardly surprising in a director so preoccupied with memory as Trier. It is an interest he has spoken about publicly, sharing that he collects photography books and that his sister is a photographer.[7] In his work, his interest in the relationship between visual media and memory can be traced as far back as the short films he made as a student at the National Film and Television School. *Pietà* (2000) opens with a photograph of a child and an adult narrator saying that his first memory was of his mother taking his picture. *Still* (2001) is a dying photographer's look back on his life, and this work, too, is filled with a mixture of moving and still images. In *Procter* (2002), the protagonist witnesses a suicide that is also caught on video, a video he takes home and watches over and over. As discussed in Chapter 1, *Oslo, 31. August* begins with a montage of recounted memories and archive footage of Oslo in the 1970s and 80s.

An image can take us back to the very first day of school, to a certain summer, or to exactly how a loved one looked the very first, or last, time we saw them. The photograph as a form of expression is, however, intimately connected not just with memories, but with death. As such, it is a well-suited lens through which to explore bereavement, arguably the very core of *Louder Than Bombs*. Since its invention, photography has kept company with death, Susan Sontag writes in *Regarding the Pain of Others*, a work that has inspired Trier.[8] Because a photograph is created with the help of a camera, it is 'literally, a trace of something brought before the lens', and this objective property of the new medium made it a superior means of producing portraits or mementos, Sontag argues.[9] Similar wording can be found in Roland Barthes' writings on the photograph.[10] A photograph is an image of something or someone that *was there*. It is, in other words, directly anchored to a specific time and place. To Barthes, the very essence of photography was exactly this – that it points back to something that was, or, more precisely, that a photograph can show us something 'that has been' a peculiar combination of presence and absence.[11]

All photographs are thus memento mori, Sontag writes, and to take a photograph is, 'to participate in another person's (or thing's) mortality, vulnerability, mutability. Precisely by slicing out this moment and freezing it, all photographs testify to time's relentless melt'.[12] Further, she claims that 'Photographs state the innocence, the vulnerability of lives heading towards their own destruction, and this link between photography and death haunts all photographs of people'.[13] These passages from Sontag echo with the very type of mood and motif running through all of Trier's films: 'remembrances of things past', attempts to freeze and keep hold of time. Barthes has described photographs as 'more memorable than moving images, because they are a neat slice of time, not a flow'.[14]

Isabelle is present in *Louder Than Bombs* through the other characters' fragmented memories of her. To Conrad, she is also present as virtual images in his dreams and fantasies. The film as a whole is more or less a collage of different, individual memories of who Isabelle was: a mother who was simultaneously loving and absent, a parent to be proud of during college visits, a wife who liked to challenge the way her husband saw her.

Retrospection and personal recollection are also central in Roland Barthes's book *Camera Lucida*, which he wrote while mourning his mother's death. As such, it has much in common with one of the core themes of *Louder Than Bombs*. Barthes often dreamt of his mother, he writes, but in dreams she was never quite *her*: 'I dream about her, I do not dream *her*.'[15] Barthes describes digging through family albums to find the mother he remembered: 'Now, one November evening shortly after my mother's death, I was going through some photographs. I had no hope of "finding" her, I expected nothing from these "photographs of a being before which one recalls less of that being than by merely thinking of him or her".'[16] Paradoxically, Barthes does rediscover the mother he knew and remembered in a childhood photo of her – a picture taken before he himself existed. This old, somewhat tattered photograph of her sets Barthes on the trail of what he believes is the 'essence of the Photograph', its ability to capture what has been. Multiple theorists have highlighted how a core difference between movies and photographs lies in our experience of time. Film scholar Laura Mulvey, for instance, has called the difference between a narrative film and a photograph a temporal one: the film has a sense of 'here and now', the photograph always provides a feeling of 'then'.[17]

One scene in *Louder Than Bombs* is reminiscent, in a way, of Barthes's hunt for the truth in his photo albums. Jonah is looking not for pictures of his mother, but pictures taken by her, to include in the exhibition. He finds a memory card in her room which he browses through on her computer. On it are pictures from her final work trip away from her family, before she put her career on the shelf: the view from her hotel room, mirror selfies, but also a sombre portrait of her, bare shouldered in the hotel bed, taken by someone else. His half-naked reflection in the background reveals that her colleague Richard is behind the camera. This image thus suggests that they were lovers. Jonah deletes these pictures, which show a side of his mother he does not wish to see, or for others to see. But they have given him a different, perhaps truer, view of her.

Trier's exploration of the photograph is, however, not limited to a study of the portrait or the nostalgic retrospective, which were Barthes's main interests. On the contrary, a surprising number of aspects of the photographic medium are touched on in the film, both playfully and with the gravest reverence. Throughout *Louder Than Bombs*, photography is represented in numerous forms: as negatives in plastic charteques; as small paper copies; as files on a digital memory stick; as images on computer screens; as large exhibition objects; as still images from a documentary film within the film. In the film's universe, photography functions informatively, as a feature of news reporting, scientifically, as an x-ray, ceremonially, at an awards ceremony, and documentarily, when proud grandfather Gene shows images of Jonah's new baby off to his colleagues on his phone. In other words, the presence of photography in the film mirrors its role in the lives of people today.

Not every image of war, crisis, or tragedy has the same impact. Sometimes news photography fails, at least to captivate its audience. In one scene, Isabelle sees the pictures she has so worked hard to capture in Afghanistan make it to the front page of the New York Times – only to be all but ignored by the reader swiftly flipping past them. Trier is conscious of how the modern reader and viewer is seemingly becoming desensitised to news photography's depictions of other people's grief, other people's crises: 'It's easy to get cynical these days and we've become numb to these kinds of photographs because there's so much of it thrown at us all the time'.[18] Photographers and film directors share some common challenges in this, and Trier has talked about the importance of not reducing human beings to clichés, and how one must strive for the images one creates to contain real insight into people's fates. All the more in a time where competition is brutal, perhaps especially for news media, from myriad impressions, swift changes, easy clicks. In the director' own words: 'In this time and age, war photography of that sort which takes time and is contemplative, and is put into a context is not being prioritized as much as the immediacy. Here it is right now: explosion, death!'.[19]

While preparing to make his film, Trier spent a lot of time immersing himself in the work of multiple war photographers. And in interviews, he is full of praise for Susan Sontag's *Regarding the Pain of Others*, calling it a 'wonderful book' that 'ponders upon the representation of other people's grief and how to convey those things without being patronizing or vulgar'.[20] To Trier's mind, this is also a question for filmmakers to ponder: 'As Susan Sontag would wonderfully describe: how do we regard the pain of others? How do we deal with other human stories'.[21] Sontag's book has directly inspired some of Isabelle's musings on war photography in the film as well: 'As she says in the film, under normal circumstances you wouldn't walk into a house of someone who is grieving and take their photo. So why do we do that, and what does it mean?'.[22] Sontag describes the act of observing another's suffering from a distance as a uniquely modern experience, enabled by the invention of the photograph. War has become a thing we can watch from the comfort of our own living rooms, also when we are not ourselves at or affected by war.[23]

The effect of all these horrible images, readily available to us in our own homes through newspapers, online media, or television, is, however, unclear; they can generate both compassion and numbness. To Sontag, however, the crucial thing is not whether images inspire compassion, but that they are 'an invitation to pay attention, to reflect, to learn'.[24] Although an image can only capture part of reality, the photograph holds fundamental reminders of human pain, and of evil:

The images say: This is what human beings are capable of doing – many volunteer to do, enthusiastically, self-righteously. Don't forget. This is not quite the same as asking people to remember a particularly monstrous bout of evil ('Never forget'). Perhaps too much value is assigned to memory, not enough to thinking.[25]

It is surely no coincidence that when Renate Reinsve was preparing to play a photographer in *The Worst Person in the World*, she carried a copy of Sontag's *On Photography* around with her on set.[26] And likewise, it seems meaningful that Trier and Vogt have Julie end up as a unit photographer on a film set. According to Trier, Julie ends up trying to actually see people 'in the moment, as they are, rather than that idealization that she's been trying to escape for most of the film, if that makes sense. At some point she's just documenting. I think there's something there that I'm very intrigued by'.[27]

Although photography is clearly singled out, *Louder Than Bombs* also explore the possibilities and limitations inherent in different media more generally. In the film, we see media that bring people together, and somehat keep people apart. However, several of the media represented serve as both communicative hindrances *and* communicative possibilities. The most illustrative example of this might be the mobile phone: When his father is attempting to get in touch with him, Conrad can choose to shut down the conversation, or to simply not answer the call (as is the case when he spends a night out and Gene is worried). Similarly, the music in Conrad's headphones works as a barrier between him and other people, but the sound of music also serves as a conversation starter for him and his older brother. Media facilitates meetings, can serve as common ground, like when Jonah and Conrad laugh at embarrassing YouTube clips of their father, or play computer games together.

Gaming itself also has this duality, because while it can serve as a point of contact for Conrad and his brother, it is also a world in which he closes himself off with virtual friends. For a long while the spectator is led to believe that Conrad is deeply miserable, perhaps even approaching depression and a potential violent outburst, an assumption shared by his brother, who at one point asks him: 'You are not gonna shoot up a school, are you?' Gene, in an attempt to connect with his aloof, hostile son, makes an effort to learn how to play *The Elder Scrolls Online*, but all he achieves is, ironically, for his character to be killed by Conrad's, who has no idea that this is an act of patricide. Gene's disappointment aside, this scene can be read as a rather positive depiction of video games as a medium; the game allows Conrad to express feelings (here his hatred towards his father) that he cannot, to the same extent, voice or act on in other areas of his life. Seen in this light, the video game is as expressive, and perhaps liberating, as literature is. In his own writing, Conrad describes how he enjoys changing between the different avatars, and how role playing different characters gives him access to different skills. Conrad's gaming could also be compared with Isabelle's photography, and her dangerous but exciting life as a war photographer.[28] *Louder Than Bombs* is consequently not only a film about (troubled) relations between people, it is very much a film about the relationship between human beings and media.

Louder Than Bombs shows us two sons and a husband with vastly different recollections of *who* Isabelle was, and *what* she was to each of them. Photography theorist Mette Sandbye as described a photograph as 'a fragment of a fractured whole'.[29] And considered in this way, the kaleidoscopic structure of the film can be interpreted as a mosaic of pieces that together form a whole, make up the entire trauma of Isabelle's death.

This chapter may leave an impression of *Louder Than Bombs* as a sombre, traumatic film, but it is also, at times, both optimistic and playful. While the collage depicting Isabelle is mournful and serious, the other montage, Conrad's diary is a playful cornucopia of different media, including photographs (see also chapter two). In investigating what photographic images are and do, *Louder Than Bombs* also becomes a study of what film can do, and how the two media, cinema and photography, can work together, and how art and media interact with our perceptions of identity and reality.

NOTES

1. Elissa Suh, 'A Stick, a Stone, the End of the Road: Joachim Trier Discusses "The Worst Person in the World"', MUBI, https://mubi.com/notebook/posts/a-stick-a-stone-the-end-of-the-road-joachim-trier-discusses-the-worst-person-in-the-world.
2. Andrew Bundy, 'Joachim Trier Talks The Inspiration For "The Worst Person In The World", His Love Of Graphic Novels & More', *The Playlist*, 2 February 2022, https://theplaylist.net/joachim-trier-talks-the-inspiration-for-the-worst-person-in-the-world-interview-20220202/.
3. Ibid.; Suh, 'A Stick, a Stone'.
4. Walter Wehus, 'Her er tegneserien *Gaupe* fra Verdens verste menneske', *Empirix*, 31 December 2021, https://www.empirix.no/her-er-tegneserien-*Gaupe*-fra-verdens-verste-menneske/.
5. See also Jørgen Bruhn and Anne Gjelsvik, *Cinema Between Media: An Intermediality Approach* (Edinburgh: University Press, 2018).
6. I also write about this in Anne Gjelsvik, 'Analysen: Louder Than Bombs (2015)', *Montages*, 5 October 2015, http://montages.no/2015/10/analysen-louder-than-bombs-2015/;
7. Gemma Gracewood, 'The Power of the Still: The Photography Behind the Scenes', *Journal: A Letterboxd Magazine*, 20 March 2022, https://letterboxd.com/journal/power-of-the-still-unit-photography/.
8. Susan Sontag, *Regarding the Pain of Others* (New York: Farrar, Straus and Giroux, 2003), 26.

9. Ibid.
10. Roland Barthes, *Camera Lucida: Reflections on Photography*, Vintage Classics (London: Vintage Books, 2000).
11. Ibid., 77.
12. Susan Sontag, *On Photography*. (London: Penguin, 2002).
13. Ibid., 170.
14. Barthes, *Camera Lucida*, 17.
15. Ibid., 66.
16. Ibid. Barthes is here referencing Proust, but I have not been able to find the original.
17. Laura Mulvey, *Death 24x a Second: Stillness and the Moving Image* (Chicago: Reaktion Books, 2006), 57.
18. Kee Chang, 'Q&A with Joachim Trier', *Anthem*, 21 May 2015, https://anthemmagazine.com/qa-with-joachim-trier/.
19. Jose Solis, 'Joachim Trier Interview', StageBuddy.com, 12 April 2016, https://stagebuddy.com/film/interview-director-joachim-trier-new-york-music-playing-cinematic-form-louder-bombs.
20. Ibid.
21. Nicholas Rapold, 'Interview: Joachim Trier', *Film Comment*, 11 April 2016, https://www.filmcomment.com/blog/interview-joachim-trier/.
22. Solis, 'Joachim Trier Interview'.
23. Sontag, *Regarding the Pain*, 17, 21.
24. Ibid., 117.
25. Ibid., 115.
26. Gracewood, 'The Power of the Still'.
27. Ibid.
28. Dag Sødtholt, 'Louder Than Bombs: Joachim Trier's Play on Perspective', *Montages International Edition*, 16 January 2016, http://montagesmagazine.com/2016/01/louder-than-bombs-joachim-triers-play-on-perspective/; Bruhn and Gjelsvik, *Cinema Between Media*; Solis, 'Joachim Trier Interview'.
29. Mette Sandbye, *Mindesmærker: Tid og erindring i fotografiet* (Copenhagen: Politisk revy, 2001), 51.

CHAPTER 8

Voices and Words

'A film in 12 chapters, a prologue and an epilogue'. This is how *The Worst Person in the World* is introduced. We then meet its protagonist, first shown as young woman in medical school, while a mature, female voice-over tells us: 'Julie disappointed herself. This used to be easy.' The narration continues: 'This was wrong. This was not her'.

Trier's approach to filmmaking has sometimes been described as novelistic.[1] Elements like the ones described above – a structure based on 'chapters' and voice-over narration – contribute to that. These are techniques that are often considered literary. Off-screen narration, or voice-over, is, however, a recurring feature in Trier's work. Sometimes it takes the form of an external narrator (as in the openings of *The Worst Person in the World* and *Reprise*), sometimes what we hear is the internal voice of one of the characters (most notably in *Louder Than Bombs*).

Words are important to Trier not just as a tool, but also as a subject in and on itself. While the previous chapters have shown how his work is often visually innovative, he is also, I would argue, breaking new ground verbally. He is notable, for instance, for his lengthy, emotional dialogue scenes. Some recurring themes in his work are the ways we use language to define ourselves; our inherent need to express ourselves as human beings; and how we tell the stories of our lives. Four of the films feature young people aspiring to be or attempting to become writers: whether novelists (Erik and Phillip in *Reprise*), magazine writers (Anders in *Oslo, August 31st*) or literary diarists (Conrad in *Louder Than Bombs*). Two of these films (*Reprise* and *Louder Than Bombs*) have clear parallels with the Künstlerroman, the literary genre dedicated to chronicling a young (often male) character's path to becoming an artist (often a writer).[2]

Julie writes as well. In one scene, we see her composing her piece 'Oral sex in the age of #MeToo', and hear her inner voice speaking some of the words. We see her boyfriend Aksel reading and responding to her work. Finally, we hear the external narrator describing her blog post's online success. Her words are represented both visually (as letters on the screen) and aurally (through Julie's voice). The value and quality of her words is appraised and commented on by both Aksel and the unnamed narrator. This short scene, without much particular relevance to the general plot of *The Worst Person in the World*, is in other words used to explore how the written word can be communicated on film.

This chapter will investigate the prominence of words, writing, and voices in Trier's films. Drawing on the published scripts (all co-written with Eskil Vogt), I will look at the roles played by words, and the inventive and varied uses of voice-over. I will attempt to show that merely describing these techniques as 'literary' is a bit of an oversimplification. Both Trier and Vogt have bristled at suggestions that their way of writing and making films is non-cinematic. 'But are those things not film too?' Trier said when I inquired about his repeated use of stream of consciousness.[3] My aim is to say something about how Trier's (and his co-author Vogt's) explorations of words and voices are also explorations of cinema – what it is or can be.

Oslo, August 31st features an unusually long dialogue sequence in which Anders and his friend Thomas discuss a range of different subjects. Anders has unexpectedly shown up at Thomas's doorstep after a long estrangement. Their conversation flows continuously for twelve minutes, as they move through several physical locations, and covers subject matter like addiction, love, children, the Battlefield games, how there are never enough hours in the day, happiness, and the fact that Anders is considering suicide. In an interview that was published along with the script, Eskil Vogt explains how pushing the boundaries of what can be done with cinematic dialogue was part of what interested them during their work on this film together. Vogt, who writes the lion's share of the dialogue in their collaborations, stresses the importance of 'exploring dialogue for its own sake, letting it have its own value'.[4]

Among other things, this means indulging in repetition and pauses, letting hurtful remarks hang in the air, have the time to take their full effect. Letting dialogue go on for this long challenges convention, and moves the on-screen conversation closer to what an everyday exchange might sound like in real life. In the script, this scene spans twenty-five pages, but in the finished film, the two actors Anders Danielsen Lie and Hans Olav Brenner – close personal friends in real life – have reshaped and coloured it. Some of the most famous lines from the film are their own twists on what had been written. This focus on the importance of words springs directly from the two scriptwriters' opposition to the notion that a lot of dialogue is inherently anti-cinematic.[5]

Even in their first film, Trier and Vogt were self-aware in their concern with the difference between telling and showing. *Reprise* features a somewhat sarcastic, detached narrator, providing commentary on what the characters are thinking and doing. In the companion interview to the published script, the pair discuss the purist position that rejects the use of voice-over in film, the notion that showing things visually should always be the ideal.[6] The archetypal representative of this view is perhaps screenwriting guru Robert McKee as played by Brian Cox in *Adaptation* (2002). The film's protagonist, Charlie Kauffman (played by Nicholas Cage) is struggling with writer's block and signs up for one of McKee's famous 'Story' seminars. While Charlie listens to McKee's lecture on what a script should be, we hear his own inner monologue as a voice-over, deriding him as pathetic, worthless, a loser. Charlie's internal narration mingles and intertwines with the words of the lecture, and just as he, panicked, considers leaving the hall, McKee thunders: 'God help you if you use voice-over in your work, my friends. God help you! It is flaccid, sloppy writing. Any idiot can write voice-over narration to explain the thoughts of a character.'

The arguments against the use of voice-over are many. There is the view that it is a redundant legacy from literature, that film should primarily be a visual medium. In Hollywood especially, the 'show, don't tell' ideal looms large, along with the notion that cinema should be immersive. The voice-over can be seen as unnecessarily distancing, or, as in *Adaptation*, as shoddy, sloppy work. To this, Vogt and Trier say that all narrative responsibility should not be foisted onto the visual, that the voice-over offers the filmmaker many possibilities beyond mere illustration, that it does not need to be superfluous. It can reveal a character's secret mind, transform the mood, the style, or the tempo of the film, inject humour, and so much more.[7] According to Trier, the voice-over 'let us do more with the images than just tell a story'.[8]

A number of words can be used to describe Vogt and Trier's use of the voice-over, but 'sloppy' is not among them. In fact, they employ this tool so extensively and in so many ways that it can be difficult to chart or typologise. In *Invisible Storytellers*, Sarah Kozloff argues against the prejudice against sound and intertitles, and in favour of a re-evaluation of voice-over narration, including in classical narrative cinema.[9] In Kozloff's definition of voice-over narration, 'all three words are fully operative'.[10] By this she means that we can hear someone speaking (voice) who is not visible in the image the viewer is watching as they speak (over), and the third element, narration 'relates to the content of the speech: someone is in the act of communicating a narrative – that is, recounting a series of events to an audience'.[11] Kozloff has been a key voice in opposition to the visual and more conservative school of thought represented by McKee, but even her perspectives cannot fully account for what is happening in Trier's films.

Kozloff is only concerned with the voice-over as narration, and her definition can therefore not be applied to all instances of voice-over in film.[12] The voice-over can have several functions beyond narrating. Her definition: 'oral statements, conveying any portion of a narrative, spoken by an unseen speaker situated in a space and time other than that simultaneously being presented by the images on the screen' will, among other things, exclude scenes in which the speaker is visible in the frame.[13]

In *Oslo, August 31st*, we at one point see Anders walking the streets alone, having been stood up by his sister. We chiefly follow him from behind and from a distance. We simultaneously hear his voice speaking about his parents, but we do not see his lips move, nor any person that he might be saying these things to. We hear him make a long list of statements: 'He taught me how to ride a bicycle', 'She taught me to always floss', 'He taught me that people who consider the army a worthwhile experience are most likely utterly uninteresting', 'She held a tolerant view on drugs', 'They respected my privacy. Maybe too much sometimes', 'They never taught me to cook', 'She said I could do whatever I wanted, decide what to be, who to love, where to live'. This sequence consists of three parts, where the first emphasises images of Oslo following the line 'They were both from Oslo. Remembered places we passed'. In other words we are hearing, through the voice-over, what would seem to be an internal monologue from a character we are also watching in real time.

Richard Raskin has created a typology of the most common forms of voice-over in fiction film, and the first, the inner voice, is described as follows: 'Inner thoughts of a character shown on screen with his or her lips not moving'.[14] On the face of it, this definition might seem to fit our example from *Oslo, August 31st*. But what Anders is saying in this voice-over does not seem like the actual thoughts he is thinking in the moment we are watching. On the contrary, something about his voice and turns of phrase make it seem like these lines are being spoken out loud to someone else. One could just as well, in other words, interpret the Anders we hear as 'situated in a space and time other than' the Anders we see.[15] There is at the very least some ambiguity, if not directly a temporal discrepancy between the words and images in this scene, and what we hear is never actually explained or given any context. This monologue also lacks the intimacy of Anders's conversation with his friend Thomas. The lines spoken almost sound like answers to interview questions, like some private parallel to his failed job interview from before perhaps. More precisely, it sounds like someone reading out a list, point by point. This is another form of ambiguity that Vogt and Trier like to explore, forms existing somewhere in the space between written and spoken word. We can find it several places in this and their other films.

In a scene shortly before this monologue occurs, Anders sits in a café, listening in on other people's conversations and observing passers-by. Here, too, there is a disconnect between what we see and what we hear. Anders, and the camera, may focus on a man walking down the street as he (and we) listens to an exchange from the next table over. Here, many voices mingle with his own thoughts, stealing his, and our, attention. These snippets of conversation function as commentary to his own musings, but also as a demonstration of the discrepancy between his and their lives. The other people in the café are on dates, have just had babies, lament commonplace problems. A group of young girls have him smiling, in spite of himself, as they, giggling, discuss how Kurt Cobain committed suicide by shooting himself in the head with a shotgun. He hears another girl reading out a bucket list to a friend.[16]

Here, too, the written and the oral are mixed. The girl is reading out a list she has previously written down. She runs through a long list of trivial desires, like learning how to cook, reading a book she will remember for the rest of her life, and going ice swimming, but her list ends with 'And to be loved!' Again, the contrast between what we see and what we hear is played for effect, because as she reads out this final point, the camera is tracking a woman passing by outside, clearly not happy, but struggling. This scene thus also becomes an illustration of a typical discrepancy between what people say (we are happy) and how things actually look (many, like Anders, are not).

Anders has no bucket list anymore, and this girl's dreams only serve to solidify this, for both him and the viewer. When we hear him list his parents' traits later on, though, we carry with us the bucket list in the café, as an echo or a mirror. My own interpretation of his voice-over is that it is a flashback to a therapy exercise he took part in during his treatment. Earlier in the film, we see Anders in a group therapy setting in the clinic, and he tells Thomas about role playing he had to do while there. Still, there is no way to know for sure whether such a therapy session is what is being played for us as he is walking around. His narration being intercut with images of Oslo streets also brings back an echo of the chorus of voices talking about their memories of Oslo in the prologue.

Raskin defines two other forms of voice-over by a character within the fictional universe, but neither of these fit here either: 'Lines spoken by a character looking back at earlier events that are shown on screen' and 'Lines spoken by a character to another at moment when the events are shown on screen'.[17] What we hear, though not what we see, is a looking back of sorts. But it is not, I would claim, Anders who looking back, but rather some unknown narrating entity, one that we, per Seymour Chatman, might call the cinematic narrator.[18] These scenes do not tell us Anders's thoughts as he is walking by himself, but offer a number of other things, some of them informative (context about how his parents were supportive of him), some of them emotional. They represent the longest stretches of time in which we see Anders alone, and they underline both his outsiderness and his difficulty putting words to his relationships. They are also typical of how Trier and Vogt work with voice-overs.[19]

There are sometimes discrepancies between what is seen and heard, and understanding who is speaking is not always straightforward. In summary, we might say that there is a sense of ambiguity, both temporal and spatial, about this form of voice-over. This type of ambiguity is also found in Trier's use of third person narrators, or, as Raskin defines them: 'lines spoken by an unseen, anonymous narrator'.[20] This type of voice-over is perhaps most closely associated with classical adaptations of literary works (like Stanley Kubrick's *Barry Lyndon* (1975)) but was also notably used in films like *Casablanca* (1942) or *Amélie* (2001). In Trier's films, this external, unknown narrating voice is employed in unusually transgressive ways, however. *The Worst Person in the World* and *Reprise* both open with complex montages (see Chapter 2) featuring omniscient external narrators with what seems like a full overview of both events and characters' inner realities.

In *Reprise*, the narrator in the opening sequence describes not only what has happened, but also something that might (possibly) happen in the future. As Phillip and Erik have just sent off their respective manuscripts, exclaiming 'This is when it all begins', the narrator takes over. Over images of two thick manila envelopes being opened, he can be heard saying, 'Their manuscripts would be accepted immediately'. As he says, 'They would be published the next fall', we see the printed versions of the books, and then portraits of each fresh author on the backs of them, as he continues, 'Finally, after years of hard work, they would at last be able to call themselves authors'. As he says this, their images come alive, and we see that they, too, can hear the narrator(!), we see them react to his statements about poor sales and a subsequent cult following. As the story

Figure 8.1 Erik and Phillip when it all begins.

of these two writers goes on, the narrator changes his mind repeatedly, most notably as he relates how they reunite after some time spent apart: 'They would meet by chance at a café – no, on the street. On the Metro . . . at an airport – No, in the Luxembourg Gardens'. The black and white images follow along with these jumps between different versions of the story, letting us see the two friends run into one another again and again, each time in a new place.

Then, following this prologue, we get a repeat of the opening line and the envelopes being posted, but subsequently stay in the present of the narrative, without any further predictions about the future. After a title sequence, the narrator returns to tell us that only Phillip's book was accepted for publication. As this is the version of events we are shown from here on out, it is fair to assume that this is the version viewers will be inclined to believe as true. As Seymour Chatman, among others, demonstrates in his books on narratology: seeing is believing.[21]

As pointed out by Audun Engelstad, there is a duality to the male narrator in *Reprise*. His voice is authorial and authoritative, but he also 'undercuts his superiority by opening up uncertainty about the status of events'.[22] Even as he, seemingly impulsively, changes his mind about what actually happens in his story, his delivery has a tenor of written prose. This can give the audience a sense that they are participating in a creative process where a writer is writing and deleting things from a manuscript in real time.[23] It is as if the narrator himself, just like the protagonists, is an author. Engelstad therefore compares this narrational voice to 'a typical nineteenth-century literary narrator', and considers him a pastiche, or a meta-fictional representation existing only in the imaginations of Erik and Phillip. Not least, he says, because the story is so much like a romantic tale of what it means to be an author. Alternatively, Engelstad suggests, we can consider 'the narratorial voice as that of a de facto narrator, which entails being in charge of, more or less, the whole fictional universe'.[24]

A good opening scene gives the audience an immediate sense of what a film is going to be about, as well as of its style and modes of narration. While part of the opening story in *Reprise* is pure fancy, it also contains important clues to what is actually happening with Phillip (his mental illness) and Erik (his romantic conflicts and struggles with his writing). Film scholar Tarja Laine therefore describes the prologue as 'the complete film in a nutshell'.[25] To Laine, the voice-over featured here is more than just Trier playing around with conventions of the medium, it strikes at the heart of the film's exploration of time and opportunity. She describes the narration as not quite in the future tense, but as something that, like the core tale of *Reprise* itself, is 'structured in an if-only mode'.[26] An example: if only the two young men could get their books published, then they would become famous and renowned authors. As a whole the film consistently mixes different conditionalities; *Reprise* explores the relationship between coincidence and fate. In Laine's words: 'The present (what-is) characterized by coincidence, is constantly in collusion with the future (if-only), which is characterized by fate. Therefore in my view the film is about the coexistence of fate and coincidence'.[27]

Audun Engelstad, too, argues that the voice-over in *Reprise* gets straight to the core of its themes: 'On one hand, the story deals with overcoming – or perhaps just accepting – the burden of the past as well as projecting (and even recreating) cherished moments of the past on the present'.[28] As the title also suggests, the organisation of time is crucial both to how the characters' 'experiences and states of mind' are depicted in the film, and to the modernist film story that inspired it.[29] The narrator is thus, like the film itself, both self-aware and meta-reflexive. This kind of voice-over narration, functioning as a distancing feature, insisting, almost, that the viewer be aware of just how the film is told, is found again in *The Worst Person in the World*. Here, too, the voice-over is paired with fast-paced, intricate montages.

While *Reprise*'s narration begins with a story of what could have happened, the external narrator in the prologue of *The Worst Person in the World* is somewhat more conventional. The female voice-over recounts Julie's background up until the point of the film's present. Her (Ine Jansen's) voice returns sporadically throughout the film. During Julie's thirtieth birthday celebration, she interrupts the eating of the cake to offer us a light, sarcastic overview of the lives of Julie's mother, grandmother, and several female ancestors, describing where they each were at age thirty, and placing particular emphasis on how many children previous generations would have by the time they reached that age. The relationship between Eivind and Sunniva (Maria Grazia Di Meo – the woman he is with when he and Julie meet) is also elaborated on through this narrator, who caustically describes Sunniva's pursuit of her Sami identity and how her climate-change anxiety forces Eivind to nod along and forget about flying to New York. When he encounters and falls for Julie at a party, the narrator says, sardonically: 'He felt he was betraying Sunniva. Betraying the Sami people. He felt like the world's worst person but couldn't resist'. This part of the story takes place in the chapter 'Finnmark Highlands' ('Finnmark-koduottar') and is the only section of the film not told from Julie's point of view. As such, it feels like something of a detour. But the voice-over narration here offers comic relief, a necessary reference to the film's title, and, not least, keen observations about contemporary society and questions of identity that are central to the overarching story.

In this film, too, the voice-over goes a step beyond merely supplying background information. In the midst of an emotional argument between the two, the narrator comments on both Julie's and her partner Aksel's lines, in real time, as they are speaking them, and verbalises some of Julie's own thoughts about what is being said. After Julie meets Eivind a second time, she initiates a breakup with Aksel by saying, 'Aksel, we need to talk.' When she hesitates, the narrator jumps in, drowning out the conversation between the couple, saying, 'Julie said she'd been thinking about it for a while now.' We then hear Julie, more softly, say, 'There's something I've been thinking about a while.' 'It wasn't his fault, it's not like there was anything he could have done differently', the narrator continues; 'It's not anything you did, or your fault, or anything like that', Julie says.

Then the narrator's version plays the dominant part for a while before Julie and Aksel's own lines again become more prominent. In this dialogue, or argument, which takes place over a long stretch of time and features several narrative pauses, the narrator repeatedly jumps in with remarks like 'Julie said he deserved someone more put together, someone who wouldn't flake out every six months', and 'Aksel said that he liked her flaky'. Aksel says that if she still loves him, they will be able to figure out that other stuff. Julie responds: 'Yes, I do love you. And I don't love you'. The narrator re-enters to say, 'Julie felt that in this sentence, the way she said it, her emphasis, she somehow summed up the impossibility of the whole situation.' Throughout this emotional scene, the sound design alternates between favouring the argument being played out before us and the cooler, more articulate narrator speaking over it. This alternation peaks when the fight is nearing its end and the voice-over says, 'She said she was terrified of being alone. Terrified of living without him. That when she went out the door she'd be like Bambi on the ice. And that was precisely why she had to do it.' As these words are spoken, we watch Julie drop out of her conversation with Aksel and smile thoughtfully through her tears as, the narrator says: 'She was thinking about how at the age of thirty, she'd just compared herself to Bambi.'

Interestingly enough, the cool, distant narrator and the intricate alternation between voices do not actually create a sense of distance between us as viewers and this break-up. It is actually a very emotional and affecting scene. Part of this is of course down to dramaturgy, as well as Renate Reinsve and Anders Danielsen Lie believably acting out all the complex emotions of this relationship. The dialogue here is also highly reflective of each of the two main characters; it allows the audience to sympathise with both. It puts a number of their problems into words, but also holds a number of things back, keeps them hidden; indeed, Julie is lying when she says there is no one else. And the narrator adds a temporal aspect to it all: the way she describes what is happening makes everything feel almost preordained, like we are watching an unavoidable tragedy. In other words: the voice-over functions as a playful and distancing element, but simultaneously adds some dramatic weight to the breakup scene; it injects a nostalgic touch and a sense of the past, of something that was, but went away; making us feel, like Aksel argues, what she is about to do and thus to lose. Here too, though, the narrator's actual status is ambiguous and unresolved. Does she represent Julie's inner voice, or something external? This is not clear, which, as mentioned is typical of Trier's voice-overs. We cannot always place them in time or space, nor know exactly what they represent.

While the narrators in both *Reprise* and *The Worst Person in the World* have an almost insistent presence – they feel like they are willing the viewer to focus on them – the use of voice-overs in *Louder Than Bombs* is more subtle. More subtle, however, does not mean less sophisticated. Here, there is no external narrator, but several different internal ones, all being used in different ways. *Louder Than Bombs* is about a family of four where the mother, Isabelle has passed away before the story begins, though she is present through various flashbacks. We are first introduced to her in a memorial video in which an anonymous narrator, her colleague Richard's voice, and her own voice, all briefly describe who she was in her working life. Her husband Gene does not have any voice-overs in the film, but also gets to tell his version of his family's story and struggles to his co-worker and lover (Amy Ryan). Most prominent, in terms of the narration and in other ways, is the voice of youngest son Conrad. In Chapter 1, I described how a recitation from a novel in his classroom morphs into a stream-of-consciousness depiction of his own inner reality. The words read out by his classmate Melanie gradually become words describing what he feels inside, taking the form of his memories and fantasies of, among other things, his mother's death. This is an internal narrator (Melanie) reading something an external (unknown) author has written, but that we perceive as an expression of Conrad's thoughts and imaginations.

Melanie's voice-over returns towards the end of the film, in a scene where Conrad, who is in love with her, walks her home after a party, because she is drunk. Aside from being unhappily infatuated, he feels particularly lonely and fragile on this particular evening, as he has just found out that his mother's fatal car accident was the result of an intentional act on her part. His father and brother Jonah both found this information too difficult to share with him; he has accidentally stumbled upon it in a newspaper and been forced to process it all by himself. Melanie is the most popular girl in class, and barely knows who he is, but this night, when she is drunk and alone, he can connect with her in a way he never has before. As they walk towards home and daybreak, we do not hear them speak to each other, just Melanie's voice on the soundtrack, along with Ola Fløttum's exquisite music, recounting Conrad's memories in the third person:

> He could still, many years from now, recall this scene in odd detail. The lock of hair she carefully placed behind her ear. The way the washing label stuck out from the neck of her tank top. The streetlights that went out as they passed Kevin Anderson's house. That strangely familiar smell of damp earth that he could not quite place. As a stranger passed, he glanced at them as he went by, probably thinking they were a couple.

> She had said she wanted to have lunch with him Tuesday after English. He knew that this would never happen. That she would feel differently Monday back in school. But at that moment he just enjoyed that she felt like saying this to him. That she maybe really felt like having lunch with him. That while they were walking there like that having lunch together at school seemed to her like a perfectly natural thing to do.

Again, the use of voice-over is blurred, almost paradoxical. It is the voice of young, present-day Melanie expressing what is seen, felt, and then remembered by a Conrad from an unspecified point in the future (many years from now). Just like with the narrator in *Reprise*, the words we hear here come across as written prose being read out loud. Because the voice we hear is Melanie's, we are reminded of the scene where she read from the novel at school, but the two texts are also linked by how they both concern memories and remembering. This passage, though distinctly representing Conrad's thoughts and experiences, was also written in the third person, and is as such a little clearer and less ambiguous than our previous encounter with Melanie's voice. We get the impression that this is the work of a far more mature, maybe published writer, a feeling that is helped along by the way Melanie reads it, in a much more self-assured and rhythmic manner than when she was reading before.[30] It being Melanie's voice, as opposed to Conrad's own, makes the scene feel even more intimate, more romantic and nostalgic.

We are shown, through several scenes, that Conrad possesses a much richer and more complex inner life than his brother and father think, as they observe him shutting himself in to play *The Elder Scrolls Online* or shooter games. When he shares his journal with his older brother who is home for a visit, Trier lets him speak both through written words (on a computer screen) and spoken ones. We watch Jonah reading from the screen and hear Conrad's voice reading out those same words on the soundtrack. Along with the words, his journal is represented visually by YouTube clips and scenes from his own life. His text is a series of reflections on and questions about himself: How many people are called Conrad, how many pairs of socks and underwear does he own, how many books and films, what does he like (real stuff, like goosebumps), and what does he not like (people who try to be funny). His journal entries are rich and imaginative, but also eclectic (what colour of M&M he prefers) and at times dark (how his father smothers him, the way animal carcasses decompose in different climates). Both his specific reflections and his turns of phrase are evocative of James Joyce's *A Portrait of the Artist as a Young Man* (1916), one of the most famous Bildungsroman in literary history. Like Joyce's autobiographical novel, *Louder Than Bombs* shifts, through its modes of narration, between identification and distance. And like Joyce, Trier is exploring the ways in which he, through his medium, can render people's inner worlds. While

Joyce's stream-of-consciousness is literary, Conrad's diary is highly cinematic. But in it, too, words are important, as they are in all of Trier's films, and to most of his characters.

In Julie and Aksel's fight, discussed above, she accuses him of thinking that being strong is synonymous with being good at verbalising things. She, who struggles to define even herself, feels trapped by his need for language that will describe exactly what she is and feels.[31] And, indeed, mid-fight, he yells at her to 'Shut up and I will tell you!' As she casts around for words, he practically throws them in her face. Julie is, interestingly, the freest version of herself when she lies about who she is (pretending to be a doctor at the party she crashes), and also the happiest. The act of defining who we, and others are, is a recurring theme in Trier's work, as is the ability to 'put things into words'.

Aksel represents a certain kind of character, a verbal, intellectual man, commonly found in Trier's film's (academics like Jonah in *Louder Than Bombs* or Thomas in *Oslo, August 31st*, but also Phillip and Erik and several of their friends in *Reprise*). And as Anders in *Oslo* says of his parents: 'They made me contemptuous of the less eloquent.' Characters who hold power over words seem important to Trier and Vogt both; they have described their own writing process as comprised of months of conversation and discussion'.[32]

Julie is a more emotional, intuitive person, but she is attracted to Aksel's way with words, and she basks in his praise for her own writing. And this ends up becoming something she misses in Eivind, for whom she leaves him. While Aksel is the more lingual and rhetorical person in his and Julie's relationship, Eivind is less capable of verbalising his feelings than Julie is. And just as Julie has experienced before him, he finds that the person with the words is the person with the power. Julie writes two separate pieces over the course of the film, one that Aksel reads, and one when she is with Eivind, which he finds and reads unprompted. Aksel's praise is delivered with authority, they are the sort of words Julie wants to hear; their conversation about her essay leads to connection, and to sex. Eivind can't find the right words to compliment what he has just read and stumbles his way through empty phrases like 'proper', 'real', 'like', 'I mean, it's good', as he attempts to find her wavelength. He eventually gives up, saying he doesn't know what to do, and leaves the room, leaving her to sit alone.

The narrator is most prominent in the first part of the film, she follows Julie into her new relationship with Eivind, but does not stay for long. She notes that Julie and Eivind were both hesitant to have children, and then she disappears.[33] This can be seen as Julie breaking free from one kind of inner, governing voice; she no longer needs that mental and verbal support to be able to say who she is or what she is feeling.

When conducting an auteur study, one looks for commonalities across films, but in this case, variety, arguably, is the signature. The simplest way of summarising Trier and Vogt's approach to words in general, and to voice-overs in particular, is to say that it is incredibly varied. To put it differently: words function in too many ways in Trier's films for it to make sense to attempt to categorise them, so, in closing, I will limit myself to running through the different forms of voice-over used.

Trier's films employ both external and internal narrators, in several forms. External, third-person narration is not limited to a singular voice, it can be performed by multiple narrators, as with the chorus of anonymous voices in the prologue of *Oslo, August 31st*. External narrators may be authorial and omniscient, fully aware of the happenings of the story or the minds, motives, and actions of its characters, both in the past (*The Worst Person in the World*) and in the future (*Reprise*). The external narrator can also, as we have seen, be intrusive – offer direct commentary on action, thoughts or feelings (most fully developed in the relationship between young Julie and her more mature narrator). Trier's external narrators are, among other things, used for efficient narration of longer stretches of time (*The Worst Person in the World*), for setting the tone or establishing the themes of a film (*Oslo, August 31st*), or for providing commentary on the plot (*The Worst Person in the World*) or the themes and subject matter of a film (*Reprise*).

The internal narrators, or character narrators, serve to provide insight into the characters' inner worlds (*Louder Than Bombs, Oslo, August 31st*), but Trier does this with different voices, and situates them on different temporal planes. When what we can see and what we can hear appears out of sync, different moods – and both intimacy and distance – are created. When Phillip and Kari in *Reprise* reunite after his mental breakdown, the Kari we see does not speak, while the one we can hear describes not knowing quite what to do. The film cuts between different scenes and conversations that are sometimes synced up, but often not. This technique serves to reflect the way in which these former lovers have fallen out of sync with each other, leaving them uncertain as to whether or not they should attempt a reprise of their romance. One narrating voice can also be expressing the thoughts of another character (as when Melanie speaks for Conrad in *Louder Than Bombs*), and voices may come to us from another time or place than the one depicted on screen. Both internal and external narrators may be used to create moods or evoke certain emotions. In Trier's films they add vulnerability, melancholy, and humour.

In summary, we might say that in Trier's films, voice-overs are used to direct the viewer's attention one way or another: sometimes in order to create a feeling of closeness, other times to keep us at a distance. Sometimes we are directed towards the characters and their inner lives, other times towards the formal aspects of the film and the medium itself. Though these creative approaches to the voice-over have a number of effects and are each a little different, they all represent a playful exploration of the inherent possibilities of the film medium.

Voices and words are important in all of Trier's films. Both the spoken and the unspoken words are important in all of his characters' lives. Putting feelings into words, defining roles and personalities, and separating truth from lies are all thematic throughlines in his work. But so is a meta-perspective: how can and do we tell stories in cinema? This is why dialogue, monologue, and narrative voice-overs are such important components of Trier's storytelling style.

NOTES

1. Susannah McCullough, 'Ask the Director: Joachim Trier on Personal Cinema, the Close-Up and "Louder than Bombs"', *The Take*, 7 April 2016, https://the-take.com/read/ask-the-director-joachim-trier-on-personal-cinema-the-close-up-and-louder-than-bombs; Jørgen Bruhn and Anne Gjelsvik, *Cinema Between Media: An Intermediality Approach* (Edinburgh: University Press, 2018), 51–69; C. Claire Thomson, 'Louder Than Films: Memory, Affect and the "Sublime Image" in the Work of Joachim Trier', *Arts* 8, no. 2 (2019), https://doi.org/10.3390/arts8020055.
2. Bruhn and Gjelsvik, *Cinema Between Media*.
3. See Epilogue, 154.
4. Bjarte Breiteig, Eskil Vogt, and Joachim Trier, 'Oslo gjennom mørkt glass – Eskil Vogt og Joachim Trier i samtale med Bjarte Breiteig', in Eskil Vogt and Joachim Trier *Oslo, 31. August. Filmmanus.* (Oslo: Tiden Norsk Forlag, 2011), 170.
5. Ibid.
6. Bjarte Breiteig, Eskil Vogt, and Joachim Trier, 'Overskudd og ambivalens. En samtale rundt tilblivelsen av *Reprise* mellom Bjarte Breiteig, Eskil Vogt og Joachim Trier', in Eskil Vogt and Joacim Trier, *Reprise. Et filmmanuskript* (Oslo: Tiden Norsk Forlag, 2007), 231.
7. Ibid., 232–6.
8. Ibid., 233.
9. Sarah Kozloff, *Invisible Storytellers: Voice-over Narration in American Fiction Film* (Berkeley: University of California Press, 1988).
10. Ibid., 3.
11. Ibid., 4.
12. Richard Raskin, 'Five Types of Voice-over in Feature Film Storytelling', *16:9 filmtidsskrift*, 18 October 2020, http://www.16-9.dk/2020/10/five-types-of-voice-over/.
13. Kozloff, *Invisible Storytellers*, 5.
14. Raskin, 'Five Types of Voice-over'.
15. Ibid.
16. According to Trier the bucket list was taken from a radio broadcast (Joachim Trier, 'Masterclass with Joachim Trier in Conversation with Anne Gjelsvik'. Department of Art and Media Studies, NTNU, 18 September 2017).
17. Raskin, 'Five Types of Voice-over'. Out of Raskin's five most common forms of voice-over, 'lines ostensibly spoken by the filmmaker, not visible in the act of speaking them' is the only one never used by Trier.

18. Seymour Chatman, *Coming to Terms: The Rhetoric of Narrative in Fiction and Film* (Ithaca: Cornell University Press, 1990). The question of the narrating entity in film is a complicated one, with too many theoretical branches to fully explore here. Accordingly, for simplicity's sake I will follow Seymour Chatman, who distinguishes between the cinematic narrator and the voice-over narrator by establishing the cinematic narrator as the one who 'does the showing': *Coming to Terms*, 133–4. This showing also includes 'the telling', which is done by a narrating voice, and is part of the film's discourse. The cinematic narrator is not synonymous with the filmmaker – it is a non-human entity. This narrator, or agent (a term preferred by others) can, in Chatman's words, be defined as the 'principle within the text to which we assign the inventional tasks', 133. An audience may sometimes (mistakenly) perceive a voice-over as the cinematic narrator, or, as Kozloff puts it, 'We put our faith in the voice not as created but as creator', Kozloff, *Invisible Storytellers*, 45.
19. In Eskil Vogt's own debut feature *Blind* (2014), which he both wrote and directed, he also utilises voice-over narration. The film is about Ingrid (Ellen Dorrit Pedersen), who has recently lost her sight. It opens in all black, with Ingrid's voice saying 'I'll start with something simple. A tree, for instance.' Then, the images appear, showing us different examples of trees, and eventually dogs, as Ingrid is picturing them. The film was inspired by a novel about a blind woman, which sparked Vogt to imagine how one might visually represent what it is like not to see. Here, the narrator is something like an omniscient but internal narrator.
20. Kozloff, *Invisible Storytellers*, 20; Raskin, 'Five Types of Voice-over'.
21. Chatman, *Coming to Terms*. In Danish film *Copenhagen Does Not Exist* (2022), written by Vogt, there is a fully unreliable narrator.
22. Audun Engelstad, 'The Concept of Time in Joachim Trier's Reprise', *Journal of Scandinavian Cinema* 9, no. 2 (1 June 2019): 197–202, at 199; https://doi.org/10.1386/jsca.9.2.197_1.
23. Eskil Vogt does something similar in *Blind*, where we hear protagonist Ingrid's narrating voice describing her husband meeting an old friend in a café. Suddenly, we see the two not in a café but on a tram. Ingrid says 'No, I'm getting mixed up . . .' and we briefly see her erasing lines she has written from her computer.
24. Engelstad, 'The Concept of Time', 199.
25. Tarja Laine, *Feeling Cinema: Emotional Dynamics in Film Studies* (New York: Continuum, 2011), 58.
26. Ibid. In other words, a form of conditionalist tense.
27. Ibid.
28. Engelstad, 'The Concept of Time', 197.
29. Ibid.
30. Bruhn and Gjelsvik, *Cinema Between Media*.
31. Renate Reinsve has stated in interviews that she had this line added because she felt like 'Eskil and Joachim had romanticised the way Aksel defined Julie'.
32. Breiteig, Vogt, and Trier, 'Oslo gjennom mørkt glass'; Vogt and Trier, 'Overskudd og ambivalens'; Eskil Vogt, Joachim Trier, and Mattis Øybø, 'Kunsten å oppnå

sekvensiell nytelse', in *Verdens verste menneske. Filmmanus.* (Oslo: Tiden Norsk Forlag, 2021), 277–304.
33. In the script, the narrator has the final word – a comment about how Julie, for the first time in a long while, thinks of her dead ex-boyfriend Aksel. This line did not make it through the cutting room.

CHAPTER 9

Moments and Movements

'Misfits, miscommunication and melancholy'. These words open *Little White Lies*'s video essay, 'A Beginner's Guide to Joachim Trier'.[1] They fit all of Trier's films, or, to paraphrase Julie from *The Worst Person in the World*: they fit and they do not. All three elements are found in all films, but though he keeps returning to darker themes, Trier's work is never quite as gloomy as such a summary might suggest. Even when thematically melancholy and sad, his films are, aesthetically speaking, full of light and play, of creativity and humour. They are playful, poetic and personal. As Hillary Weston puts it:

> His films are poetic and haunting, honest and visceral, telling stories of friendship, illness, love, ambition, foolishness, and intellect that are both playful in their style and striking in frankness. Shot beautifully, Trier's work swerves in and out of deep states of sadness and melancholy yet are never bleak.[2]

We see this when Anders, over the course of the night before the 31st of August, spirals into darkness. Having stolen money from the guests at Mirjam's party, he buys a quantity of heroin, more than enough to overdose on. He seeks out his acquaintance from the party, Petter (Petter Width Kristiansen) who is out on the town, and parties on with him and two girls. In the scenes that follow, the music is sombre, the camera movements jittery, the rooms dark. Anders picks a fight with a guy he suspects his ex-girlfriend Iselin cheated on him with, drinks (despite his newfound sobriety), makes out with random girls, shoves one of them in the face, and retreats, alone, into a backyard. But then the others find him, and he continues on into the night with them. Petter is playing around with a stolen fire extinguisher, and then we see the four of them heading down an empty Oslo street on two bicycles. The girls are cycling, each with one of the guys on the back. Every now and then, Petter lets out a spurt from the fire extinguisher with a potent 'ptsssssssh', the white powder joining the yellow lines on the asphalt and the green traffic lights in illuminating the night. The camera starts out trailing behind the cycling foursome, but eventually slides up close along Anders' side. He lets his head rest against the leather jacket of the girl he is riding with, closes his eyes. Her hair flutters in the wind, the streetlights blink. It is unnaturally quiet; we see the girl laughing, but hear no sound. As Ola Fløttum's poetic score emerges, Anders tilts his head back slightly, and the light from a street lamp falls across his face. An instance of pure bliss. This scene lasts a mere thirty seconds, but is an unforgettable moment from Trier's filmography.

Figure 9.1 A short glimpse of bliss.

Watching Trier's melancholy, existential films is not solely a sombre, heavy experience, and these moments play a key part in that. So does the fact that Trier, like Julie, is a visual person. In a masterclass given to students at the Department of Art and Media Studies at NTNU (the Norwegian University of Science and Technology) in 2017, Trier spoke of the value of – or, rather, the joy in – gazing: 'being allowed to gaze upon something is highly important'.[3] He elaborated by referencing a research project in which children in nursery were given video cameras and instructed to film. When asked to tell the researcher something, they were confused. Asking them, instead, to show her something, yielded several fresh perspectives and unexpected captured moments: anything from a favourite toy or place to a rat's secret hideout caught on video. What these children did, according to Trier, was to 'show their world'. He wrapped up his anecdote saying, 'that is cinema to me'.[4]

As both this anecdote and the example from *Oslo, August 31st* show, the joy in the visual side of his medium, and in looking – gazing – are important motivators for Trier. His approach to filmmaking can be compared to that very childlike one he shared with the students: he is showing us his world. What is it like to be in an Oslo bar, or to cycle down a road in the middle of a summer night? What is the light, and the darkness, of those city streets like?

The film that most explicitly tackles what it means to see, how our choice of perspective affects what we see and how we understand it, is *Louder Than Bombs*. In this film, each member of the family has their own secrets, but what is concealed may be revealed if only one knows where to look (behind a closed door, or on a hidden memory stick, for instance). Jesse Eisenberg's Jonah asks multiple thetorical questions like, 'What are we looking at here?', 'What is this?', or 'What are we watching here?'. These lines could just as well be used to epitomise Trier's way of exhibiting his world and his perspectives. To him, as to so many artists, it all comes down to the art of seeing.

Joachim Trier is, above all else, an observer of people, and this becomes evident in how he portrays them, and how he works with actors. Those skills of observation are what lets him capture the summer fling that cannot quite give life meaning after all, or the ways in which people end up making the wrong choices. They enable him to render those moments of awkwardness, like the summer party in *The Worst Person in the World*, or the fumbling hands of a person wishing to touch another for the very first time, like when Thelma brushes Anja's arm under the pretence of studying her tattoos. They are what make him include and show the effects of words, on the speaker and the listener both, in difficult conversations, be they between friends, lovers, or family members.

When Trier, as a young director with a single feature film under his belt, got the opportunity to make a film in the United States, he knew he wanted it to be an 'actor film'.[5] Interviews, as well as the films themselves, make it clear that Trier loves working with his actors, and that the feeling is mutual. Renate Reinsve's first film role was a small part in *Oslo, August 31st* (one of the girls Anders spends time with during the night). Reinsve has described the set of that film as a safe and fun place to be, and related how later experiences with directors with a less functional and considerate communication style came as a bit of a shock to her.[6] Anders Danielsen Lie's first role as an adult actor was in Trier's debut feature, and has, more than anyone else, become the face of Trier's filmography, and an essential piece of the Oslo trilogy.[7] Acting, Danielsen Lie says, does not always feel like a creative profession to him, but in his work with Trier, he always feels like a creative collaborator.[8] Trier has himself placed great import on his collaboration with his favourite leading man, stating that he and Vogt will write parts specifically for Danielsen Lie (the same way the role of Julie was written for Renate Reinsve). All of Danielsen Lie's parts have something of Trier's own experiences and personality in them, Trier says – an example of how his films, though never autobiographical, are always personal. Of Danielsen Lie, he has also said that 'I like to see him growing older throughout my films. . . We can see time in his face from film to film.'[9] Casting and directing actors are crucial parts of Trier's work. He will have long conversations about the concept and idea behind each film with his casts and play music on set meant to create the ideal atmosphere for them to express themselves in.[10]

In one interview, Trier described his way of making film as a cinema of intimacy, meaning that he seeks to really get inside the people he portrays.[11] But the term cinema of intimacy is also descriptive of other aspects of his process and work, including his affinity for the close-up. Close-ups are important to Trier because of the sense of intimacy they create between the audience and the characters, but also because, as images, they feel especially tactile.[12] Nowhere else do we get as close to the human face as when we experience one that has been shot in close-up on a big cinema screen. And accordingly, Trier will argue (in line with several film theorists) that the close-up is purely cinematic:

> When people say the close-up is made for television, I think, no, no, you can't have a cinematic close-up on TV. You can't watch *Persona* by Bergman on TV and get the same effect as on the big screen, because you see into the eye of Liv Ullman differently. That way to perceive a close, intimate, sometimes brutally intimate view of humans is very cinematic.[13]

His love of the close-up places Trier firmly within a Scandinavian cinema tradition, with directors like Danish Carl Dreyer and Swedish Ingmar Bergman as important forebears. In Trier's own words: 'I come from a tradition of Scandinavian fascination for the close-up and the paradox of the close-up which is that you can both be extremely close in a cinematic close-up and yet often it's impenetrable'.[14] This aesthetic, with an extensive use of close-ups, with and without accompanying words, fits both Trier's wish to let his actors shine and his interest in exploiting the unique characteristics and possibilities of the film medium.

The intimacy of Trier's close-ups is demonstrated in a long, somewhat disconnected, close-up portrait of Isabelle Huppert in *Louder Than Bombs*. This remarkable shot occurs just after a sequence in which Gene seeks out Isabelle's colleague Richard and asks him if he was having an affair with her. Richard confirms the two were lovers while travelling together, but says that, in the end, Isabelle wished to stay with her husband and children. The conversation between the two men is broken up by flashbacks with Isabelle in a home where she felt like an outsider, a bystander to her family's habits and quirks; an observer of their lives. The voices of Richard, Gene, and Isabelle flow over these muted images, forming a mosaic of a maladjusted woman. This perspective on her is reinforced by the oral stories from Richard and Isabelle about how they are struggling to combine their roles as war reporters with the personal lives they step in and out of. Isabelle's own descriptions are supplemented with images of her husband and sons, both retrospective (with her watching them from a distance) and from the film's present (after she is gone). As the line 'They don't need you' is spoken, the long take (a close-up held for thirty-seven seconds) of Isabelle Huppert cuts in. She stares straight into the camera, never blinking. Her face barely moves at all, and less than the camera, which has a slight shake.[15] She looks like she might cry, but never does; she appears only to be pulled ever further into her own thoughts. When the scene is cut, we see Gene bringing in the paper that will reveal the secret: that Isabelle took her own life.

In an analysis of Trier's use of close-ups, Anne Jerslev argues that the mediated face in fiction film can function on a number of levels: 'First, it is general (an iconic, filmic face); second, it is the face of a specific actress (e.g. a well-known star); and third, it is the face of a specific filmic character (a role)'.[16] Traditionally, the aim is for the audience to mainly notice the third level and empathise with the character portrayed; the actor's work is a secondary part of the experience. But with this long take, that balance is disrupted, Jerslev claims. Because of this close-up's 'unusually sustained duration', we not only meet the gaze of Isabelle, but also make unusually 'intimate contact with (the face) of French actress Isabelle Huppert'.[17] The long take places Huppert's face both within and outside of the diegesis: she is Isabelle Reed, but she is also Isabelle Huppert, with all the baggage from film history that that entails.[18] Jerslev,

Figure 9.2 Isabelle Huppert as Isabelle and herself in the long close-up.

accordingly, calls this and other Trier close-ups autonomous moments.[19] It is a moment of intimacy and intensity, but also a moment where the image seen is detached from the film's story and spatial–temporal continuity. And yet it is itself a reminder of time, this recurring, crucial theme of Trier's.

I dwell on this moment because I believe it captures something of Trier's essence as a filmmaker. One could argue that, more than anything, Trier's films are character-driven or character studies. He is nearly always looking for ways to show his character's inner lives. But his films are both specific, psychological portraits of individuals, and, simultaneously, universal reflections on the significance and meanings of words and language, of imagery and the cinematic language. In this sequence with Isabelle Huppert (shot by Trier himself),[20] for instance, he breaks a number of the unwritten rules of filmmaking: Do not let your actor look straight into the camera, do not use voice-overs, do not let your cuts draw attention to themselves. It is also typical that he will add this kind of shot not because it is needed for the plot, but for the value of the shot in itself.

In her review of *The Worst Person in the World*, Danish critic Lone Nikolajsen describes how Trier often keeps his audience at something of a distance from his characters. We possibly never get to fully understand Isabelle, Anders, or Julie; Trier's characters remain (despite all the close-ups, narrators, and visual streams-of-consciousness) somewhat secretive. And though these characters may move or aggravate audiences, Trier is perhaps more unique for how he tells his stories than what or who they are about:

> Generally speaking, Joachim Trier has a talent for imaginative exploitation of the film medium, and varying his modes of narration, so it is the staging itself, the way it is all shot and cut, which creates the dynamics, rather than plot twists and surprises'.[21]

The critic points out that highlighting the contrast between parenthood and childlessness could in itself feel banal, but becomes interesting when as keenly observed and deftly executed as in *The Worst Person in the World*.

When Trier explores his medium and challenges conventions, he does so in ways that may seem and feel intuitive. And his descriptions of both his writing process with Eskil Vogt and the way he instructs actors make clear how spontaneity and improvisation run through much of his work. Cinematographer Kasper Tuxen has described Trier as 'a flexible perfectionist', he spends a long time on meticulous preparation, but is open to pursuing new ideas and impulses as they emerge.[22] Jakob Ihre, his usual cinematographer, relates how intentional Trier is with his visuals – for instance whether a take needs to move calmly and fluidly, or be handheld: 'Every shot is planned, everything has a purpose, a sound and a beat, the rhythm of the shot'. The meticulous planning of just how the light should hit the office building where Phillip seeks out Kari at work is a good example of this, as is the way they tested the lift he rides up to see her, ahead of shooting, in order to find just the right angles. 'What should the shot feel like?', Ihre finishes.[23] The meticulous way of working can come into play in seemingly understated scenes like the ending of *Oslo, August 31st*, when Anders overdoses in his parents' apartment. It is calm and quiet, but also a long dolly-shot, more than eight minutes, that captures every movement through the apartment as Anders places his last call to Iselin, plays the piano, and takes his own life. But the approach is also valuable in technical complex sequences such as the car crash in *Louder Than Bombs* and the epilepsy scene in *Thelma*.

Trier's ability to be both the perfectionist (in search of the perfect light) and a flexible on-set director (collaborating with the actors he directs) is founded in his lifelong cinephilia. Any Trier interview will contain a number of asides about the inspiration he has found in other filmmakers; such as Yasujiro Ozu's way of creating close-ups of two people together, Stephen Frears's work with actors, or Andrei Tarkovsky and Alain Resnais's ways of structuring their films.[24] Trier has never concealed his delight in classical American film either and has cited titles like *The Breakfast Club* (1985), and directors like Woody Allen and George Cukor as being among his favourites. It is also typical of him as a filmmaker to fluctuate between these and other different cinematic influences. *The Worst Person in the World* is, for instance, both romantic and comedic, and sits comfortably within a tradition comprising both American and European role models (*Holiday* (1938), *Annie Hall* (1977), *The Age of Innocence* (1993), *Frances Ha* (2012), *The Green Ray* (1986) *Notting Hill* (1999)). *Louder Than Bombs* and *Thelma* have obvious roots in American cinema, while *Reprise* and *Oslo, August 31st* fall closer to the director's European favourites. Undoubtedly, part of Trier's appeal to his many cinephile fans is just how all these influences can be traced in his work, whether he is cutting like Alain Resnais, shooting close-ups like Ingmar Bergman or creating montages like Mike Mills.

Another appealing trait is how, in spite of all the different inspirations, his films always feel genuinely Trieresque, and simultaneously unpredictable and surprising. They always have something recognisable and something new. *Little White Lies's* video essay from 2022 ends on the comment 'With Trier's star rising fast, we're excited to see what he does next'.[25]

As this book is being finished, Trier's next film, with the working title *Sentimental Value,* is still in pre-production. In the spring of 2023, The Norwegian Film Institute (NFI) announced that what they at the time called 'Trier's sixth film' had received the highest production funding support they have ever granted (20 million Norwegian kroner), an indicator of the status and credibility held by Trier in contemporary Norwegian cinema. The film was described as 'an ambitious yet playful family drama set in Oslo. An intimate, moving and often funny film about family, memory and how we need to rewrite the stories we tell about ourselves in order to survive'.[26] It was granted funding by the NFI based on a so-called artistic evaluation, and their film commissioner described the new film as an ambitious generational portrait featuring artfully crafted characters, with different histories and resolves, chasing moments of human acknowledgement. He concluded his evaluation: 'Through inventive storytelling techniques weaving together past and present, Trier's sixth film will be an intimate, touching, and humorous film about loneliness and family, and on the reconciling power of art'.[27]

The sixth feature is once again based on a script by Trier and Vogt and will be set in Oslo. *Sentimental Value* will be produced by Andrea Ottmar (Eye Eye productions, who also produced *The Worst Person in the World*) and Norwegian producer Maria Ekerhovd (Mer Film), along with, among other international co-producers, French mk2.[28]

Trier himself describes the film as a study of the family, in which he and Vogt wish to dig deeper into the role family plays in shaping who a person becomes. What is inherited from preceding generations? Why do siblings turn out so different? The story begins when the father of the family (Gustav), formerly a successful director, returns to Norway to shoot a film and repair his relationship with his two adult daughters, Nora and Agnes. He offers Nora, who is a theatre actor, a role in his new film. One core element of *Sentimental Value* will be the family home in Oslo, the value and significance of a house and a home. Another will be the creation of art – how to do it well – and the part art can play in reconciliation.[29]

If I were to craft a description of a prototypical Joachim Trier film, it would feature many of the exact words from both Trier's and the NFI's description of this project. Both the themes (character portraits, family, Oslo, loneliness, memory, art, cinema) and the aesthetic properties (inventive storytelling, interwoven past and present) mentioned are characteristic of Trier as a filmmaker, as this book has shown. Still, I expect to be surprised by this film too, because I expect Trier to continue pursuing new ways of developing his medium. In this project, for the first time, one of Trier's main characters will be a director, enabling him, perhaps, to add yet another meta-perspective on the film medium into the mix.

A phrase often used by Trier himself is 'that is cinema to me' – and it can serve to describe him as a director too. The phrase shows up in a number of interviews with him, not always in the same context or referring to the same type of thing. It can be about showing or depicting a particular world, or creating a mood, or compiling something like a hit album, or spectacular set pieces, and the list could go on (see also the Epilogue). But his preoccupation with discovering what cinema is, and what is uniquely cinematic, can be used to epitomise him as a filmmaker.

My grandfather, Erik Løchen, was a director. His film *Jakten* was in competition in Cannes in 1959. In my family there was this discussion with my parents and in the little bit I remember, as a child, about 'what is uniquely cinematic. One of the things my grandfather said was "Tati". He said: 'You cannot do that in a theatre, you cannot do that in a book, it's not a song, it's cinema'. And that is what I'm yearning for. It's to try to find something very personal that keeps going around in my head and I try find a form that I hope is cinematic.[30]

Trier is also a director who will compare filmmaking to both skateboarding and Proust. And so another word one might employ to sum up what makes his work unique is his and Vogt's own writing mantra: contrast. The contrast between the intimate and the grand, between the long, intense dialogue and the drawn-out silence. Between the romantic ballad and the aggressive rock song, the blending of the intellectual with the emotional, the melancholy with the playful; colourful cheerleaders floating through the air in slow motion in one moment, the sped-up decomposition of fruit, rabbits, and human bodies in the next. The contrasts are what make the individual moments stand out.

Figure 9.3 Cheerleaders in *Louder Than Bombs*.

And when we think of Trier's films, individual scenes, images, or moments are often what stand out as most striking about them and what we remember. I asked a number of friends and acquaintances with an interest in film to name any scenes or sequences of Trier's of which they had particularly fond or strong memories. The resulting list was a lot like the string of nostalgic 'I remember' memories from the opening of *Oslo, August 31st*: plentiful, varied, and atmospheric. This very prologue recurred in many of the responses I got, particularly from those with close ties to Oslo, – people who live or are from there, those that have moved to the city and those who have escaped it.

But people also remembered everything freezing in *The Worst Person in the World* and Julie visiting her cancer-ridden ex-boyfriend Aksel in hospital. They remembered Thelma teleporting her little brother under the sofa, images of cheerleaders, Anders sitting alone in a café and listening to the voices around him. They remembered how Phillip and Kari's fraught reunion was cut so as to leave the sound and images out of sync, and yet somehow flowed seamlessly. Some remembered poignant portraits, like the half-caricature of a publisher (Henrik Mestad) in *Reprise*, or perfectly captured situations, like the awkward job interview in the same film, or the holiday in the summer house in *The Worst Person in the World*. Others remembered Conrad's journal, or the dialogues: between Anders and Thomas in the parks of Oslo; between Eivind and Julie when his praise for her writing only pisses her off; between Thelma and her father. People had memories of songs: of Aksel playing air drums along with Turbonegro's 'Back to Dungaree High'; how a-ha's 'I've Been Losing You' opens up the world as the camera exits a tunnel; Joy Division's 'New Dawn Fade' taking over from a marching band at the Constitution Day celebration in the opening of *Reprise*. Some had memories of the close-ups of Isabelle Huppert, of the images of Thelma's first encounter with university, and her being with Anja. There were memories of the lads in *Reprise* ribbing each other by the sun-soaked Oslo fjord, and of Anders walking the streets, talking about his parents; of the montages about Julie's past and Phillip and Erik's future, and of the sound of Melanie's pee trickling along the asphalt and hitting Conrad's shoe the night he learns the truth about his mother's death. People remembered the sound of a fire extinguisher going off in the summer night.

One way of taking stock of Trier as a filmmaker is through these brief, unique moments. His films are made up of many of them, moments standing out from the whole, often as specific images, but sometimes as lines, sounds, or songs. Moments swerving between lightness and darkness, created by the underpinning structures within each film, and between all of his films. Misfits, miscommunication and melancholy, yes, but also moods, movements and moments.

NOTES

1. Will Webb, 'A Beginners Guide to Joachim Trier', *Little White Lies*, https://www.youtube.com/watch?v=_wOLVOAj6tU&ab_channel=LittleWhiteLies 2022.
2. Hillary Weston, 'The Quiet Allure of Joachim Trier's "Oslo, August 31st"', 1 February 2013. http://hillaryweston.squarespace.com/new-page-17/.
3. Joachim Trier, 'Masterclass with Joachim Trier in Conversation with Anne Gjelsvik'. Department of Art and Media Studies, NTNU, 18 September 2017.
4. Ibid.

5. Ibid. *Louder Than Bombs* was supposed to be Trier's second film, but when they encountered a delay in the funding process, Trier and Vogt rapidly wrote and finished *Oslo, August 31st* instead.
6. Alex Heeney and Orla Smith, *Existential Detours. Joachim Trier's Films of Indecisions and Revisions*, vol. 5.1 (Toronto: Seventh Row, 2024). Reinsve, who was never happy with the roles she had previously gotten in Norwegian film and television, has after the success of *The Worst Person in the World* been cast in several Nordic and international productions.
7. Anders Danielsen Lie's actual debut was in the titular role in *Herman* (1990) when he was only eleven years old.
8. Heeney and Smith, *Existential Detours*. Despite combining his acting career with one as a medical doctor, Anders Danielsen Lie has appeared in a number of Norwegian and international productions. Chief among these are perhaps his roles as terrorist Anders Behring Breivik in Paul Greengrass's Netflix feature *22 July* (2018) and Mia Wasikowska's love interest in Mia Hansen Løve's *Bergman Island* (2021). The latter premiered in Cannes at the same time as *The Worst Person in the World*.
9. Serge Kaganski, 'Joachim Trier on The Worst Person in the World', Norwegian Film Institute, 5 July 2021, https://www.nfi.no/eng/news/2021/joachim-trier-on-the-worst-person-in-the-world.
10. Nicholas Rapold, 'Interview: Joachim Trier', *Film Comment*, 11 April 2016, https://www.filmcomment.com/blog/interview-joachim-trier/; Trier, 'Masterclass'.
11. Jackson Wald, 'Joachim Trier's Cinema of Intimacy', *Interview Magazine*, 7 February 2022, https://www.interviewmagazine.com/film/joachim-trier-cinema-of-intimacy .
12. Trier, 'Masterclass'.
13. Elise Nakhnikian, 'Interview: Joachim Trier Talks Louder Than Bombs', *Slant Magazine*, 6 April 2016, https://www.slantmagazine.com/film/interview-joachim-trier-talks-louder-than-bombs/.
14. Rapold, 'Interview'.
15. Trier has described how he and Huppert discussed what he calls one of cinema history's greatest close-ups, from *The Piano Teacher*, also a close-up of Huppert, ahead of shooting; Rapold, 'Interview'. Critic Benjamin Yazdan has described this close-up as an echo of Ingemar Bergman's cinematographer Sven Nykvist's finest close-ups in Benjamin Yazdan, 'Minner, identitet og nærbilder i Joachim Triers Louder Than Bombs – en humanistisk film', *Montages*, 20 October 2015, http://montages.no/2015/10/minner-identitet-og-naerbilder-i-joachim-triers-louder-than-bombs-en-humanistisk-film/.
16. Anne Jerslev, 'Joachim Trier's Close-Ups and Autonomous Moments', *Journal of Scandinavian Cinema* 9, no. 2 (1 June 2019), 221; https://doi.org/10.1386/jsca.9.2.219_1.
17. Ibid. Jerslev's article also provides an excellent overview of theoretical reflections on the mediated face and the closeup in film, from classical theorists like Béla Balázs and Jean Epstein to modern ones like James Elkins and Mary Ann Doane.
18. Huppert has received the Best Actress award at Cannes twice (for *Violette Nozière* (1978) and *The Piano Teacher* (2001)), and a number of other awards and nominations, including an Honorary Golden Bear at the Berlin film festival

in 2022. She has worked with many highly renowned directors, such as Claude Chabrol, Francois Ozon, Paul Verhoeven, and Mikael Hanke. Trier has said about her that: 'I think in film history there are very few faces as interesting as Isabelle Huppert's.' Nakhnikian, 'Interview'.
19. Jerslev, 'Joachim Trier's Close-Ups', 221.
20. Rapold, 'Interview'.
21. Lone Nikolajsen, '"Verdens værste menneske" er en suverænt velfortalt skildring af længsel', *Information*, 15 June 2022, https://www.information.dk/kultur/anmeldelse/2022/06/verdens-vaerste-menneske-suveraent-velfortalt-skildring-laengsel.
22. Lindsay Pugh, 'An Interview with Kasper Tuxen', in *Existential Detours: Joachim Trier's Cinema of Indecisions and Revisions* (Toronto: Seventh Row, 2024).
23. Jakob Ihre, 'Masterclass with the Emmy Award Winner Jakob Ihre, Director of Photography' (Kulturakademin Gotenburgh Studios, 2020), https://www.youtube.com/watch?v=b2ZzPRLeL_g. Production designer Jørgen Stangebye Larsen has revealed that they looked at 150 apartments before deciding on Thomas's apartment in *Oslo, August 31st*; Orla Smith, 'Designing a Journey through Oslo', Seventh Row, 31 August 2021, https://seventh-row.com/2021/08/31/jorgen-stangebye-larsen-oslo-august-31st-production-design-interview/.
24. Heeney and Smith, *Existential Detours*; Alex Heeney, 'With Thelma, Joachim Trier Continues to Develop his Dirty Formalism", Seventh Row, 25 November 2017, https://seventh-row.com/2017/11/25/thelma-dirty-formalism/; Andrew Bundy, 'Joachim Trier Talks The Inspiration For "The Worst Person In The World", His Love Of Graphic Novels & More', *The Playlist*, 2 February 2022, https://theplaylist.net/joachim-trier-talks-the-inspiration-for-the-worst-person-in-the-world-interview-20220202/; Colleen Kelsey, 'Joachim Trier's Family Dynamics', *Interview Magazine*, 6 April 2016, https://www.interviewmagazine.com/film/joachim-trier.
25. Will Webb, 'A Beginners Guide'.
26. Elsa Keslassy, 'MK2 Films Reteams With Joachim Trier on New Movie – Variety', *Variety*, 16 May 2023, https://variety.com/2023/film/global/mk2-films-joachim-trier-worst-person-in-the-world-1235614625/.
27. NFI, 'New Joachim Trier Feature Receives NFI Funding', Norwegian Film Institute, 9 May 2023, https://www.nfi.no/eng/news/2023/new-joachim-trier-feature-receives-nfi-funding.
28. Keslassy, 'MK2 Films'. Mer Film founder Maria Ekerhovd is one of Norway's major film producers today. Ekerhovd's recent Norwegian productions count *War Sailor* (*Krigsseileren*) (2022), *Let the River Flow (Ellos eatnu/La elva leve)* (2023) and Eskil Vogt's *The Innocents* (*De Uskyldige*) (2021). She has also been a co-producer for several international collaborations, including Oscar nominee *Flee* (*Flukt*) (2021). Andrea Berentsen Ottmar has, after *The Worst Person in the World*, also produced *Sick of Myself* (*Syk Pike*) (2022), which was featured in the Cannes Un Certain Regard programme in 2022. Mk2 also co-produced *The Worst Person in the World*.
29. This information is from a conversation with Joachim Trier on 11 October 2023. The names of the characters might change before the film is shot, but as of now

the two female leads have names known from Henrik Ibsen's plays, Nora (*A Dolls House*) and Agnes (*Brand*). As of October 2023, it has been announced that Renate Reinsve will play Nora, but the other two main characters are as yet uncast.

30. Tarik Khaldi, 'Interview – Joachim Trier: "I Yearn to Find Something Very Personal and Uniquely Cinematic"', Festival de Cannes, 24 May 2014, https://www.festival-cannes.com/en/2014/interview-joachim-trier-i-yearn-to-find-something-very-personal-and-uniquely-cinematic/.

EPILOGUE

An Interview with Joachim Trier

This interview was conducted in Oslo in August 2022. When I met with Trier, he had spent nearly a year promoting *The Worst Person in the World* all over the world, from Cannes to Hollywood, and was in the process of writing a new script with his partner Eskil Vogt: a script that half a year later was put into motion when Trier received funding for his new project by the Norwegian Film Institute; it is scheduled for release in 2025.

I asked him to pick the place, and he chose the bar at Frogner kino – a renovated 1926 neighbourhood cinema situated on Oslo's westside, in what he himself calls his 'hood'. We met in the afternoon, the day before the cinema was, fittingly, to have an 8 am(!) screening of a 35mm version of Francois Truffaut's *The 400 Blows*.

AG: Often when you give interviews, you have a new film out. But I would like for this conversation to take a wider view, beyond individual movies. And so I want to ask you: what is it about the medium that makes cinema so important to you?
JT: That's interesting, because there are two ways to answer that question. There's what fascinates me about cinema as a visual art form, things that captivated me even as a child. And then there are certain personality traits of mine. A mixture of things I'm not so good at. I have a form of dyslexia, and I'm not confident when it comes to writing – I couldn't have been just a writer. I come from a family where my great-grandfather and grandfather were painters, but I don't have that talent.

So why in the world would you become an artist, you might ask? But I saw that there were things about me that suited film. I understood how to position the camera in fun ways, I was fascinated with movement and stunts and all that. Like how Buster Keaton or vaudeville lets you be transported out into some cityscape, or a forest, or a railway station, and then someone will fall down from something, or sit in front of the train. As a kid, I did a lot of stunts with my skateboard and a camera. I'm a restless person, and more concerned with people and collaboration than most. I like to direct, and I need to watch that I don't do too much of that in my personal life (laughs). That's the great art form, the great game. I think the Icelandic word for director is 'leikstjóri' – the person who controls the game, or play. As a child I got to visit movie sets, and I saw how these adults had this . . . fellowship of play.

And as I've met many other filmmakers, I've understood that we share some traits, it's not something everyone can, should, or want to be doing. Being a director is an eccentric life choice. As Claire Denis said in a public conversation many years ago: 'It is a lifestyle'.

AG: You seem to be choosing two approaches that are distinct, but also interconnected here: One is the process, the act of directing, the other is the product, the art. And now you're focused more on play?
JT: Maybe it was just the way you phrased the question. There must be something more personal, something about *me*, in my reasons too. But film . . . I'm still so childish, really; I just saw *Top Gun: Maverick*, and I thought that was so much fun!

AG: Like how old block busters used to be . . .
JT: Yes, and that's what it's about: now the drones are here, do we really need these veterans in airplanes – yes, we do! We *need* Tom Cruise doing his own stunt work, we need the physical action movie. *But*, as I walk out of the cinema, and everyone is all sweaty and weird and red-faced, and you can see how excited people are about what they've just experienced, something in me feels childishly proud to be allowed to make movies. I have given my life to this craft, and it really means a lot to me.

I'm in love with film, and I have been since I was a kid: [I saw] *E.T.* three times in the cinema when I was nine – 'Please, let me go again!!' – and *The Pinchcliffe Grand Prix*, which my dad took part in making, and I was endlessly proud of. We had bits of it on Super-8, that I could show off at birthday parties. There's this scene in one of the races, where the camera swoops down a hill in this ingenious way, everyone feels it in their stomachs, it's this physical experience brought on by an image. And that moment for me, that is cinema. It's magical – it is magic – playing with the audience's emotions. And then, eventually, you understand how advanced, complex, and ambivalent cinema can get; these emotional spaces that are simultaneously very thought out and constructed, and so open.

AG: You're obviously a film fan, and when talking about it, you quickly turn to examples of works you enjoy. But you're mentioning everything from action

flicks to these intimate, Bergmanesque interpersonal dramas. That's quite the range. Are you able to see yourself from the outside, see what kind of director you are yourself?
JT: That is a very difficult question for me to answer myself. For the longest time, I dreamed of becoming this sort of director, or that, but along the way, I became something else. I've recently become more comfortable seeing that I'm trying to combine character and psychological intimacy with a greater, visual ambition. In a way, I'm extremely interested in Stanley Kubrick and Tarkovsky, the monumental, the powerful, great works. All of Kubrick's films . . . they were *whole*, entire, stand-alone works, and a lot of time passed between each of them. A whole philosophical paradigm had to take form, in another time or a separate universe. Autonomous works, that's always been my dream.

But I'm being pulled in two directions, because I also love Woody Allen and the Bergmanesque, the quick, the messy, the human, and the exploration of character intimacy. I've understood, after *Thelma*, that I don't want to be Brian de Palma – though I do love him! I feel I have much further to go with these interpersonal things.

It is not enough for me to make films about 'that's why mum or dad was mean' or 'that's why that relationship was dysfunctional.' It's got to be about something existential, some greater ideas – time, identity, existence. It's not enough to make this cute story that is realised. I'm sorry, but it has to connect with time and death to be worth making.

AG: But insisting on making humanist dramas with existentialist themes is perhaps a bit out of sync with the current times?
JT: Yes, but maybe that's a good thing? Many of the artists I've admired did things that were maybe a bit out of sync. Fellini's *8 ½* and Antonioni and Bergman's contemporary observations: 'what does it mean to be a human being right now?' There's something there that I'm instinctively drawn to in my time. Characters that don't need to be allegorical or representative of everyone, but that I believe could be real, that I believe in and know.

AG: And you're often highlighted as a Norwegian director, not least when you have international successes like *The Worst Person in the World*, but would you call yourself that?
JT: Yes and no, and ambivalently. That's a personal question too, I grew up with a Danish father who was never truly content with living so many of his years in Norway. In my family, Copenhagen was this continental ideal. My mother, who is Norwegian, got a bit fed up with this idealisation of European and Danish culture, and would tell him: 'But you can't get lost in the woods in Denmark'. And it's true, in Denmark you'll always eventually end up at a bar or a pub or a highway. In Norway, I could walk out my front door in Oslo and

end up somewhere I might freeze to death. That's a powerful cultural experience, it's a beautiful and terrible possibility, but it is a distinctly different way of relating to the world, as a person.

AG: But I also mean in relation to Norwegian film production?
JT: No, I felt completely 'othered' there. Ran off, Eskil and I – him to France and me to London. Perhaps traumatised by my grandfather's experience of not making it in Norway, not feeling seen or supported. And we've got that same struggle, with this New Public Management approach to film policy. I feel like I'm in the same conversations my grandfather, my mum, and my dad told me about. I believed from very early on that what I wanted to do, I couldn't accomplish in Norway. I was reckless, ambitious, naïve, a dreamer. At eighteen, I was counting it out, and at that time (the 1990s) we were maybe five billion people in the world, and out of those maybe only two hundred directors worldwide were working in the manner I wanted to work in, as freely, artistically, and singularly as that. And what were the odds of becoming one of them? So I've been keeping track of directors' careers all along; it might sound cynical, but I think it's crucial.

AG: Does that mean that the first leg of your career – going to London to study and make short films before returning to make your debut feature *Reprise* – was part of the plan?
JT: No, *Reprise* was my break with the plan. I didn't think it possible. I was very young, twenty-three, when I got into the National Film and Television School. I was pretentious, but scared too, and I couldn't see a way forward. I thought I'd be the new genre guy, the guy who made these cerebral thrillers that would the potential inherent in cinematic language, but be catchy and exciting too.

And then I started writing *Reprise* sort of on the side. And it got made a little while before I'd had enough training to, craft-wise, achieve everything I wanted to do with it. And it turned into a film that I thought of as more Norwegian, but that others considered un-Norwegian. That's a paradox I've been inhabiting since. I do feel like *Reprise* is culturally specific, but I also get anxious about people coming at me saying 'There are so many people in Oslo it doesn't represent!' I know. I know. I can only do a qualitative study, not some broad, statistical one, and my study is of one person, or maybe two. I can attempt to say something true about Erik and Phillip. I can't say something about everyone in the world, everyone in Oslo, everyone of a certain generation. And I've never claimed otherwise. That's not my job, my job is to let the story of one friendship – ambitions and dreams and lost dreams, responsibilities, all of that – be enough.

And then I'm suddenly that Norwegian guy who made a film in Norway. And that was validating and good! And Miramax bought it. But I particularly enjoyed people from all over the world saying they found it relatable, because that was such a personal movie. A lot of the rock bands I grew up with had this sound that started out as just their unique, weird taste, but then they took off and people got it.

I've got to tell you something, yesterday my good friend Øystein Greni in Bigbang played their first album, *Waxed* from 1995, live at Parkteateret in Oslo with the original lineup. And the first song on that record, which he wrote when he was seventeen [or] eighteen, when we were in school together, it's called 'Bus Ride'. It's so naïve, so beautifully banal. He sings:

> Sitting on a bus going downtown
> Thinking how great it would be
> To write a great song that could tell people how I feel

And he did, and I was at those shows, ages before it was released, thinking: that's my dream also.

AG: So that's what you and Eskil Vogt did with *Reprise*?
JT: Yes, we tried to 'write a great song', to get people to catch all our obscure references. And when it premiered at the Norwegian film festival in Haugesund, I met the Norwegian film industry. And I don't mean to be smug, but looking back, I don't think a lot of people dared stand up for that film. It's become something of a cult hit, even though *Oslo, 31. August* is more well-respected. But *Reprise* has this energy, this formal ambition. And I still encounter people who say 'Shit, can you believe you opened with that?'

AG: As a debut film, it does stand out.
JT: It's a very ambitious debut film, and childishly cinephilic. Filled with references and high jinks. Not many people dare do that with their first work. And everyone would nit-pick or offer advice or say things like 'It's so French'. It's no masterpiece, but it's a film that dared to be what it wanted to be. And that's when it suddenly became possible for me to believe I could be a film director in Norway.

AG: And now you're in a position where your scripts are published by a major Norwegian publishing house. Can you talk a bit about how you and Eskil Vogt write together, and what he has meant to you and for your films throughout many years of collaboration?
JT: Utterly crucial, incredibly important. In terms of process, he's the deciding factor in bringing things together, getting them done. We write together, but I'm more fanciful and talkative, Eskil is more introverted, more contemplative. I'm often the initiator, and it's my privilege to decide in the end what the thing

is going to be. What's the concept, what type of film is this? But we have to work our way through lots of dreams and debates. He likes to say that people tend to think we each do our defined thing, but that we're actually pretty good at some of the same things. We care about composition and structure as something personal, we've not been very concerned with textbook definitions of what is right, just with what works for us.

AG: I've thought that you are very bold when it comes to structure. Perhaps most obviously in The Worst Person in the World, with the title pages announcing each chapter, but *Louder Than Bombs* is structured extremely ambitiously, with tricky point-of-view shifts. What shapes your choices about these things when you are working?
JT: Lots of reading. Read, write, read. Reading is a bit like playing a piece of music and getting a sense of where there's a dull part, where it builds. That whole structuring thing is incredibly important to us. That's our thing, that's very well spotted.

When you talk to musicians about a tune, they might say, 'God, how do they shift the rhythm from that to that?' Things like that, in film, we're super nerdy about, doing those runs, the point-of-view shifts, formal chapters, mixed emotions. I'll say to Eskil that we need an emblematic close-up here, or some mise-en-scène trick there, even as we're writing. Take that scene with Conrad in the classroom, in *Louder Than Bombs*.

AG: But that means that more is planned out in the writing room than what ends up on the page?
JT: Yes, much more. And Eskil trusts me. During the writing process, he can be stubborn in terms of ideas, but in the end, he is very loyal and generous. If, say, I lose faith in the editing room.

AG: But he is not usually on set with you?
JT: No, he may be the only person who actually intimidates me a bit there. Let's say I've worked through the text with my actors, exploring things – if he's there, he'll know what the plan was, but maybe not what I've done with the actors to make the scene work. And then my mind is sort of pulled in two directions.

AG: I've thought about something as I've rewatched the films after reading the scripts . . .
JT: This I'm curious about!

AG: There are often things in your scripts that don't make it into the final feature, which is common, of course. But I'm struck by how your films always end up tighter, the thesis always clearer, once they're done.

JT: I'm glad to hear that. And things do happen in collaboration with the actors, like Anders Danielsen Lie, whom I've worked with the most; I like encouraging the actors to let things happen.

AG: This ties in with something we've already talked about, the value of collaboration. You have quite a few collaborators you've been working with for a long time. Is it important to you to find the right people?
JT: Yes, and that's a process, not just finding the good people, but the people who are right for this project, who can work together. That's my job, getting the team to jive optimally. This is an important part of artistic work, how the actors' frame of mind, their courage and focus, is steered throughout the day. From when they're picked up in the morning, through their time in the makeup chair, and so on. All of this is art. We don't talk much about that. I hope this is something I'm good at, and I'm irritated, disgusted even, when I hear actors talk about directors who don't work with this kind of sensitivity. Respecting creativity is important to me, it's an ideal.

AG: But there are other recognisable traits in your approach to filmmaking too, visible patterns, signatures. Like the way you use voice-overs, or the tight, playful montages that make up such an important part of *Reprise*, *Louder Than Bombs*, and *The Worst Person in the World*. These are recurring elements – how conscious are you about there being a repertoire of tools and features that are yours?
JT: Those montages are so much fun to do! Narration techniques like Conrad's diary. It's the sort of thing done in novels. I remember reading Jonathan Franzen's *Freedom*, which opens with that sort of objective observations on a street. It spans many years, but it's very short. There's a diary entry from a woman who has moved there, and then I think you get her husband's story. And then her son. And, God, what a network. Franzen is one of many who do this stuff. There's something about *Sans Soleil* by Chris Marker that is just the coolest thing ever, essayistic films like that. *Hiroshima Mon Amour* is the best film ever made, maybe. That's my *Citizen Kane,* it's a film that employs everything. Poetry, documentary, true musical sequences, silence, faces, places. That's art. Those are my ideals, shape-shifting and playing. I'm standing on a bunch of shoulders when it comes to exciting cinematic language, and that gives me so much energy. I've heard a rumour that Sam Levinson, who makes *Euphoria*, has taken some of what we've done and done it another way. I'm so happy when I hear that he and his crew allegedly enjoyed *Reprise*. I'm rooting for everyone who plays around with form, telling human stories. And if I accept your premise, that this is typically us, then that makes me proud.

AG: Stretching the limits of the cinematic seems to be a motivator for you, I think. One can imagine a filmmaker asking, 'how can I best portray this so

the audience will experience what I want them to; should I use this or that technique or feature?', but in your films, I get the feeling that playing around with techniques, with modes and methods of narration, can itself be the goal?
JT: Quite right. Yes, that can be my motivation. Like that scene with Melanie and Conrad in the classroom. She reads a book out, which creates these associations in his mind, and his imaginings, memories, and reconsiderations of his mother are guided by the voice of this girl he has an erotic interest in. It exists on a notepad from a few years before, just this idea that it would be fun if someone was reading aloud from a book to someone else, and then that became the voice-over in this stream of thoughts.

And just like that, I have a lot of strange ideas that suddenly become relevant. And then Eskil can step in and make sure everything is clear enough; we need to step out of the scene and see that he is an outsider in his class, we have to get that he doesn't know how his mother died. But that's sneaking plot information into a scene we really just wanted to make. So, you're right, form often guides what we want to narrate.

AG: That's interesting, but this scene is also one where people say these are literary techniques, stream-of-consciousness, modernist literature . . .
JT: But are those things not film too? Isn't it the case that literature, those delicious, mutated forms of the novel, Joyce and Proust and all that experimentation, reveals possibilities that film, too, in its way, can realise? I once read that cinema came about too late to truly ever be modernist. But there is something inherently meta-textual about film that comes into play – you can play around with mimesis and reality and falsehood. When people call them 'literary films', I know that's meant as a compliment, but I dearly hope they don't feel like literature, literature is so wonderful in itself.

AG: What about themes that are important to you? Time seems to be a recurring one, throughout all your work. Is that right?
JT: Yes, absolutely. It's hard to talk about time, but it easily comes into play once you formulate some specific ideas. I'm a very existentially oriented person; as an atheist, I believe this life is the one. And I think I've been shaped a bit by the fact that when I was between the ages of seven and ten, a number of my older relatives passed away. Boom, boom, boom, and they're gone. And that gave me a clear sense that. . . there is no answer to this. Fantasising about death, about what death is . . . time comes into play there.

AG: Are your films a means of reflecting on existential questions?
JT: Yes, things like grief and loss. I've been letting the emotional side of things take up more space. But I haven't been entirely conscious of it, it's snuck in. When I stepped into *The Worst Person in the World*, I was at one stage in life,

and when I stepped back out, I was somewhere else – I'd met and had a child with someone who was in the same place as me. With that film, I sort of walked in Julie's shoes for a bit, recognised myself in my late twenties, and then, as I was coming out of the film, life had changed.

AG: You often describe your films as personal. Say that you draw on personal experience.
JT: Yes, I see that now. *Reprise* . . . being young, wanting to succeed, trying to be friends, trying to find love. Many people wondered, out of Eskil and me, who was Erik and who was Phillip, but it's not that simple.

Thelma might be my weirdest film, but I've struggled with that thing of owning and coping with who you are, taking responsibility for yourself and your stuff. And Thelma has full responsibility. She can destroy, or she can create, as I can. Do I dare be who I am? That's applicable to me as well. I don't write things where I can't relate to what my characters are working through, even if it's a supernatural movie, or they're an American family.

And creating a mood is a very personal thing, I have to say. Moods are like music. Creating spaces, emotions, lighting. The sense of melancholy about 'oh God what a wonderful time we're having, but I know it's going to end, it's ephemeral'. There's that time thing. I'm trying to make it precious, not just sentimental, to give it force and a sense of true meaning. I spoke to a young musician who had experienced a lot of heartbreak, and used to write sad love songs, but he told me that right now he was happy. But then I told him, 'There's always death!' There's always something irreconcilable, this fracture in reality, we should try to be happy, but there's always some loss. The world is so far from perfect.

AG: And we see that in your films too, these great shifts, from great infatuation to a sudden loss just around the bend.
JT: Yes, this is true, the great shifts. Life is shocking! I'm confronted with the fact that my films are about people who have roofs over their heads, food, and cool clothes, in a world that is otherwise on fire. And it's a question one should ask oneself, but I think that even an ostensibly safe, Norwegian middle-class life is shockingly dramatic. Shockingly. I've seen so many people go under. Substance abuse, mental illness, suicide, siblings who can't even talk to each other, parents and children who can't reconcile. Utterly dramatic, some of the biggest, worst, most painful things that can happen to a person. That's drama enough for me. And that stuff also happens within these frameworks where things very well might have been lovely. And I want to champion the idea that these stories are found everywhere. That's my role. You can't do everything, but you must do what you can.

AG: Because you have been criticised about representation, challenged on the fact that your characters are all urban, middle-class people? Do they have to be?

JT: Sure, but it's not entirely true either, not everyone in *Reprise* is that, nor *Thelma*, although she pursues a university education in the city. So . . . one film. But of course, if we place this people on a Bourdian map, these are the people I understand. I'm also interested in the sociological terms 'somewheres' and 'anywheres'. Why is it that I, as a person who makes movies for people all over the world – Turkey, Canada, Mexico – get a lot of feedback, on Instagram, say, from people saying they relate to my work? But you're challenging me to see myself from the outside, which is something I may not be so good at, though we're all born into a certain context too.

AG: But would you say relational stuff is more interesting to you than, say, politics?
JT: I'm very interested in politics. Olivier Bugge Coutté and I always talk world politics when we're editing, and he is very knowledgeable. But we had a project about Dag Hammarskjold that was never realised, we haven't been able to make it happen. These human, relational stories are easier. But we haven't given up.

AG: One thing I think all your films are about, is art. There is a lot about different art forms in your work, photography in *Louder Than Bombs*, literature in *Reprise*, Aksel's comics in *The Worst Person in the World*. And music is important. Would it be accurate to say that you're exploring art and its value as well?
JT: It's accurate, but if you'd asked us about that after *Reprise*, we'd be ashamed. We'd say we used artistic longing to verbalise existential questions. And then dusted it with literary references for fun. So, there's humour in that too.

But we're very concerned with the importance of art, within democracy. I feel bad for Aksel when he's on that talk show. And the woman accusing him of sexism is right, too. If we were to look at *Gaupe* (the comic strip from the film), the way we imagine it, it would be full of women with big breasts, and other nonsense. Aksel thinks he's an ally to the marginalised, and then, suddenly, he's told he's the man with all this power punching down, ridiculing women. The boys in *Reprise* are like that too. I've seen it a lot, and I've inhabited that sort of masculine culture, been the cool guy heading to the party without the dumb girls. I've tried to confront that in myself. And so I'm letting Aksel be confronted with it there, but he also says something I agree with. He says that art is supposed to be this messy space where you can test and explore. I want to protect art as an artificial, constructed room for thought, where things can be unclear or dangerous, a little uncomfortable. That is its value.

AG: When working, you do a lot of research into all these fields as well. Studying Charlie Christensen's comic books, or different photographers.
JT: Yes, and I like that. That's about representation too. Art is about capturing those tricky things, that which cannot so easily be represented, parts of life and

reality that are difficult. The languageless, the traumatic, the sublime. And this is where the war photograph plays a different role from Aksel's urge to break all the rules. But they're related too, just as the guys in *Reprise* are trying to write novels that will say something that has never been said before.

There's this desire for borderline, boundary-pushing experiences in art. Perhaps because reality is strange and we don't quite know where we belong in it. Art is so important. I believe in that. And I'd want for everyone to have some relationship with it, whether they sing or tell each other stories.

AG: The final bullet point on my list is Oslo, and its significance.
JT: Oslo is my matter. Like a sculptor's medium. It's not loaded with meaning beyond . . . being what it is. Oslo is that 'Oslo-ness', the material is the message, and I know its moods. I know what the light is like on a certain street at a certain time. We work with Sun Tracker, this software that knows where the sun will be, and incorporate that into our production plans. We strive to find this visual mood in certain places, and they end up being places I know well.

AG: So, it's the hunt for the mood.
JT: Yes, that's well put. The hunt for the mood. That's cinema to me. That's the thing.

FILMOGRAPHY

Joachim Trier's films*

Note: The filmography includes all films that have been made available digitally. Some student and amateur productions are not included.

Pietà (2000) (short)
Writers: Eskil Vogt and Joachim Trier
Producer: Teun Hilte
Cinematography: David Luther
Editing: Olivier Bugge Coutté
Composer: Tara Creme
Cast:
Julian: David Birkin
Jacob: Dick Fontaine
Julian's mother Rebecca: Caroline Langrishe

Still (2001) (short)
Writers: Eskil Vogt and Joachim Trier
Producer: Anna Wulff
Cinematography: David Luther
Editing: Olivier Bugge Coutté
Composer: Quentin Thomas
Cast:
Walter 70: James Bradley
Walter 25: Peter Bayliss

Procter (2002) (short)
Writers: Eskil Vogt and Joachim Trier
Producer: Marie Farquharson
Cinematography: Jakob Ihre

Editing: Helle le Fevre
Composer: Graham Slack
Cast:
Charles Procter: John Joyce

Reprise (2006)
Writers: Eskil Vogt and Joachim Trier
Producer: Karin Julsrud
Cinematography: Jakob Ihre
Editing: Olivier Bugge Coutté
Composer: Ola Fløttum, Knut Schreiner
Sound design: Gisle Tveito
Production design: Roger Rosenberg
Costume design: Maria Bohlin
Cast:
Phillip: Anders Danielsen Lie
Erik: Espen Klouman Høier
Kari: Victoria Winge
Hanne, Phillip's mother: Elisabeth Sand
Johanne: Rebekka Karijord
Mathias Wergeland: Torbjørn Harr
Jan Eivind: Henrik Mestad
Morten: Odd-Magnus Williamson
Lars: Christian Rubeck
Henning: Henrik Elvestad
Geir: Pål Stokka
Sten Egil Dahl: Sigmund Severed
Narrator: Eindride Eidsvoll

Oslo, August 31st (*Oslo, 31. August*) (2011)
Writers: Eskil Vogt and Joachim Trier, based on the novel by Pierre Drieu La Rochelle
Producer: Sigve Endresen
Cinematography: Jakob Ihre
Editing: Olivier Bugge Coutté
Composers: Ola Fløttum, Torgny Amdam
Sound design: Gisle Tveito
Production design: Jørgen Stangebye Larsen
Costume design: Ellen Dæhli Ystehede
Cast:
Anders: Anders Danielsen Lie
Thomas: Hans Olav Brenner
Rebekka: Ingrid Olava
Petter: Petter Width Kristiansen
Tove: Tone B. Mostraum
David: Øystein Røger

Mirjam: Kjærsti Odden Skjeldal
Johanne: Johanne Kjellvik Ledang
Renate: Renate Reinsve

Louder Than Bombs (2015)
Writers: Eskil Vogt and Joachim Trier
Producers: Thomas Robsahm, Joshua Astrachan
Cinematography: Jakob Ihre
Editing: Olivier Bugge Coutté
Composer: Ola Fløttum
Sound design: Gisle Tveito
Production design: Molly Hughes
Costume design: Emma Potter
Cast:
Jonah: Jesse Eisenberg
Conrad: Devin Druid
Gene: Gabriel Byrne
Isabelle: Isabelle Huppert
Melanie: Ruby Jerins
Hannah: Amy Ryan
Erin: Rachel Brosnahan
Richard: David Strathairn

Thelma (2017)
Writers: Eskil Vogt and Joachim Trier
Producers: Thomas Robsahm
Cinematography: Jakob Ihre
Editing: Olivier Bugge Coutté
Composer: Ola Fløttum
Sound design: Gisle Tveito
Production design: Roger Rosenberg
Costume design: Ellen Dæhli Ystehede
Cast:
Thelma: Ellie Harboe
Anja: Kaya Wilkins
Father: Henrik Rafaelsen
Mother: Ellen Dorrit Petersen
Thelma 6 years old: Grethe Eltervåg
Doctor Paulsen: Anders Mossling
Nevrolog: Marte Magnusdotter Solemn

The Other Munch (*Den andre Munch*) (2018)
Co-directed with Emil Trier.
Producers: Nicolai Moland, Thomas Robsahm
Cinematography: Jon Gaute Espevold, Magnus Flåto, Petter Holmern Halvorsen, Fred Arne Wergeland.

Editing: Christian Siebnherz
Composer: Ola Fløttum
With:
Joachim Trier (himself)
Karl Ove Knausgård (himself)

The Worst Person in the World (*Verdens verste menneske*) (2021)
Writers: Eskil Vogt and Joachim Trier
Producers: Thomas Robsahm, Andrea Berentsen Ottmar
Cinematography: Kasper Tuxen
Editing: Olivier Bugge Coutté
Composer: Ola Fløttum
Sound design: Gisle Tveito
Production design: Roger Rosenberg
Costume design: Ellen Dæhli Ystehede
Cast:
Julie: Renate Reinsve
Aksel: Anders Danielsen Lie
Erlend: Herbert Nordrum
Sunniva: Maria Grazio Di Meo
Ole Magnus: Hans Olav Brenner
Karianne: Helene Bjørneby
Julie's mother Eva: Marianne Krogh
Julie's grandmother: Thea Stabell
Julie's father Per Harald: Vidar Sandem
Narrator: Ine Jansen

Sentimental Value (No Norwegian title yet) (2025)
Writers: Eskil Vogt and Joachim Trier
Producers: Maria Ekerhovd, Andrea Berentsen Ottmar
Cast: Renate Reinsve, Stellan Skarsgård, Elle Fanning and Inga Ibsdotter Lilleaas

Filmography

400 Blows (*Les quatre cents coups*) (François Truffaut), 1959
8 1/2 (Federico Fellini), 1963
20th Century Women (Mike Mills), 2016
22 July (Paul Greengrass), 2018
Adaptation (Spike Jonze), 2002
The Age of Innocence (Martin Scorsese),1993
Amélie (Jean-Pierre Jeunet), 2001
Annie Hall (Woody Allen), 1977
Autumn Sonata (*Höstsonaten*) (Ingmar Bergman), 1978
Barry Lyndon (Stanley Kubrick), 1975
Before Midnight (Richard Linklater), 2013
Before Sunrise (Richard Linklater), 1995
Before Sunset (Richard Linklater), 2004
Beginners (Mike Mills), 2010
Bergman Island (Mia Hansen-Løve), 2021
Blind (Eskil Vogt), 2014
The Breakfast Club (John Hughes), 1985
Carrie (Brian De Palma), 1976
Casablanca (Michael Curtiz), 1942
C'mon C'mon (Mike Mills), 2021
Citizen Kane (Orson Welles), 1941
Congo Murders (*Mordene i Kongo*) (Marius Holst), 2018
Copenhagen Cowboy (Nicolas Winding Refn), 2023
Copenhagen Does Not Exist (*København finds ikke*) (Martin Skovbjerg), 2023
Cries and Whispers (*Viskningar och rop*) (Ingmar Bergman), 1973
Don't Look Now (Nicolas Roeg), 1973
E.T. (Steven Spielberg), 1982
Euphoria (Sam Levinson), 2019 – to date

Fanny and Alexander (Ingmar Bergman), 1983
Ferris Bueller's Day Off (John Hughes), 1986
The Fire Within (*Le feu follet*) (Louis Malle), 1963
Flee (*Flugt*) (Jonas Poher Rasmussen), 2021
The French Connection (William Friedkin), 1971
Frances Ha (Noah Baumbach), 2012
The French Dispatch (Wes Anderson), 2021
Game of Thrones (David Benioff and D. B. Weiss), 2011–2019
Gravity (Alfonso Cuarón), 2013
The Green Ray (*Le rayon vert*) (Eric Rohmer), 1986
Herman (Erik Gustavson), 1990
Hannah and Her Sisters (Woody Allen), 1986
The Hunt (*Jakten*) (Erik Løchen), 1959
High and Low (*Tengoku to jigoku*) (Akira Kurosawa), 1963
Hiroshima Mon Amour (Alain Resnais), 1959
Holiday (George Cukor), 1938
The Ice Storm (Ang Lee), 1997
Infinitely Polar Bear (Maya Forbes), 2014
Insomnia (Erik Skjoldbjærg), 1997
Insomnia (Christopher Nolan), 2022
The Innocents (*De uskyldige*) (Eskil Vogt), 2021
Jules and Jim (*Jules et Jim*) (Francois Truffaut), 1962
Junk Mail (*Budbringeren*) (Pål Sletaune), 1997
Let the River Flow (*Ellos eatnu/La elva leve*) (Ole Giæver) 2023
Louder Than Bombs (Joachim Trier), 2015
Manchester By the Sea (Kenneth Lonergan,), 2016
The Matrix (Lilly and Lana Wachowski), 1999
The Mirror (*Zerkolo*) (Andrei Tarkovsky), 197.
Mission Impossible (Brian de Palma), 1996
Next of Kin (*Arven*) (Anja Breien), 1979
Notting Hill (Roger Michell), 1999
Ordinary People (Robert Redford) 1980
Oslo, 31. August (*Oslo, August 31st*) (Joachim Trier), 2011
The Other Munch (*Den andre Munch*) (Emil and Joachim Trier), 2018
Persona (Ingmar Bergman), 1966
The Philadelphia Story (George Cukor), 1940
The Piano Teacher (*La Pianiste*) (Michael Haneke), 2001
Pietà (Joachim Trier), 2000
Pinchcliffe Grand Prix (*Flåklypa Grand Prix*) (Ivo Caprino), 1975
Procter (Joachim Trier), 2002
Remonstrance (*Motforestilling*) (Erik Løchen), 1972
Reprise (Joachim Trier), 2006
Rosemary's Baby (Roman Polanski), 1968
Sabrina (Billy Wilder), 1954
Sans Soleil (Chris Marker), 1983
Sentimental Value (Joachim Trier), forthcoming 2025

Sick of Myself (*Syk pike*) (Kristoffer Borgli), 2022
Silver Linings Playbook (David O. Russell), 2012
Singin' in the Rain (Stanley Donen and Gene Kelly), 1952
Still (Joachim Trier), 2001
The Sweet Hereafter (Atom Egoyan), 1997
Thelma (Joachim Trier), 2017
Through a Glass Darkly (*Såsom i en spegel*) (Ingmar Bergman) 1961
Top Gun: Maverick (Joseph Kosinski), 2022
Triangle of Sadness (Ruben Östlund), 2022
Two Days, One Night (*Deux jours, une nuit*) (Jean-Pierre Dardenne and Luc Dardenne), 2014
Vertigo (Alfred Hitchcock), 1958
Violette (*Violette Nozière*) (Claude Chabrol), 1978
Virgin Mountain (*Fúsi*) (Dagur Kári), 2015
War Sailor (*Krigsseileren*) (Gunnar Vikene), 2022
Wild Strawberries (*Smultronstället*) (Ingmar Bergman), 1957
The Worst Person in the World (*Verdens verste menneske*) (Joachim Trier), 2021

Bibliography

ADAA. 'Symptoms: Anxiety and Depression Association of America, ADAA'. no date. https://adaa.org/understanding-anxiety/panic-disorder-agoraphobia/symptoms (accessed 26 November 2023).

Aguilar, Carlos 'How Joachim Trier's Unplanned Oslo Trilogy Became a Cinematic Masterpiece in Three Distinct Parts'. *IndieWire*, 1 February 2022. https://www.indiewire.com/2022/02/joachim-trier-oslo-trilogy-interview-1234695516/ (accessed 26 November 2023).

Bahr, Oda 'Ti år som kjedet kvinnen'. *Rushprint*, 1 January 2010.

Bakke Andresen, Christer. *Norwegian Nightmares: The Horror Cinema of a Nordic Country*. Edinburgh University Press, 2022.

———. 'Thelma: Empathic Engagement and the Norwegian Horror Cinema'. *Journal of Scandinavian Cinema* 9, no. 2 (1 June 2019): 227–33. https://doi.org/10.1386/jsca.9.2.227_1 (accessed 26 November 2023).

Barthes, Roland. *Camera Lucida: Reflections on Photography*. Vintage Classics. London: Vintage Books, 2000.

Bechdel, Alison. *Dykes to Watch Out For*. Boston: Mariner Books, 1986

Beckhurst, Gabriella. '"Intra-Active" Desire in Joachim Trier's "Thelma"'. *Another Gaze: A Feminist Film Journal*, 18 January 2019. https://www.anothergaze.com/intra-active-desire-joachim-trier-thelma-feminist-lesbian/ (accessed 26 November 2023).

Bigelow, Benjamin. 'Acts of Remembering, Acts of Forgetting: Architecture, Memory and Recovery in Oslo, August 31st'. *Journal of Scandinavian Cinema* 10, no. 1 (1 March 2020): 7–24. https://doi.org/10.1386/jsca_00011_1 (accessed 26 November 2023).

Birkvad, Søren. 'Analysen: Oslo, 31. August (2011)'. *Montages*, 14 September 2011. http://montages.no/2011/09/analysen-oslo-31-august-2011/ (accessed 26 November 2023).

———. 'In Search of the Antagonist: On Inner Struggles and Soft Parental Power in Joachim Trier's Films'. *Journal of Scandinavian Cinema* 9, no. 2 (1 June 2019): 203–10. https://doi.org/10.1386/jsca.9.2.203_1 (accessed 26 November 2023).

Bjørkly, Arnstein. 'Psykogen bedehusmagi'. *Le Monde diplomatique*, 7 September 2017. https://www.lmd.no/2017/09/psykogens-bedehusmagi/ (accessed 28 November 2023).

Bjørnødegård, Vilde. 'Film og sanselighet: Affektfremkallende egenskaper i "Louder Than Bombs" (Joachim Trier, 2015)'. Oslo, Universitetet i Oslo, 2018. https://www.duo.uio.no/handle/10852/63219 (accessed 26 November 2023).

Bloomer, Jeffrey. 'Director Joachim Trier on the Problem With His Movies and Louder Than Bombs' Curious Ending'. *Slate*, 8 April 2016. http://www.slate.com/blogs/browbeat/2016/04/08/louder_than_bombs_interview_with_joachim_trier_on_the_movie_s_ending_and.html (accessed 26 November 2023).

Blum, Sophie. 'Interview: Joachim Trier, Director of Oslo, August 31st'. *Film Comment*, 23 May 2012. https://www.filmcomment.com/blog/interview-joachim-trier-director-of-oslo-august-31st/ (accessed 26 November 2023).

Boym, Svetlana. *The Future of Nostalgia*. New York: Basic Books, 2001.

Brady, Tara. 'Making The Worst Person in the World, an Oscar-Nominated "Unromantic Comedy"'. *The Irish Times*, 19 March 2022. https://www.irishtimes.com/culture/film/making-the-worst-person-in-the-world-an-oscar-nominated-unromantic-comedy-1.4824526 (accessed 26 November 2023).

Breiteig, Bjarte, Eskil Vogt, and Joachim Trier. 'Oslo gjennom mørkt glass – Eskil Vogt og Joachim Trier i samtale med Bjarte Breiteig'. In Eskil Vogt and Joachim Trier, *Oslo, 31. August. Filmmanus*. Oslo: Tiden Norsk Forlag, 2011, pp. 161–83.

———. 'Overskudd og ambivalens. En samtale rundt tilblivelsen av Reprise mellom Bjarte Breiteig, Eskil Vogt og Joachim Trier'. In Eskil Vogt and Joachim Trier, *Reprise. Et filmmanuskript*. Oslo: Tiden Norsk Forlag, 2007, pp. 208–37.

Brody, Richard. '"The Worst Person in the World" is a Sham, Except for Its Lead Performance'. *The New Yorker*, 7 February 2022. https://www.newyorker.com/culture/the-front-row/the-worst-person-in-the-world-is-a-sham-except-for-its-lead-performance (accessed 26 November 2023).

Bruhn, Jørgen, and Anne Gjelsvik. *Cinema Between Media: An Intermediality Approach*. Edinburgh: Edinburgh University Press, 2018.

Buder, Emily. '"Thelma": Joachim Trier on Shooting the Norwegian "Carrie" on Cinemascope'. *No Film School*, 14 November 2017. https://nofilmschool.com/2017/10/joachim-trier-thelma-interview (accessed 26 November 2023).

Bulie, Kåre. '– Av å se film lærer man mye om det å være menneske og om hverandre'. https://www.dn.no/d2/film/joachim-trier/eskil-vogt/filmfestivalen-i-cannes/-av-a-se-film-larer-man-mye-om-det-a-vare-menneske-og-om-hverandre/2-1-1076331 (accessed 27 November 2023).

Bull Thorvik, Hannah. 'Hun kjeder meg voldsomt'. *Dagbladet*, 25 October 2021. https://www.dagbladet.no/kultur/hun-kjeder-meg-voldsomt/74450358 (accessed 26 November 2023).

Bundy, Andrew. 'Joachim Trier Talks The Inspiration For "The Worst Person In The World", His Love Of Graphic Novels & More'. *The Playlist*, 2 February 2022. https://theplaylist.net/joachim-trier-talks-the-inspiration-for-the-worst-person-in-the-world-interview-20220202/ (accessed 26 November 2023).

Carrasco, Salvador. 'Anatomy of a Breakup or Her Life to Fix: The Worst Person in the World'. *Senses of Cinema*, 2022. http://www.sensesofcinema.com/2022/

feature-articles/anatomy-of-a-breakup-or-her-life-to-fix-the-worst-person-in-the-world/ (accessed 26 November 2023).

Chang, Kee. 'Q&A with Joachim Trier'. *Anthem*, 21 May 2015. https://anthemmagazine.com/qa-with-joachim-trier/ (accessed 26 November 2023).

Chatman, Seymour. *Coming to Terms: The Rhetoric of Narrative in Fiction and Film*. Ithaca: Cornell University Press, 1990.

Chen, Nick. 'Director Joachim Trier Selects Ten of His All-Time Favourite Romcoms'. *Dazed*, 2 March 2022. https://www.dazeddigital.com/film-tv/article/55580/1/joachim-trier-worst-person-in-the-world-ten-romcoms-top-ten (accessed 26 November 2023).

Croll, Ben. 'Joachim Trier On Rounding Out His Oslo Trilogy With "The Worst Person in the World"'. *Variety*, 9 July 2021. https://variety.com/2021/film/news/joachim-trier-on-rounding-out-his-oslo-trilogy-with-the-worst-person-in-the-world-1235012245/ (accessed 26 November 2023).

Dargis, Manohla. 'For Your Consideration, Academy'. *New York Times*, 3 January 2009. https://www.nytimes.com/2009/01/04/movies/awardsseason/04oscars.html (accessed 26 November 2023).

———. 'Two Friends, Two Novels, One Mailbox: Lives at the Speed of Ambition'. *The New York Times*, 16 May 2008. https://www.nytimes.com/2008/05/16/movies/16repr.html (accessed 26 November 2023).

Eidsvåg, Terje. 'Glødende om fortvilelse'. *Adresseavisen*, 31 August 2011. https://www.adressa.no/kultur/i/KzyPb4/glodende-om-fortvilelse (accessed 26 November 2023).

Engelstad, Audun. *Film og fortelling*. 2nd edn [AU]. Bergen: Fagbokforlaget, 2022.

———. 'The Concept of Time in Joachim Trier's Reprise'. *Journal of Scandinavian Cinema* 9, no. 2 (1 June) 2019: 197–202. https://doi.org/10.1386/jsca.9.2.197_1 (accessed 26 November 2023).

Eriksen, Ulrik. 'En storbysymfoni'. *Morgenbladet*, 26 August 2011, https://morgenbladet.no/kultur/2011/en_storbysymfoni (accessed 26 November 2023).

Faldalen, Jon Inge. 'Utfor vestkanten'. *Vinduet* 2, 2011, 92–101.

Gjelsvik, Anne. 'Analysen: *Louder Than Bombs* (2015)'. *Montages*, 2015. http://montages.no/2015/10/analysen-louder-than-bombs-2015/ (accessed 26 November 2023).

———. 'In Focus: Joachim Trier'. *Journal of Scandinavian Cinema* 9, no. 2 (1 June 2019): 191–96. https://doi.org/10.1386/jsca.9.2.191_1 (accessed 26 November 2023).

———. 'Openings and Closures: Mental Health in Joachim Trier's Cinematic Universe'. *Journal of Scandinavian Cinema* 9, no. 1 (1 March 2019): 75–88. https://doi.org/10.1386/jsca.9.1.75_1 (accessed 26 November 2023).

———. 'Sculpting Time: Joachim Trier's *The Worst Person in the World*'. *Montages International Edition*, 17 December 2021. https://montagesmagazine.com/2021/12/sculpting-time-the-worst-person-in-the-world/ (accessed 26 November 2023).

Gracewood, Gemma. 'The Power of the Still: The Photography Behind the Scenes'. *Journal: A Letterboxd Magazine*, 20 March 2022. https://letterboxd.com/journal/power-of-the-still-unit-photography/ (accessed 26 November 2023).

Hamsun, Knut. *Hunger* (trans. Robert Bly). New York: Farrar, Straus and Giroux, 1967.
Haugros, Sigrid. 'Triers Oslo'. *Z Filmtidsskrift*, no. 2, 2012: 64–75.
Heeney, Alex. 'With *Thelma*, Joachim Trier Continues to Develop his Dirty Formalism'. *Seventh Row*, 25 November 2017, https://seventh-row.com/2017/11/25/thelma-dirty-formalism/ (accessed 26 November 2023).
Heeney, Alex, and Orla Smith. *Existential Detours. Joachim Trier's Films of Indecisions and Revisions*, vol. 5.1. Toronto: Seventh Row, 2024.
Heti, Sheila. 'Second Selves'. *The New York Times*, 18 January 2013. https://www.nytimes.com/2013/01/20/books/review/missing-out-by-adam-phillips.html (accessed 26 November 2023).
Hindse, Casper. 'Ordleg med Joachim Trier'. *Filmmagasinet Ekko*, 30 November 2017. https://www.ekkofilm.dk/artikler/joachim-trier-/ (accessed 27 November 2023).
Hobbelstad, Inger Merethe. 'Bevegende bysommer'. *Dagbladet*, 18 May 2011. https://www.dagbladet.no/kultur/bevegende-bysommer/63687380 (accessed 26 November 2023).
'How Frozen-In-Time Scenes Are Shot For Movies And TV'. *Movies Insider: Insider.* (2022) https://www.youtube.com/watch?v=OrgbZD2sRnU (accessed 26 November 2023).
Huser, Aleksander. 'Mike Mills og "C'mon C'mon": En fabel som imiterer livet'. *Cinema*, 7 April 2022. https://cine.no/2022/04/08/mike-mills-og-cmon-cmon-en-fabel-som-imiterer-livet/ (accessed 26 November 2023).
Ihre, Jakob. 'Masterclass with the Emmy Award Winner Jakob Ihre, Director of Photography'. *Kulturakademin Gotenburgh Studios*, 2020. https://www.youtube.com/watch?v=b2ZzPRLeL_g (accessed 26 November 2023).
Iversen, Gunnar. 'Lyden av Oslo, 31. August'. In Iversen and Tiller (eds), *Lydbilder: Mediene og det akustiske*. Oslo: Universitetsforlaget, 2014: 101–17.
———. *Norsk Filmhistorie*. Oslo: Universitetsforlaget, 2011.
———. 'Tiden leger ingen sår Reprise'. In *Den norske filmbølgen: Fra Orions belte til Max Manus*. Oslo: Universitetsforlaget, 2010: 267–90.
Iversen, Gunnar, and Asbjørn Tiller. *Lydbilder: mediene og det akustiske*. Oslo: Universitetsforlaget, 2014.
Jakobsen, Svenn. 'Lyden av Oslo, 31. August'. *Rushprint*, 19 March 2012. https://rushprint.no/2012/03/lyden-av-oslo-31-august/ (accessed 26 November 2023).
Jerslev, Anne. 'Joachim Trier's Close-Ups and Autonomous Moments'. *Journal of Scandinavian Cinema* 2019, no. 2: 219–25. https://doi.org/10.1386/jsca.9.2.219_1 (accessed 26 November 2023).
'Joachim Trier's DVD Picks'. 2016. https://www.youtube.com/watch?v=qF3qYnnuGxI (accessed 26 November 2023).
Johansen, Guro. 'Sted og selvrefleksivitet : en adaptasjonsanalyse av Oslo, 31. August og Le feu follet'. 2012. Oslo, Universitetet i Oslo. https://www.duo.uio.no/handle/10852/38132 (accessed 26 November 2023).
Joyce, James. *A Portrait of the Artist as a Young Man*. New York: B. W Huebsch, 1916.
Kaganski, Serge. 'Joachim Trier on *The Worst Person in the World*'. Norwegian Film Institute, 5 July 2021. https://www.nfi.no/eng/news/2021/joachim-trier-on-the-worst-person-in-the-world (accessed 26 November 2023).

Kasman, Daniel. 'Representation of Self: Discussing "Louder Than Bombs" with Joachim Trier'. MUBI, 29 May 2015. https://mubi.com/notebook/posts/representation-of-self-discussing-louder-than-bombs-with-joachim-trier (accessed 26 November 2023).
Kelsey, Colleen. 'Joachim Trier's Family Dynamics'. *Interview Magazine*, 6 April 2016. https://www.interviewmagazine.com/film/joachim-trier (accessed 26 November 2023).
Kemp, Ella. 'Cool World: Norway's Capital Through the Eyes of the Oslo Trilogy'. *Journal: A Letterboxd Magazine*, 28 March 2022. https://letterboxd.com/journal/cool-world-oslo-norway-capital-trier-vogt/ (accessed 26 November 2023).
Kerr, Eino Aleksander. *Minner og melankoli en auteurstudie av den norske filmskaperen Joachim Trier*. Trondheim: Institutt for kunst og medievitenskap, NTNU, 2013.
Keslassy, Elsa. 'MK2 Films Reteams With Joachim Trier on New Movie – Variety'. *Variety*, 16 May 2023. https://variety.com/2023/film/global/mk2-films-joachim-trier-worst-person-in-the-world-1235614625/ (accessed 27 November 2023).
Khaldi, Tarik. 'Interview – Joachim Trier: "I Yearn to Find Something Very Personal and Uniquely Cinematic"'. Festival de Cannes, 24 May 2014. https://www.festival-cannes.com/en/2014/interview-joachim-trier-i-yearn to find something-very-personal-and-uniquely-cinematic/ (accessed 26 November 2023).
Knapstad, Marit, Ove Heradstveit, and Børge Sivertsen. 'Studentenes helse- og trivselsundersøkelse 2018 [Students' Health and Wellbeing Study 2018].' Oslo: Studentsamskipnaden i Oslo og Akershus, 2018.
Kodak. 'DP Kasper Tuxen DFF Lenses a Modern-Day Love Story on 35mm for Joachim Trier's 2021 Cannes Contender "The Worst Person in the World"'. Kodak, 8 July 2021. https://www.kodak.com/en/motion/blog-post/the-worst-person-in-the-world (accessed 26 November 2023).
Kozloff, Sarah. *Invisible Storytellers: Voice-over Narration in American Fiction Film*. Berkeley: University of California Press, 1988.
Kristeva, Julia. *Black Sun: Depression and Melancholia, European Perspectives*. New York: Columbia University Press, 1989.
Laffy, Tomris. 'Film Review: "Thelma": Film Journal International'. *Filmjournal*, 11 2011. http://www.filmjournal.com/reviews/film-review-thelma (accessed 5 November 2018).
Laine, Tarja. *Feeling Cinema: Emotional Dynamics in Film Studies*. New York: Continuum, 2011.
———. 'Trauma, Queer Sexuality and Symbolic Storytelling in Joachim Trier's Thelma'. *Journal of Scandinavian Cinema* 12, no. 3 (1 September 2022): 291–305. https://doi.org/10.1386/jsca_00077_1 (accessed 26 November 2023).
Larsen, Vegard. 'Joachim Trier'. *Drivkraft*, 12 October 2021.
Lie, Truls. 'Joachim Trier on Being a Director'. 16 September 2015. https://vimeo.com/140561626 (accessed 26 November 2023).
Lim, Dennis. 'Joachim Trier's "Reprise": Cinematic Life in Oslo (Where Else?)'. *The New York Times*, 11 May 2008. https://www.nytimes.com/2008/05/11/movies/11lim.html (accessed 26 November 2023).
Lismoen, Kjetil. 'Et svært sterkt skuespillerløft'. 19 May 2011. https://www.aftenposten.no/oslo/byliv/i/GnVV/et-svaert-sterkt-skuespillerloeft (accessed 26 November 2023).

Lyngar, Marius. 'Fra Revolt Til Reprise? – Joachim Trier og den franske nybølgen'. *Z Filmtidsskrift*, 6 October 2011. http://znett.com/2011/10/fra-revolt-til-reprise-joachim-trier-og-den-franske-nybolgen/ (accessed 27 November 2023).

Lysne, Anders. 'Manifestations of Dread in Thelma'. *Journal of Scandinavian Cinema* 9, no. 2 (1 June 2019): 235–39. https://doi.org/10.1386/jsca.9.2.235_1 (accessed 26 November 2023).

McCullough, Susannah. 'Ask the Director: Joachim Trier on Personal Cinema, the Close-Up and "Louder than Bombs"'. *The Take*, 7 April 2016. https://the-take.com/read/ask-the-director-joachim-trier-on-personal-cinema-the-close-up-and-louder-than-bombs (accessed 26 November 2023).

McDaniel, Kym. *Why Can't I Be Who I Am: A Queer Disabled Analysis of Joachim Trier's 'Thelma'*. New York: School of Professional Studies, City University of New York, 2021.

McHenry, Jackson. '*The Worst Person in the World* Held Up Oslo for Its Freeze-Frame Sequence'. *Vulture*, 17 February 2022. https://www.vulture.com/2022/02/behind-the-worst-person-in-the-worlds-freeze-frame-sequence.html (accessed 26 November 2023).

Mills, Mike. 'Speed of Life: *The Worst Person in the World* Director Joachim Trier Interviewed by Mike Mills'. *Filmmaker Magazine*, 18 January 2022. https://filmmakermagazine.com/112885-interview-mike-mills-joachim-trier-worst-person-in-the-world/ (accessed 26 November 2023).

Mitchell, Wendy. 'Joachim Trier on his Existential Romantic Comedy "The Worst Person in the World"'. *Screen Daily*, 9 July 2021. https://www.screendaily.com/features/joachim-trier-on-his-existential-romantic-comedy-the-worst-person-in-the-world/5161391.article (accessed 26 November 2023).

Mohr, Emil. 'Mike Mills: – Jeg betrakter mammaer som mer avanserte vesener'. *www.dn.no*, 7 April 2022.. https://www.dn.no/d2/film/joaquin-phoenix/kino/joachim-trier/mike-mills-jeg-betrakter-mammaer-som-mer-avanserte-vesener/2-1-1165287 (accessed 26 November 2023).

Mongaard, Christian. 'Fortællingen om den dobbelte skam'. *Information*, 26 October 2011. https://www.information.dk/kultur/2011/10/fortaellingen-dobbelte-skam (accessed 26 November 2023).

Moreno, Victor. 'Joachim Trier in the Wheelhouse'. *Metal Magazine*, 2015. https://metalmagazine.eu/en/post/interview/joachim-trier-in-the-wheelhouse-victor-moreno (accessed 27 November 2023).

Mulvey, Laura. *Death 24x a Second: Stillness and the Moving Image*. Chicago: Reaktion Books, 2006.

———. 'Visual Pleasure and Narrative Cinema'. *Screen* 16, no. 3 (Autumn 1975): 6–18.

Murphy, Mekado. 'Watch Time Stand Still in "The Worst Person in the World"'. *The New York Times*, 4 February 2022, sec. Movies. https://www.nytimes.com/2022/02/04/movies/worst-person-in-the-world-clip.html (accessed 26 November 2023).

Myrstad, Anne Marit. 'Soft Strength, Mild Mystery: Female Characters in the Films of Joachim Trier'. *Journal of Scandinavian Cinema* 9, no. 2 (1 June 2019): 211–18. https://doi.org/10.1386/jsca.9.2.211_1 (accessed 26 November 2023).

Nakhnikian, Elise. 'Interview: Joachim Trier Talks *Louder Than Bombs*'. *Slant Magazine*, 6 April 2016. https://www.slantmagazine.com/film/interview-joachim-trier-talks-louder-than-bombs/ (accessed 26 November 2023).
Neumann, Birgit. 'The Literary Representation of Memory'. In Astrid Erll and Ansgar Nünning (eds), *Cultural Memory Studies: An International and Interdisciplinary Handbook*. Berlin: De Gruyter, 2008, pp. 333–43.
NFI. 'New Joachim Trier Feature Receives NFI Funding'. Norwegian Film Institute, 9 May 2023. https://www.nfi.no/eng/news/2023/new-joachim-trier-feature-receives-nfi-funding (accessed 26 November 2023).
Nikolajsen, Lone. "Verdens værste menneske" er en suverænt velfortalt skildring af længsel'. *Information*, 15 June 2022. https://www.information.dk/kultur/anmeldelse/2022/06/verdens-vaerste-menneske-suveraent-velfortalt-skildring-laengsel (accessed 26 November 2023).
Nipen, Kjersti. 'Joachim Trier: – Alt jeg gjør, er ekstremt personlig'. 14 September 2017. https://www.aftenposten.no/amagasinet/i/92Gxd/joachim-trier-alt-jeg-gjoer-er-ekstremt-personlig (accessed 26 November 2023).
Novrup Redvall, Eva. 'Sidste omgang i Oslo'. *Information*, 26 October 2011. https://www.information.dk/kultur/anmeldelse/2011/10/sidste-omgang-oslo (accessed 26 November 2023).
O'Malley, Sheila. '*The Worst Person in the World*: Lost and Found'. The Criterion Collection, 2022. https://www.criterion.com/current/posts/7844-the-worst-person-in-the-world-lost-and-found (accessed 26 November 2023).
Phillips, Adam. *Missing Out: In Praise of the Unlived Life*. London: Penguin, 2013.
Phipps, Keith. 'An Insider's Guide to the Oslo of "The Worst Person in the World"'. Substack newsletter, *The Reveal* (blog), 15 February 2022. https://thereveal.substack.com/p/an-insiders-guide-to-the-oslo-of (accessed 26 November 2023).
Pugh, Lindsay. 'An Interview with Kasper Tuxen'. In *Existential Detours: Joachim Trier's Cinema of Indecisions and Revisions*. Toronto: Seventh Row, 2024.
Radstone, Susannah. 'Cinema and Memory'. In *Memory. Histories Theories, Debates*, edited by Susannah Radstone and Bill Schwarz, pp. 325–42. New York: Fordham University Press, 2010. https://www.jstor.org/stable/j.ctt1c999bq.26 (accessed 26 November 2023).
Rapold, Nicholas. 'Interview: Joachim Trier'. *Film Comment*, 11 April 2016. https://www.filmcomment.com/blog/interview-joachim-trier/ (accessed 26 November 2023).
Raskin, Richard. 'Five Types of Voice-over in Feature Film Storytelling'. *16:9 filmtidsskrift*, 18 October 2020. http://www.16-9.dk/2020/10/five-types-of-voice-over/ (accessed 27 November 2023).
Rees, Ellen. 'Norwave: Norwegian Cinema 1997–2006'. *Scandinavian–Canadian Studies* 19 (1 December 2010): 88–110. https://doi.org/10.29173/scancan51 (accessed 26 November 2023).
Reumont, Francois. 'Kasper Tuxen, DFF, Discusses the Shooting of "The Worst Person in the World", by Joachim Trier'. *Afcinema*, 15 August 2021. https://www.afcinema.com/Kasper-Tuxen-DFF-discusses-the-shooting-of-The-Worst-Person-in-the-World-by-Joachim-Trier.html (accessed 26 November 2023).
Robinson, Tasha. 'Joachim Trier on His Dreamy Gay Coming-of-Age Superhero Story'. *The Verge*, 10 November 2017. https://www.theverge.com/2017/11/10/16635068/

joachim-trier-thelma-interview-behind-the-scenes-academy-award-submission (accessed 26 November 2023).

Rushprint (ed.). '"Jakten" er tidenes norske kinofilm'. *Rushprint*, 21 December 2011. https://rushprint.no/2011/12/jakten-er-tidenes-norske-kinofilm/ (accessed 26 November 2023).

Saito, Stephen. 'Interview: Joachim Trier & Eskil Vogt on Finding Their Power in "Thelma"'. *The Moveable Fest*, 4 December 2017. https://moveablefest.com/joachim-trier-eskil-vogt-thelma/ (accessed 26 November 2023).

Sandbye, Mette. *Mindesmærker: Tid og erindring i fotografiet*. Copenhagen: Politisk revy, 2001.

Scott, A. O. '"The Worst Person in the World" Review: Oslo, Her Way'. *The New York Times*, 3 February 2022. https://www.nytimes.com/2022/02/03/movies/the-worst-person-in-the-world-review.html (accessed 26 November 2023).

Shunyata, Kaiya. '*The Worst Person In The World* Perfectly Captures the Rawness of Young-Adulthood'. *Obscur* (blog), 10 March 2022. https://obscurmagazine.co.uk/the-worst-person-in-the-world-the-rawness-of-young-adulthood/ (accessed 1 August 2023).

Simpson, Don. 'Joachim Trier (Oslo, August 31st): Interview'. *Smells Like Screen Spirit*, 21 May 2012. http://smellslikescreenspirit.com/2012/05/joachim-trier-oslo-august-31st-interview/ (accessed 2 June 2018).

Smith, Orla. 'Designing a Journey through Oslo'. Toronto: *Seventh Row*, 31 August 2021. https://seventh-row.com/2021/08/31/jorgen-stangebye-larsen-oslo-august-31st-production-design-interview/ (accessed 26 November 2023).

Sødtholt, Dag. 'Alt skal glemmes, men ikke Oslo, 31. August'. *Montages*, 21 September 2011. http://montages.no/2011/09/alt-skal-glemmes-men-ikke-oslo-31-august/ (accessed 26 November 2023).

———. 'Focus of Faith: Joachim Trier's *The Worst Person in the World*'. *Montages International Edition*, 27 March, 2022. https://montagesmagazine.com/2022/03/focus-of-faith-joachim-triers-the-worst-person-in-the-world/ (accessed 26 November 2023).

———. 'Joachim Trier's Thelma, Part III: The Epilepsy Test'. *Montages International Edition*, 9 December 2017. http://montagesmagazine.com/2017/12/joachim-triers-thelma-part-iii-the-epilepsy-test/ (accessed 26 November 2023).

———. '*Louder Than Bombs:* Joachim Trier's Play on Perspective'. *Montages International Edition*, 9 January 2016. http://montagesmagazine.com/2016/01/louder-than-bombs-joachim-triers-play-on-perspective/ (accessed 26 November 2023).

———. 'Touchstones – a Guide to Joachim Trier's Cinematic Universe'. *Montages International Edition*, 7 December 2021. https://montagesmagazine.com/2021/12/touchstones-a-guide-to-joachim-triers-cinematic-universe/ (accessed 26 November 2023).

———. 'Tre enigmaer av Joachim Trier'. *Montages*, 27 August 2015. https://montages.no/2015/08/tre-enigmaer-av-joachim-trier/ (accessed 27 November 2023).

Solis, Jose. 'Joachim Trier Interview'. StageBuddy.com, 12 April 2016. https://stagebuddy.com/film/interview-director-joachim-trier-new-york-music-playing-cinematic-form-louder-bombs (accessed 7 December 2023).

Sontag, Susan. *On Photography*. London: Penguin, 2002.

———. *Regarding the Pain of Others*. New York: Farrar, Straus and Giroux, 2003.

Steinkjer, Mode. 'Triers lavmælte triumf'. *Dagsavisen*, 31 August 2011.

Suh, Elissa. 'A Stick, a Stone, the End of the Road: Joachim Trier Discusses "The Worst Person in the World"'. MUBI, 2022. https://mubi.com/notebook/posts/a-stick-a-stone-the-end-of-the-road-joachim-trier-discusses-the-worst-person-in-the-world (accessed 26 November 2023).

Tarkovsky, Andrei. *Andrei Tarkovsky: Interviews*. Conversations with Film Makers Series. Jackson: University of Mississippi Press, 2006.

———. *Sculpting in time: reflections on the cinema*. London: The Bodley Head, 1986.

Thomson, C. Claire. '*Louder Than Films:* Memory, Affect and the "Sublime Image" in the Work of Joachim Trier'. *Arts* 8, no. 2 (2019). https://doi.org/10.3390/arts8020055 (accessed 26 November 2023).

Thomson, David. 'A Small Norwegian Film and the Critic Who Praised It'. *The New Republic*, 12 September 2012. https://newrepublic.com/article/107141/thomson-oslo (accessed 26 November 2023).

Tinkham, Chris. 'Joachim Trier. Co-Writer and Director of Reprise'. *Under the Radar*, 2 May 2008. https://www.undertheradarmag.com/interviews/joachim_trier_interview_052008 (accessed 26 November 2023).

Trier, Joachim. *Behind the Scenes Criterion Collection*. DVD, 2021.

———. 'Masterclass with Joachim Trier in Conversation with Anne Gjelsvik'. Department of Art and Media Studies, NTNU, 18 September 2017.

Tweedie, James. 'The *Mise-En-Scène* of Modernity: The French New Wave, Paris, and the Global 1960s'. In James Tweedie (ed.), *The Age of New Waves: Art Cinema and the Staging of Globalization*. Oxford: Oxford University Press: pp. 45–82. https://doi.org/10.1093/acprof:oso/9780199858286.003.0002 (accessed 26 November 2023).

Vestmo, Birger. 'Reprise: En dristig og spennende debutfilm'. NRK (Norwegian Broadcasting Corporation) P3, 8 September 2006. https://p3.no/filmpolitiet/2006/09/reprise/ (accessed 26 November 2023).

Vicente, Álex. 'Joachim Trier: "The Monogamous Are the Real Romantic Heroes of Our Time"'. *El País* English, 17 March 2022. https://english.elpais.com/culture/2022-03-17/joachim-trier-the-monogamous-are-the-real-romantic-heroes-of-our-time.html (accessed 26 November 2023).

Vogt, Eskil and Joachim Trier. *Reprise. Et filmmanuskript*. Oslo: Tiden Norsk Forlag, 2007

———. *Oslo, 31.august. Filmmanus*. Oslo: Tiden Norsk Forlag, 2011

———. *Thelma*. Oslo: Tiden Norsk Forlag, 2017

———. *Verdens verste menneske: filmmanus*. Oslo: Tiden Norsk Forlag, 2021.

———. *Oslo-trilogien. Filmmanus*. Tiden Norsk Forlag, 2022.

Vogt, Eskil, Joachim Trier, and Mattis Øybø. 'Kunsten å oppnå sekvensiell nytelse'. In Eskil, Trier and Øybø (eds), *Verdens Verste Menneske. Filmmanus*. Oslo: Tiden norsk forlag, 2021, pp. 277–304.

Wald, Jackson. 'Joachim Trier's Cinema of Intimacy'. *Interview Magazine*, 7 February 2022. https://www.interviewmagazine.com/film/joachim-trier-cinema-of-intimacy (accessed 26 November 2023).

Webb, Will. 'A Beginners Guide to Joachim Trier'. *Little White Lies*, 2022.

https://www.youtube.com/watch?v=_wOLVOAj6tU&ab_channel=LittleWhiteLies.
Wedding, Danny, and Ryan Niemiec. *Movies and Mental Illness: Using Films to Understand Psychopathology*, 4th edn. Boston: Hogrefe Publishing, 2014.
Wehus, Walter. 'Her er tegneserien *Gaupe* fra Verdens verste menneske'. *Empirix*, 31 December 2021. https://www.empirix.no/her-er-tegneserien-*Gaupe*-fra-verdens-verste-menneske/ (accessed 26 November 2023).
Weston, Hillary. 'Everyday Magic: Joachim Trier on Reimagining Louis Malle'. The Criterion Collection, 17 December 2017.
———. 'The Art Form of Memory: A Conversation with Joachim Trier'. The Criterion Collection, 8 April 2016. https://www.criterion.com/current/posts/4001-the-art-form-of-memory-a-conversation-with-joachim-trier (accessed 26 November 2023).
———. 'The Quiet Allure of Joachim Trier's "Oslo, August 31st"'. Hillary Weston, 1 February 2013. http://hillaryweston.squarespace.com/new-page-17/ (accessed 26 November 2023).
WHO, 'Data and Resources. Prevalence of Mental Disorders'. 28 May 2018, http://www.euro.who.int/en/health-topics/noncommunicable-diseases/mental-health/data-and-resources (accessed 28 May 2018).
With, Anne Lise. 'Det levende og det fryste: Noen betraktninger omkring "Verdens verste menneske"'. *Montages*, 6 January 2022. https://montages.no/2022/01/det-levende-og-det-fryste-noen-betraktninger-omkring-verdens-verste-menneske/ (accessed 26 November 2023).
Yazdan, Benjamin. 'Å se med og på – det fenomenologiske blikket i Joachim Trier og Eskil Vogts filmer'. *Montages*, 2014. http://montages.no/2014/03/a-se-med-og-pa-det-fenomenologiske-blikket-i-joachim-trier-og-eskil-vogts-filmer/ (accessed 26 November 2023).
———. 'Minner, identitet og nærbilder i Joachim Triers *Louder Than Bombs* – en humanistisk film'. *Montages*, 2015. http://montages.no/2015/10/minner-identitet-og-naerbilder-i-joachim-triers-louder-than-bombs-en-humanistisk-film/ (accessed 26 November 2023).

Index

actors, 136–7, 153
adverts, 22
Aguilar, Carlos, 62
art
   art-identity connection, 106, 108–9, 110, 156–7
   cinema as, 147–8
   comic art in *The Worst Person in the World*, 106, 107–8, *108*, 156
   in *Louder Than Bombs*, 106
   representation through, 156–7
   in *Reprise*, 106
   in Trier's films, 5, 106–7, 156
   Trier's interest in comic art, 107, 156
   Vigeland Sculpture Park, 73, 108
   see also photography

Bakke Andresen, Christer, 19, 34, 35
Barthes, Roland, 111, 112, 113
Bergman, Ingmar, 31, 73, 137, 149
Bigelow, Benjamin, 16, 17, 67
Birkvad, Søren, 95
Boym, Svetlana, 17
Brenner, Hans Olav, 119
Brody, Richard, 48
Bugge Coutté, Olivier, 6, 38, 156
Byrne, Gabriel, 24

Carrasco, Salvador, 53
characters
   actors' experiences of working with Trier, 136–7, 153
   close-ups, 137–9
   coming-of-age periods, 91
   existential crisis of Trier's characters, 5, 22, 73, 81, 90–1, 92, 102–3, 149, 154–5
   importance of character development, 5
   interior lives, 98–9, 130–1, 139
   Oslo, 60, 64, 69–70
   seeking to understand themselves, 73, 81
   Trier's observational skills, 136
   Trier's personal experiences and, 154–5
   Trier's portrayal of female characters, 98–100
   urban, middle-class characters, 68, 155–6
Christensen, Charlie, 107, 108, 156
close-ups, 137–9

Danielsen Lie, Anders, 2, 15, 21, 22, 60, 79, 119, 126, 136–7, 153
Dargis, Manohla, 2

Den andre Munch (*The Other Munch*), 2
dialogue *see* language
Druid, David, 24

Eisenberg, Jesse, 24
Engelstad, Audun, 23, 40, 124, 125

family
    in *Louder Than Bombs*, 92, 94–6
    in *Oslo, August 31st*, 76, 92
    in *Reprise*, 92
    in *Sentimental Value*, 140–1
    in *Thelma*, 93–4, 95
    in *The Worst Person in the World*, 92–3
feminist criticism, 101
Ferris Bueller's Day Off, 53–4
flashbacks
    absent/present characters, 18–20, 23–4, 81, 84–5
    in *Louder Than Bombs*, 24, 75, 137–8
    within narrative structures, 18–20, 27, 33
    in *Thelma*, 33–5, 39
Fløttum, Ola, 6, 127, 135
French New Wave
    influences in the Oslo trilogy, 66, 69
    influences in Trier's work, 4, 5, 40, 97
    urban settings, 66, 69
Freud, Sigmund, 94
friendship
    female characters/friendships, 100–2
    male friendships, 102
    in *Oslo, August 31st*, 102, 119
    in Trier's films, 5, 92

Godard, Jean-Luc, 4, 40, 69

Hamsun, Knut, 76
Harboe, Eili, 19
Hitchcock, Alfred, 95
Hobbelstad, Inger Merete, 75–6
human relationships
    depictions of falling in love, 54–5
    familial relationships, 76, 92–6, 140–1
    friendships, 100–2
    insider-outsider perspectives in *The Worst Person in the World*, 89–90
    Oedipal narratives, 94
    relational, existential dramas, 5, 22, 73, 81, 90–1, 92, 102–3, 149, 154–5
    The Scream (Munch), 63, 102
    with technology, 41, 115–16
    in Trier's films, 90, 92
    see also romantic relationships
Huppert, Isabelle, 24, 138–9, *138*

identity
    art-identity connection, 106, 108–9, 110, 156–7
    existential crisis of Trier's characters, 5, 22, 73, 81, 90–1, 92, 102–3, 149, 154–5
    the imagined life vs the reality, 55–6
    language and portrayal of self, 118, 128–9
    search for one's true self, 5, 73
Ihre, Jakob, 6, 64, 139, 140
image
    cinematic set pieces, 47–8
    voice-overs' disconnect with the visual image, 15, 121–2, 123
    see also photography
Iversen, Gunnar, 2, 3, 6, 65

Jerins, Ruby, 24
Jerslev, Anne, 138–9

Kemp, Ella, 62
Klouman Høiner, Espen, 22
Kozloff, Sarah, 120–1
Kristiansen, Petter Width, 134
Kubrick, Stanley, 123, 149

Laine, Tarja, 74, 93–4, 124–5
language
    explorations of voice and words, 119, 128–9
    and identity, 118, 128–9
    lengthy dialogue scenes, 118–19, 130

Trier and Vogt's approach to, 119, 130
writing as a profession, 118
Linklater, Richard, 18
literature
   Künstlerroman genre, 118
   memory in, 17, 22
   stream of consciousness, 42, 119, 127, 128–9, 154
   Trier's novelistic approach to film, 5, 118
   see also modernism
Little White Lies's video essay, 134, 140
Løchen, Erik, 3
Louder Than Bombs
   art in, 106
   close-ups, 137–9
   Conrad's inner worlds, 128–9
   English language, 4
   explorations of bereavement, 112–13, 114–15
   familial relationships, 92, 94–6
   flashbacks, 24, 75, 137–8
   framing in photography, 42–3
   main plot points, 5, 24–5
   memory sequences, 13, 22, 24–7, 26, 28, 75, 112–13
   mental health themes, 74–5
   montage in, 32, 41–4, 111
   narrative structure, 41
   non-chronological structure, 32–3, 75, 152
   Nordic Council Film Prize, 2
   observation in, 136
   photography, 107, 109–11, 113–15
   romantic relationships, 24, 43, 96, 97
   set pieces, 49
   stream of consciousness, 26–7, 42, 127, 128–9, 154
   technology and human relationships, 41, 115–16, 128
   traumatic memories, 20
   voice-overs, 28, 42, 127–8, 130

Malle, Louis, *The Fire Within* (*Le feu follet*), 69, 102
Meinich, Karsten, 67–8
melancholy
   in *Oslo, August 31st*, 14, 16–17, 20, 64, 70, 73, 76, 77, 86
   in Trier's films, 102, 130, 134, 155
memory
   act of remembering, 13, 14–15
   cinema as the medium of, 13, 27
   collective memories, 13, 16, 25
   connections with place, 16–17, 18, 19–20, 63
   importance of in Trier's films, 13, 27–8
   in literature, 17, 22
   in *Louder Than Bombs*, 13, 22, 24–7, 26, 28, 75, 112–13
   memories and flashbacks as plot devices, 18–20, 22, 23–4, 27, 33–5, 39, 93
   memory sequences and narrative structure, 22–5
   modernist modes of expression, 27
   non-chronological ordering, 22
   personal importance to Trier, 14–15, 112
   photography as a medium of, 13, 112
   photos as *memento mori*, 112
   private memories, 13, 14
   traumatic memories, 19, 20, 93
   see also nostalgia
mental illness
   anxiety disorders, 83–4
   depressive disorders, 77
   explored in *Oslo, 31st August*, 76–81
   explored in *Thelma*, 82–5
   feelings of meaninglessness in *Oslo, 31st August*, 77–9, 85
   in *Louder Than Bombs*, 74–5
   place-psychological state connections, 73, 74, 75, 78, 79–80, 81–2, 83, 84, 85, 86
   in *Reprise*, 22, 74
   in Trier's films, 7, 74, 85

Mills, Mike, 37–8, 42, 61
modernism
   expressions of time and chronology, 32
   self-reflectivity in, 40
   stream of consciousness, 26–7, 42, 119, 127, 128–9, 154
   in Trier's films, 106
montage
   in classical narratives, 35
   in *Louder Than Bombs*, 32, 41–4, 111
   main plot points, 50
   in Mike Mills's films, 37–8, 42
   narrative function, 32, 39–40
   non-chronological structures, 32–3
   in the prologue of *Oslo, August 31st*, 14–15, 16, 31–2, 112
   in *Reprise*, 38, 39–40, 111
   Trier's creative use of, 31–2, 43–4
   in Trier's films, 153
   voice-overs, 32
   in *The Worst Person in the World*, 32, 35–7, 38, 40, 50, 111
Munch, Edvard, *The Scream*, 63, 102
Myrstad, Anne Marit, 97, 101

narrative structure
   classical narratives (the Hollywood model), 33, 35, 107
   complexity of, 5–6
   experimentation, 3
   fractured narratives, 33
   framing in photography, 42–3
   inner realities expressed in film, 32
   of *Louder Than Bombs*, 41
   memories and flashbacks as plot devices, 20
   memory sequences and, 22–5
   prologues and montages, 31
   voice-over narration, 120–1
   in *The Worst Person in the World*, 40–1
   see also flashbacks; montage
National Film and Television School (NFTS), 4, 150
Neuman, Birgit, 17, 22, 27
Nikolajsen, Lone, 139

Nordrum, Herbert, 21
Norwegian film
   norwave, term, 2–3
   Trier's status within, 1–3, 4, 6, 150–1
Norwegian Film Institute (NFI), 4, 140–1, 147
nostalgia
   definition, 17
   in *Oslo, August 31st*, 14, 16–17, 20, 64, 70, 76, 77, 86
   in *The Worst Person in the World*, 13, 21–2, *21*, 91

O'Malley, Sarah, 55
Oslo
   the act of walking in the city, 68–9
   as a character, 60, 64, 69–70
   as a cinematic space, 60, 62–3
   collective memories, 14, 16, 32
   cultural elites, 68
   demolition of the Philips building, 63, 76
   development of on film, 63, 66–8
   images of in *The Worst Person in the World*, 59–60
   light in, 64, 70
   loneliness and alienation in, 61–2, 80
   the 'Oslo trilogy,' 18, 60–1
   the sound of, 65–6
   Trier and Vogt's portrayals of, 60, 61, 62–3, 157
   urban culture, 61–3
Oslo, August 31st
   acts of remembering, 14–15
   Anders's feelings of meaninglessness, 77–9, 85
   Anders's last 24 hours, 15–16, 17–18, 76–7
   blissful moments, 134–5, *135*
   demolition of the Philips building, 63, 76
   empty spaces of the epilogue, 17–18, 20, 22, 81
   familial relationships, 76, 92
   flashbacks, 18

forgetting, 13, 20
French New Wave influences, 4, 5
friendship in, 102, 119
Frogner Baths in summer and winter, 15, *15*, *18*, 64
lengthy dialogue scenes, 119
light in, 64
main plot points, 5, 75, 134–5
memory as a theme of, 13–14, 16
memory's connections with place, 16–17, 18
montage in the prologue, 14–15, 16, 31–2, 112
within Norwegian culture, 2
nostalgia and melancholy, 14, 16–17, 20, 64, 70, 73, 76, 77, 86
oppressiveness of Oslo, 61–2
Oslo setting, 60, 64–5, 75–6, 77, 79
within the 'Oslo trilogy,' 18, 60–1
place-psychological state connections, 75, 76–81
prologue, 14–15, 16, 31–2, 130
realism, 64–5
romantic relationships, 97
set pieces, 49
sound design, 65–6
the Vigeland Park scene, 73, 74, 77
voice-overs, 14, 61, 121, 130
voice-over's disconnect with the visual image, 15, 121–2

Petersen, Ellen Dorrit, 19
Phillips, Adam, 55
photography
    explorations of bereavement, 112–13, 114–15
    framing, 42–3
    in *Louder Than Bombs*, 107, 109–11, 113–15
    as a medium of memory, 13, 112
    photo theory, 111
    temporality, 113
    in Trier's films, 5, 112
    in *The Worst Person in the World*, 115
Pietà, 1, 112

place
    flashbacks and absent/present characters, 18–20, 23–4, 81, 84–5
    memory's connections with place, 16–17, 18, 19–20, 63
    place-psychological state connections, 73, 74, 75, 78, 79–82, 83, 84, 85, 86
Proctor, 1, 112

Radstone, Susannah, 13, 27
Rafaelsen, Henrik, 19
Raskin, Richard, 121, 122, 123
realism
    the imagined life vs the reality, 55–6
    of Oslo in *Oslo, August 31st*, 64–5
Redvall, Eva Norup, 64
Reinsve, Renate, 1, 21, 115, 126, 136, 137
Reprise
    art in, 106
    familial relationships, 92
    female characters/friendships, 101–2
    feminist criticism, 101
    flashbacks and absent/present characters, 23–4
    French New Wave influences, 4, 5
    the imagined life vs the reality, 55–6
    main plot points, 5, 22–3
    male friendships, 102
    memory sequences, 13, 22–3
    mental health themes, 74
    montage in, 38, 39–40, 111
    non-chronological structure, 32, 38–40, 41
    opening montage as a flash-forward, 32, 33, 38–9
    Oslo settings, 60, 61, 62, 74
    within the 'Oslo trilogy,' 18, 60–1
    regional and international acclaim, 1–2, 3
    romantic relationships, 96–7
    as a specifically Norwegian film, 150–1
    third person narrators, 28, 120, 123–5, 127
    time in the narrative, 40
    as Trier's directorial debut, 1–2, 3

Resnais, Alain, 140
Hiroshima mon amour, 4, 27, 63, 153
romantic relationships
  French New Wave influences, 97
  in *Louder Than Bombs*, 24, 43, 96, 97
  in *Oslo, August 31st*, 97
  in *Reprise*, 96–7
  rom-com elements of *The Worst Person in the World*, 5, 50, 53, 54–5, 140
  in *Thelma*, 19, 82–3, 96, 97–8
  in Trier's films, 96–7
  Trier's portrayal of female characters, 98–100
  tropes of hair and femininity, 97
  in *The Worst Person in the World*, 54–5, 97–8

Scott, A. O., 69–70
Sentimental Value, 140–1, 147
Singin' in the Rain, 47, 48
Sødtholt, Dag, 80, 97
Sontag, Susan, 111, 112, 114–15
Still, 1, 112

Thelma
  familial relationships, 93–4, 95
  flashbacks and absent/present characters, 18–20, 84–5
  flashbacks and memories as plot devices, 20, 33–5, 39, 93
  as a genre movie, 2, 5, 19–20, 35, 81, 82, 93
  images of Oslo, 61
  main plot points, 5, 19, 75, 81
  mental health themes, 82–5
  mood-enforcing scenes, 35
  non-chronological structure, 33
  place-psychological state connections, 75, 81–2, 83, 84, 85, 86
  queer female sexuality, 98–9
  romantic relationships, 19, 82–3, 96, 97–8
  set pieces, 49
  traumatic memories, 19, 20, 93

Trier's portrayal of female characters, 98–9
Thomson, Claire, 16–17, 27
Thomson, David, 64
time
  cinema as a time-based art form, 32, 49, 56
  as finite, 55–6
  frozen time scene in *The Worst Person in the World*, 50–6
  as a key theme in *Reprise*, 40
  non-chronological structures, 22, 32–3
  nostalgia and, 17
  set pieces, 47–8, 49
  temporality of photos, 113
  in Trier's films, 154
  see also montage
Trier, Joachim
  the act of remembering, 14–15
  actors experiences of working with, 136–7, 153
  auteur status, 4–6
  cinema as art, 147–8
  cinematic influences and inspirations, 3–4, 5–6, 38, 53–4, 140, 148–9
  collaboration with Vogt, 5, 6, 31, 151–3, 154
  collaborative work practices, 4, 5, 6, 153
  early film career, 3–4
  within European modernist film, 3, 4, 14
  family background, 3, 141–2, 147, 150
  hybridity in the cinematic style of, 31
  interest in comic art, 107, 156
  meticulous planning, 139–40
  national and international recognition, 1–2, 3, 6, 140–1
  at the NFTS, London, 4, 61, 150
  within Norwegian film history, 1–3, 4, 6, 150–1
  Norwegian identity, 149–51
  personal identity and artistic expression, 106, 156–7
  scholarship on, 6–7

unique moments of, 142–3
use of 35mm film, 49
visuality in the work of, 135–6
on what cinema is, 1, 31, 136, 141–2, 147–8, 157
work as a DJ, 106
Truffaut, Francois, 69
Tuxen, Kasper, 6, 38, 49, 139
Tveito, Gisle, 6, 65
Tweedle, James, 69

Varda, Agnes, 69
Vogt, Eskil
  Blind, 6, 132n
  on cinematic dialogue, 119, 130
  collaboration with Trier, 5, 6, 31, 151–3, 154
  contrast in cinematic style, 142
  explorations of voice and words, 119
  filmography, 6
  on human relationships in Trier's films, 90
  meeting with Trier, 4
  Oscar nomination for *The Worst Person in the World*, 31
  on *Oslo, August 31st*, 76, 79
  Oslo settings, 61, 62–3, 66–7
  regional and international acclaim, 6
  script for *The Worst Person in the World*, 40, 52
  time in film schools abroad, 4, 61, 150
  use of voice-over, 120
voice-overs
  in *Adaptation*, 120
  criticism of the use of, 120
  disconnect with the visual image, 15, 121–2, 123
  experimentation, 3
  in *Louder Than Bombs*, 28, 42, 127–8, 130
  montage sequences, 32
  as narrative devices, 5
  Oslo, August 31st, 121
  prologue of *Oslo, 31st August*, 14, 130

third person narrators, 123, 130
third person narrators in *Reprise*, 28, 120, 123–5, 127
Trier and Vogt's approach to, 130–1
in Trier's films, 118, 120, 130–1, 153
types of, 121, 122, 123
voice-over narration, 120–1
in *The Worst Person in the World*, 21, 36–7, 118, 125–7, 129, 130

Welles, Orson, 35, 111, 153
Weston, Hillary, 76, 79, 86, 134
Wilkins, Kaya, 19
Winge, Victoria, 22
women
  the Bechdel test, 100
  feminist criticism, 101
  Trier's portrayal of female characters, 98–100
Worst Person in the World, The
  Askel's work as a cartoonist, 106, 107–8, *108*, 156
  Beginners (Mills) similarities with, 37–8
  the big screen experience of, 49
  as a coming-of-age movie for grownups, 5, 91, 154–5
  critical acclaim, 1, 2
  episodic nature of, 35, 40, 89, 118, 152
  existential crisis of Trier's characters, 102–3
  explorations of voice and words, 119, 129
  familial relationships, 92–3
  female friendships, 100, 101
  frozen time scene, 48, 50–6, *51*, *52*
  human nature and behaviour in, 89–90
  images of Oslo, 59–60, 62, 69–70
  the imagined life vs the reality, 55
  main plot points, 5
  musical aspects, 53
  narrative structure, 40–1
  nostalgia, 13, 21–2, *21*, 91

Worst Person in the World, The (cont.)
  opening montage in, 32, 35–7, 38, 40, 50, 111
  Oscar nomination for Best Original Screenplay, 31
  within the 'Oslo trilogy,' 18, 60–1
  parallels with *Singin' in the Rain*, 48
  photography in, 115
  realist tensions with emotional expression, 52, 53–4
  romantic relationships, 54–5, 97–8
  rom-com elements, 5, 50, 53, 54–5, 140
  self-portrayals, 92
  set pieces challenges, 54
  soundtrack, 36
  time as finite, 55–6
  traumatic memories, 20
  Trier's portrayal of female characters, 98–100
  use of 35mm film, 49, 54
  voice-over narrator, 21, 36–7, 118, 119, 123, 125–7, 129, 130

Yazdan, Benjamin, 79

EU representative:
Easy Access System Europe
Mustamäe tee 50, 10621 Tallinn, Estonia
Gpsr.requests@easproject.com

www.ingramcontent.com/pod-product-compliance
Lightning Source LLC
Chambersburg PA
CBHW051127160426
43195CB00014B/2375